W9-BZT-237

HUNTING PIRATE HEAVEN

By the same author

Chasing the Mountain of Light:
Across India on the Trail of the Koh-i-Noor Diamond

Children of Kali:
Through India in Search of Bandits,
the Thug Cult, and the British Raj

Eating the Flowers of Paradise:
A Journey through the Drug Fields of Ethiopia and Yemen

HUNTING PIRATE HEAVEN

In Search of the Lost Pirate Utopias of the Indian Ocean

KEVIN RUSHBY

Walker & Company
New York

First published in the United Kingdom in 2001 by Constable,
an imprint of Constable & Robinson; this edition published in the United States
of America in 2003 by Walker Publishing Company, Inc.

For information about permission to reproduce selections from this book,
write to Permissions, Walker & Company, 435 Hudson Street,
New York, New York 10014

Library of Congress Cataloging-in-Publication Data
Rushby, Kevin.
Hunting pirate heaven : in search of the lost pirate utopias
of the Indian Ocean / Kevin Rushby.
p. cm.
ISBN 0-8027-1423-4 (alk. paper)
1. Pirates—Islands of the Indian Ocean—History. 2. Rushby, Kevin—
Journeys—Islands of the Indian Ocean. 3. Islands of the Indian Ocean—
History. 4. Islands of the Indian Ocean—Description and travel. I. Title.
DT468.R87 2003
910′.9165′2—dc21
2003053463

Visit Walker & Company's Web site at www.walkerbooks.com

Printed in the United States of America

2 4 6 8 10 9 7 5 3 1

I am a free Prince, and I have as much Authority to wage War on the whole World, as he who has a hundred Sail of Ships at Sea, and an Army of 100,000 Men in the Field . . . There is no arguing with such snivelling Puppies, who allow Superiors to kick them about Deck at Pleasure; and pin their Faith upon a Pimp of a Parson; a Squab, who neither practises nor believes what he puts upon the chuckle-headed Fools he preaches to.

> The pirate leader, Captain Bellamy, quoted in
> Captain Johnson's *History of the Pyrates*

A map of the world that does not include Utopia is not worth glancing at, for it leaves out the one country at which Humanity is always landing. And when Humanity lands there, it looks out, and seeing a better country, sets sail.

> Oscar Wilde, 'The Soul of Man under Socialism' in the
> *Fortnightly Review*, February 1891

Contents

Acknowledgements

A great number of good people helped me along the way on this journey, some of them utopia-seekers themselves, one or two of them a little piratical as well. In South Africa I am grateful to Anton Rousseau in Capetown, Dick Dawson of the Durban Port Control, Ashley Dee and Glynn at Tallships, Joanne Rushby, Nisaar Mohamed and Theresa Kati. In Mozambique I was helped by Captain José Carvalho and his crew on the M.V. Songo, Gareth in Nacala, Charles Gornal-Jones and Vera Viegas in Pemba. On the island of Mayotte, Vincent Forest was the epitome of generosity as were Abdulkarim Abdallah and Ibrahim Djae on neighboring Anjouan. John Guthrie and Ernst Klaar told piratical stories with all the elan of men who know the Indian Ocean intimately. Others who gave invaluable assistance with the text or translations were Tamara Castro, Jan Abegglen, Eduardo Latorre, Mike Pedley, Maggie Body, and Sophie Carr. I am also grateful to Carolyn Whitaker, Judith Rushby, and to my editor at Constable, Carol O'Brien. A few others I have left out because they prefer anonymity and a few names have been changed in the text for the same reason; to the others who I may have forgotten or whose names I never knew, I apologise for their absence here.

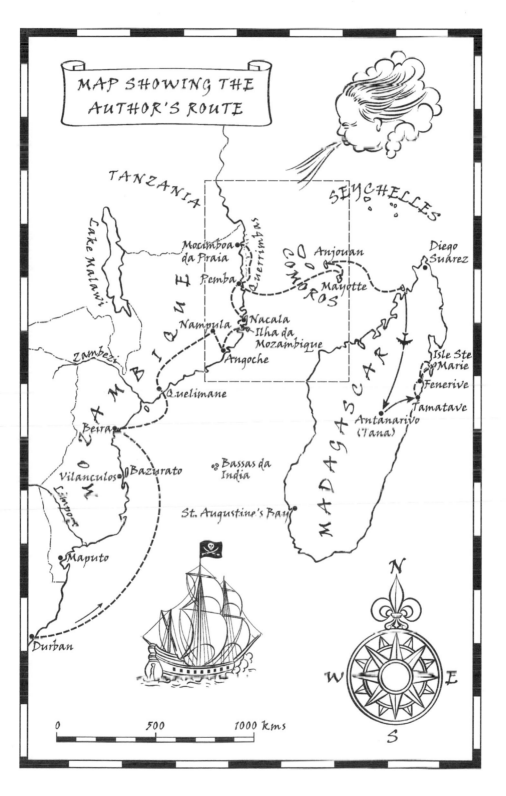

MAP SHOWING THE
AUTHOR'S ROUTE

TANZANIA

SEYCHELLES

Lake Malawi

Mocímboa
da Praia

Querimbas

COMOROS

Anjouan

Diego
Suárez

M O Z A M B I Q U E

Pemba

Mayotte

Zambezi

Nampula

Nacala
Ilha da
Mozambique

Angoche

Quelimane

Beira

Limpopo

Vilanculos

Bazurato

Bassas da
India

St. Augustine's Bay

MADAGASCAR

Isle Ste
Marie

Fenerive

Tamatave

Antananarivo
(Tana)

Maputo

Durban

0   500   1000 Kms

N

W   E

S

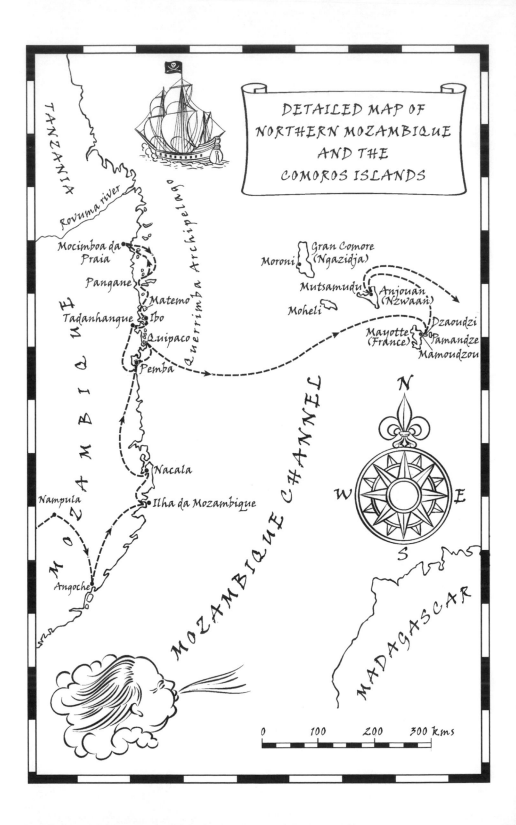

TANZANIA

Rovuma river

Mocimboa da Praia

Pangane

Matemo

Tadanhangue · Ibo

Quipaco

Pemba

Querrimba Archipelago

MOZAMBIQUE

Nacala

Nampula

Ilha da Mozambique

Angoche

DETAILED MAP OF
NORTHERN MOZAMBIQUE
AND THE
COMOROS ISLANDS

Gran Comore
(Ngazidja)

Moroni

Mutsamudu

Anjouan
(Nzwaan)

Moheli

Dzaoudzi

Mayotte
(France)

Tamandze

Mamoudzou

MOZAMBIQUE CHANNEL

N

W   E

S

MADAGASCAR

0   100   200   300 kms

1

Introduction
Cape Canaveral, AD 1601

We find after years of struggle that we do not take a trip; a trip takes us.

John Steinbeck, *Travels with Charley*

I first caught sight of him on the swing bridge at Deptford: a victim of piracy, as he later described himself, though perhaps witness would be a better word. He was wearing an old-fashioned macintosh with the collar turned up and a tweed cap pulled low against the rain. When I came alongside and stopped to look down at the creek towards the Thames, he glanced at me and I noted the long patrician nose and rather pale brown skin. There was a moment when we might have spoken then, but I was trying to balance my umbrella against the wind and at the same time see what lay below in the water. I had come down here filled with enthusiasm for all things maritime and historical: the year 2001 would mark the four hundredth anniversary of the first East India Company voyage and I was in search of the very spot where they departed. I was far too busy with my mission to register the fact that he was Indian.

The creek draws a grubby but definite borderline between the packaged heritage and cosy polished pubs of Greenwich and the very different world of Deptford. It wriggles down to the Thames through banks of wooden pilings, a few traffic cones sticking out of the grey slime like abandoned party hats. Other waterways of London have been lost inside concrete pipes or new channels, but the creek harks back to an older, less controlled, landscape: its sinuous curves and stinking mud banks carry the whiff of raw nature, if not raw sewage.

I did not linger: cars were sending clouds of fine spray across the pavement and on the far side of the bridge was a large puddle where the Indian gentleman narrowly avoided a soaking from a bus. I watched him turn right towards the river, then followed.

All around Deptford there are tiny clues to its historic past: the mulberry tree in Sayes Court garden, its gnarled trunk so aged that it lies like a giant spider on its back; the corbled doorways in Alberry Street with carvings reminiscent of ships' figureheads, and the skull-and-crossbone gateposts at St Nicholas's Church, said to be the inspiration for the Jolly Roger.

Inside the church the Jacobean pulpit is held aloft by a ship's figurehead and the walls hold tributes to the shipwrights and captains who prayed in the pews. This is a Deptford church, no soaring neo-classical lines of a Wren or Hawksmoor as you would expect to find in Greenwich, but a mongrel of brick and stone, a patched-up survivor with a charnel house in its grimy graveyard and a plaque on the wall for Christopher Marlowe, stabbed to death in a nearby bawdy house in 1593.

Then, as now, Deptford was a place for people with journeys in their boots and mysteries in mind: a rich source of material for Marlowe who had opened up the English horizons with his *Tamburlaine* and *Dr Faustus*. Like his contemporary, Shakespeare, he was fascinated by the discoveries of the New World and Old, the tales brought back by the sailors and merchants who thronged the ale-houses. It was a time when the known world was expanding at dizzying speed: every returning ship seemed to bring back fresh and ever more bizarre curiosities, and every departure was packed with ever more ambitious dreamers.

The streets now, by comparison, are deserted. If the children of the poor immigrant families play outside, they stay close to the front door. Further along I found a battered car crouched in the gutter, its bodywork patched and uneven, the back seat a mess of baby clothes, blankets and baggage. Behind it a woman was holding a toddler out over the gutter, her back hunched against the rain. She glanced up, aggressively, then turned away. Deptford was a place to start journeys, I thought, and a place to leave.

I followed the street round: on one side some dismal flats, on the other derelict riverside industrial plots. I wanted to get down to the water and after a short distance I found what I was searching for: a cobbled alleyway leading between high brick walls. It ended at an open barred gate beyond which I could see the great grey Thames sliding past. Steps led down through a deep gulch of green weedy walls to a strip of mud with a curious patch of yellow sand. That surprised me: a warm yellow strip worthy of some far-off and sunnier climate. There were no boats to be seen, no newsprint carriers unloading at Convoy Wharf next door, built on top of Henry VIII's shipyard and now the furthest point to which large vessels penetrate the Thames. There was not even a water taxi or a barge, only the shipwrecked shopping trolleys which, I suppose, is all you need to load up with the spices of the east these days. There was certainly nothing to mark the most historic stretch of river in the world, the place where Drake tied up after his circumnavigation and Elizabeth came to dub him, the place where Martin Frobisher set out for the North-West Passage, and the place where so many India-bound ships, including the first voyage, were prepared.

I had stood there for some time before I realised the gate was not locked. This was the way by which boatmen would have come for centuries: a sketch map of Deptford from 1623 shows it, sneaking down the side of the Great Dock. By that time there were a number of docks and wharves stretching in either direction, though the corner between the Thames and the creek was still largely meadowland dotted with watermills.

I pushed open the gate and went down to the yellow sand. A

[3]

vista of the river appeared: the gantry of Convoy Wharf, the cranes busy over on the far side where West India Dock had once been, and the same Indian gentleman I had seen on the bridge standing on the shingle.

He visibly jumped when I stepped forward. I suppose he thought I had come to rob him, and it was a lonely enough spot to know that a cry for help would not be heard. There was even a wallet there on the sand, empty but for an identity card belonging to an unfortunate Italian.

'I'm looking for the old docks,' I shouted, throwing the wallet down. 'But I can't find much.'

He shook his head. 'You will not,' he said. 'I remember the place as it was, but it's all changed – gone to Tilbury with containerisation.'

I picked my way across towards him. There were some big old timbers embedded in the mud here, relics of an old slipway perhaps. On the shingle were pieces of clay pipe: I bent down and picked up a bowl and mouthpiece. There were spikes of gnarled iron too, rivets from wooden ships.

'You worked here?'

The rain had stopped suddenly and the river, which had been dulled with it, now began to shine, like a clouded window that is wiped.

'Not exactly.'

'I've just been to see the skull-and-crossbone gateposts at St Nicholas's Church there,' I said to make conversation. 'There's a legend that the pirates copied it for their flag – you know, the Jolly Roger.'

'I myself was once a victim of pirates,' he said, frowning. 'We are Brahmin caste, you see.'

I made some encouraging noises, as if the logical connection was obvious, and prompted him, 'Piracy?'

'My father forbade me to become a seaman because Brahmins are forbidden to cross the sea. But post-war we were full of socialism and equality.'

[4]

'You ran away to sea?'

'I went to Madras first,' he said. 'Then got a job on deck. It was a wonderful thing – to escape to the sea. I can't tell you how marvellous a business it was. Independence for India, independence for me! But after two years, I went home and my father relented. He said if I had to do it, I should do it properly. So I was sent to college in England to study navigation and whatnot. No satellites in those days, of course. We learned the sextant and astronomy. It's all changed so much: there were no container terminals – I went on rusty freighters, British ships usually. We were carrying to Singapore and on to Hong Kong.' He smoothed his thinning hair back with an odd fluttering gesture of his hand.

'Hong Kong?' I prompted him.

'And the Middle East: Bahrain, Dubai, Muscat. I had a promotion and got myself on board a ship with a Yugoslavian captain.'

He thought for a while, getting events straight in his mind.

'One night off Madagascar, I went up to the bridge to relieve the captain and found him gagged and bound.' He frowned, as if he was seeing it all again in his mind. 'When I untied him, he said that armed men had climbed aboard and forced him at gunpoint to empty the ship's safe. Naturally, there was no trace of them by that time.'

He laughed, shaking drops of water from the end of his nose. 'A year later he retired. Do you know how it worked? He had left the company's money in the local bank at the start of the voyage, then when the pirates "emptied" the empty safe, he kept the lot for himself – $50,000 – a lot of money at that time.'

'So did the pirates ever exist?'

'I doubt it. Not unless we call the captain a pirate. I undid the rope and took off his gag for him. Afterwards I tried to think how he could have done it himself.' He shrugged. 'Possible. He had a cut over his eye too – but that would have been easy to do.'

'It seems a lot of cash for a ship to carry,' I said.

He didn't appear to mind the implication of exaggeration. 'He had everything planned, you see. It is true that normally British

[5]

ships did not carry much cash: they had so many British banks in every port for paying the men. But he chose this voyage carefully for the very lack of outlets – so we had that money, the crew's wages, on board. That is why I was a victim – I lost money from that safe too.'

'Did you stop in Madagascar?'

'Not that time, but once before. There was a tropical cyclone and we had to run for Tamatave on the east coast. Now that was the area for pirates – historically speaking. They had castles and all sorts.' He stamped his feet, looking perished. 'You know, of course, who were the first democrats of the modern era?'

I smiled. 'I think you're going to tell me.'

'The pirates, of course. They elected their leaders, took equal shares in loot, even ate from a common bowl. The great irony of it all is that these criminals, flying their skull-and-crossbones, were not only democrats but they stumbled on utopia.' He chuckled. 'All they wanted was loot – that's a Hindi word, you know – they found plenty of that, but they found paradise too – some of them.'

'Where?'

He flashed a grin at me. 'Oh! Some believe it was at Johanna – Anjouan they call it now – in the Comoros Islands, others say Madagascar, up in the jungles on the north-east coast. I really have no idea where exactly.' He shivered. 'I must be going now – my toes are numb.'

But I was reluctant to let him go. 'Pirates as heroes? Not bloodthirsty cut-throats?'

He made a face. 'Certainly, there were regrettable incidents. Torture, rape and murder.' He drew a breath. 'But there are always black sheep. To themselves, the pirates were heroes, rebels against tyranny. They freed slaves, you know. While your stately homes were being built with the profits of slave trading, the pirates were against it.'

I must have looked sceptical because he pressed on. 'Take the case of Long John Silver. A disabled man kept on as a partner in a voyage. In the Royal Navy he would have been immediately thrown out as a useless cripple.'

'He was fictitious.' The memory of a *Treasure Island* film I had seen in Thailand flitted into my mind: the ugly squawk of the parrot on Silver's shoulder, 'Pieces of Eight!', wondrously translated into a delicate simper in lisping Thai. Could it also be so simple to transmute the heroic fiend into flawed hero? I thought of my boyhood terror when reading of Blind Pew, tap-tapping his way towards the Admiral Benbow inn; a figure that seemed the very embodiment of evil.

'Naturally Stevenson used genuine individuals as models.' He muttered, looking at his feet, 'The chill is penetrating too much. I must go.'

'Do you walk along here often?'

'Very rarely.' He glanced back at the dark gully where the watergate steps began. 'There is a very nice patch of yellow sand over there which I like to see.'

'Do you miss India?'

He laughed. 'No, no, not in the least. I simply like a sandy beach.'

'But England must have been horrible and grey and cold after India?'

'You English. For you a paradise is concerned only with the weather. For me it was equality – freedom from my father's generation. I ran away to find something better. Well, toodle-oo.'

With that he waved a hand and set off around the corner. I turned back towards the river, wishing there could be a boat there waiting to carry me out to an anchored ship, trying to imagine what it had been like 400 years before when the East India ships were setting out: the *Dragon*, *Hector*, *Ascension* and *Susan*. On 13th February, 1601 they departed, setting their faces east without much clue as to what to expect but hardships, danger and possibly, with luck, a fortune and a tropical paradise. Soon behind them had gone the freebooters and pirates, fired up with stories heard in the ale-houses and alleys of Deptford.

[7]

I suddenly felt envious of the Indian gentleman; I envied him that marvellous moment of escape. I knew he was right, of course, and everything was changed now: container terminals and ro-ro ferries are not the same as tramp steamers and Surabaya, Johnny. But I felt an overpowering urge to take to the sea too and follow those pirates to their utopian lair. Until that conversation on the Deptford foreshore, the project had been an historical research idea, a possible investigation into the Honourable Company's first voyage. Now I felt a shot of adrenaline pass through me. This was about something deeper and more exciting: a lost pirate paradise in the remote jungled coasts of north-east Madagascar. Some journeys begin like that: you get on the wrong bus and realise it's the right one after all.

I began to stride along the muddy foreshore, grinning to myself: I wanted to set off immediately. A ridiculous notion as there was not even a rowing boat to be seen. If there had been, I think I would have set off right there and then, probably ending up marooned in Margate.

The sixteenth and seventeenth centuries were undoubtedly the golden age of piracy. For a while, ambitious country gentlemen could play at poachers, dashing off to the Caribbean in order to plunder the Spanish Main. These were the privateers, often given dubious letters of marque by their monarch in return for a share in proceeds; they were certainly not men who had cast themselves free of society's restraints.

The true pirates, however, were exactly that: desperadoes ready to drink the Devil's health, damn the king and laugh in the face of death. They expected no mercy when captured, and received none, usually finishing up hung in chains along the banks of the Thames at Deptford and Wapping as a warning to those who were tempted to follow.

Even by the standards of the time, they were capable of diabolical cruelty – setting fire to ships full of slaves and sewing up the lips of captives; their lives were short, passionate and often drunken;

their food was as disgusting as their language; their relations with women and cabin boys often forced. And yet, they occasionally showed great compassion and kindness to victims, even more frequently to their own kind. Pirates injured in battle could expect compensation for their disabilities – payments agreed by all the crew before setting out. The matter of who should lead them was also put to the vote. Pirate captains were elected, as was the only other 'officer', the quarter-master. When it came to prize money, these two received no more than a double share, occasionally less, but this was positively egalitarian compared to the Royal Navy where a captain and his officers took half the prize money. The lion's share of what remained went to the Admiralty, often leaving only a few shillings for the ordinary tar.

Wages for the common seaman were also poor: in 1700 an East India Company man sailing east for eighteen months might hope to earn himself £30. In stark contrast are the figures for piratical returns: an average expedition produced a staggering dividend of £500 to £3,000 per man. Risks of death were broadly similar, and though the pirate gave up any realistic hope of returning home, recruitment was never a problem.

If the pirates had discovered that crime and egalitarianism did pay, some went further and issued rousing self-justifications. In the most famous of accounts, Captain Charles Johnson's 1724 volume *A General History of the Robberies and Murders of the most Notorious Pyrates*, I discovered a description of one Captain Bellamy who declares, 'They [the rich] rob the Poor under cover of Law, forsooth, and we plunder the Rich under the protection of our own Courage, had you not better make One of us, than sneak after the Arses of those Villains for Employment.'

His fine words did him no good. After capturing and pillaging the Liverpool slave ship, *Whydah*, in 1717, Bellamy and his crew were wrecked on the Massachusetts coast, the captain drowning with all but two of his 146 fellow Robin Hoods.

According to Johnson, others had more luck. Notably, there was Captain Misson, a French filibuster who opposed slavery

[9]

and favoured equality, democracy and fraternity. 'Every man was born free,' ran his creed, 'and had as much right to what would support him as to the air he respired.' A motto which Misson, no doubt, regarded as covering the large quantities of gemstones relentlessly pillaged from his base on Johanna in the Comoros Islands. Subsequently he moved to northern Madagascar and founded the utopian colony of Libertalia where a common language was invented and a rudimentary parliament installed. This was the place all pirates dreamed of: 'some Place to call their own; and a Receptacle when Age or Wounds had render'd them incapable of Hardship, where they might enjoy the Fruits of their Labour, and go to their Graves in Peace.'

Utopian dreams and Madagascar were no strangers to each other by then. In 1640 a ship's surgeon, Walter Hamond, who had stopped at the island on a voyage east, wrote a tract entitled, *A Paradox Proving That the Inhabitants of the Isle Called Madagascar or St Lawrence (in Temporal things) are the Happiest People in the World.* In this he described a 'sluggish and slothful people' who scorn gold and silver and habitually go around naked. Like many utopians, Hamond was very interested in nudity – purely as a side effect of pre-Fall innocence.

'And what are the effects of this monstrous pride in Apparell, but the Ruine of many noble Families, the decay of Hospitality, the ushering in of Oppression, Bribery, and Extortion, Theft, Murder, Gousening and Deceit, and in the end Beggary, or which is worse, a death with Ignominie.'

It was sufficient to make a dreamer burn his breeches and head east. Hamond went on to exort his fellow countrymen to do just that (head east that is). Madagascar was, he claimed, a place where scarcely a stroke of work was required, such was the eternal abundance of the natives' land. He suggested, therefore, stealing it from them. Unfortunately, the 140 individuals that followed Hamond's advice lacked the wily determination of the pirates, dying in droves at the hands of the natives before a dozen survivors were rescued. Nevertheless, other tracts appeared, exhorting Englishmen to head for the island, and in 1688 Henry Neville, published the utopian idyll, *Isle of Pines*, a narrative larded with nudity and polygamous sex on an island mercifully uninhabited prior to the arrival of the shipwrecked utopianists.

Here was a problem even piratical dreamers were often up against: sitting tenants. Misson's Libertalia was to learn the lesson in a brutal and sudden manner. The idyllic socialist community of peace-loving pirates was abruptly brought to an end by an attack from the interior, wiping most of them out (though not the leaders – they didn't take egalitarianism too far). No trace of the settlement has ever been found and some experts now say a search is worthless because Misson never existed, neither did Libertalia, nor the universal language, nor the pirate parliament. It was all invented by Captain Johnson, and Johnson did not exist either; he was invented by Daniel Defoe.

There is certainly something ephemeral and untrustworthy about pirate history: Stevenson, Barrie and Hollywood have done their best to undermine any solid ground, and the hard facts have a habit of disappearing behind a hazy screen of wishful whitewash and unashamed embellishment. Quite simply, it is difficult to catalogue the excesses of pure evil when the image is of Errol Flynn in tights, prancing across the quarter-deck as Captain Blood.

This phenomenon, however, is not recent: it began at the very time the pirate golden age was drawing to its close in the early 1720s, its progenitor being Daniel Defoe, occasionally masquerading (but there are no hard facts on that either) as Captain Johnson. In fact, Defoe rarely signed his own works, being by nature and necessity a secretive man. Of 500 works ascribed to him, less than a dozen had his name on the original title page.

After several days' reading, I felt Defoe's presence as an almost palpable force. He stood before me, periwigged and powdered, an amused expression playing across his face. When he had produced *Robinson Crusoe* in 1719, it was as an account by the castaway himself; a year later came *The Life, Adventures and Pyracies of the Famous Captain Singleton*, again purporting to be written by the hero himself. Whole chunks of pirate history, it is alleged, were created by Defoe to further his own subtle ends in dissenting politics. The speeches of Captain Bellamy, and Misson too, were thinly disguised assaults on the English Establishment by one of its own. With a delicate flick of his pen he had forever linked pirates to our notions of outlaw heroes and, incidentally, turned the solid ground of maritime criminal history into an ocean of uncertainties.

The atlas saved me. It often does. Ever since childhood I have liked to look at maps, not as sources of information but as you might look at a picture, searching out interesting details, tracing routes through swamps and mountain ranges. My father had an atlas from his childhood which contained all sorts of countries which no longer existed by the late 1960s. There seemed no reason to link that colourful and carefully annotated diagram with any form of reality; I had no conception of what London looked like, much less Northern Bechuanaland. In particular, I liked the tribal names stretched across vast tracts of Africa. On the border of Anglo-Egyptian Condominium and Belgian Congo it read, 'Niamh-Niamh', and many years later, as a teacher in a bush school on the very same border, now transformed into that of Sudan and Zaire, I discovered that *niamh-niamh* was a phrase in the local Azande language meaning 'those people over there'.

This had not prevented the wholly imaginary Niamh-Niamh tribe from achieving some prominence during their heyday. Said to be inveterate cannibals and sorcerors, they were difficult to contact, hiding behind a haze of cartographical clangers of the 'Here be Dragons' kind. Pathologically shy of explorers, especially the map-making variety, they had slowly retreated in the face of improving knowledge, their numbers dwindling. Finally, a certain Reverend Canon, a missionary with a linguistic flair, made a dictionary of Azande and in so doing casually exterminated the brutes.

Unlike the Niamh-Niamh tribe, the pirate utopians had no legend printed across their territory – the south-western Indian Ocean. Neither were there ruined fortifications marked, castles or lonesome lookout towers. I did wonder if my Indian gentleman might have been hoaxed by an eighteenth-century genius.

And yet, looking in the atlas at the bay of Antongil in the far north-east of Madagascar, I discovered a small settlement whose name was marked as Rantabe. It triggered a memory of something I had read and I quickly went back to Philip Gosse's classic 1932 volume, *The History of Piracy*. There he mentions a pirate called John Plantain who had sailed east in 1719 with the notorious Edward England. Plantain had gone on to Madagascar and founded a settlement where he kept several native wives in fine silks and diamonds, plus a private army. This place, Gosse informed me, was known as 'Ranters Bay'.

Ranters Bay/Rantabe – I was unsure if this was the usual happy haze of Hollywood descending on me or not, but the ranters had certainly existed. They appeared in the 1650s, believing themselves incapable of sin – something they set about disproving with a vengeance, at least in the eyes of their enemies. Without a doubt they were the type of people to head out in search of utopian dreams, as were the dozens of other visionary sects thrown up by the English Civil War. But it was a tenuous link with the reality out there in Madagascar: historians noted the likeness in name and debated the democratic nature of Malagasy pirate settlements. None, however, appeared to have gone and looked for themselves, inspected ruins, or searched for descendants.

On the atlas, I marked in pencil a sea route that began at Deptford and ended at Rantabe. It touched land at St Helena, Cape Town, wriggled through the islands off Mozambique, landed in Misson's base in Johanna – now Anjouan – and rounded northern Madagascar. It was immense, at least to a landlubber, but at the end I could imagine some circle of thatched huts beneath the jungle-covered walls of a forgotten fort and old men who remembered tales their grandfathers had told them of

[13]

a pirate ancestor who had built this paradise for them to live in.

Having hatched the idea of a sea journey to remote parts of the Indian Ocean, the splendid paucity of knowledge I possessed was painful. I telephoned a friend who told me of an American sea captain who ran a tugboat in the Aral Sea. When off-duty, he locked himself in his cabin and penned erotic novels. 'They're awfully successful,' she had said. 'But strange. The last one had the hero nailing his lover's private parts to the kitchen table – and that was page one.'

The American sea captain was happy to talk. 'I ran away to sea,' he told me. 'Always wanted to. True romantic.'

This was exactly what I wanted to hear, and it got better. 'How old were you?'

'Thirty-eight.'

The same age as me. Trying to sound convincingly familiar with the ocean, I told him my plan to follow the trails of the early explorers and pirates around the Cape and into the Indian Ocean. 'Do you get seasick?' he asked.

'Never.'

'Have you been out in real weather on the real ocean?'

Real weather? Real ocean? Who was he kidding?

'I went by dhow once – from a place near Mukalla in Yemen to Socotra.'

That journey was my pride and joy. That had been real ocean. Three days, I would tell anyone (well, the journey spanned three days), on an open boat across the Indian Ocean to a remote and unvisited island. One advantage of the tale was that few people had heard of Socotra, even fewer were in any position to question the nature of the journey or know that we had experienced nothing more than gentle swells. But the American sea captain knew.

'Socotra!' He snorted dismissively. 'That's sheltered, not real ocean. Gulf of Aden. I mean real ocean like Australia to Cape Town.'

'Er, no. I haven't been anywhere like that.'

He gave a little chuckle, it was a chuckle I was to hear a lot of over the following months: the kind of mirthless clacking real sailors deploy when they watch the needless death by drowning of a greenhorn – and all through his own goddamned ignorance. 'Now that is real ocean. I was in Perth only a few months back and they wanted me to go on a freighter across to Durban in South Africa and I said NO.'

'No?'

'The ship was unseaworthy. You be careful, now. Lots of ships are unseaworthy and they just disappear.'

'How do you tell if it's a bad one?'

'Experience.'

And how does one gather such experience, I wondered, by sinking a few times?

'You get a feel for it.'

I tried a more practical approach. 'Can you tell me how I go about getting on ships? I mean, if I'm in somewhere like Durban or Maputo?'

'They don't take people,' he said emphatically. 'Those days are gone. Round the world by tramp steamer, travelling steerage, working your passage. It's all gone: the insurance people killed it by demanding high premiums on non-crew.'

There was a long silence.

'But, if I get to know a captain . . .' I had a vision of myself in a sleazy portside bar, chatting to a sea-grizzled salt.

There was more silence in which I imagined the mocking 'ping' of tobacco juice hitting the saloon bar spittoon. 'They don't carry life-saving equipment for non-crew. Boats are run like businesses nowadays. There's no spare capacity. Even if the captain wanted to take you, even if you paid him, even if you slept with him, he wouldn't take you because he'd be worried you'd stub your big toe and sue for a million dollars. It's happened.'

More silence.

'So I can't do it?'

'Nope.'

[15]

'Not a hope?'

'No.' He sighed. 'Well, I guess you might find a captain somewhere ... but I doubt it. I did it, but it was possible in those days – not now.'

Quite literally then, I had missed the boat.

I cannot really recall much of what we said after that: I felt light-headed and sick, I felt more than a bit foolish, I felt like my privates had been nailed to a kitchen table.

'Well, Kevin,' he said eventually, 'I have to go and pack. I'm off to Bhavanagar in Gujarat to pick up a boat. I wish you the best of luck. Take care now.' And he was gone.

I didn't give up entirely at that point, but I came pretty close. The thought of arranging transport through official channels, contacting head offices of shipping lines and so on, filled me with dread: nothing could have been further from the spirit of the pirates or my own love of serendipitous travel.

I toyed, very briefly, with the possibility of buying a yacht and setting out; someone offered a World War Two amphibious landing craft which needed 'minor' welding repairs. I was floundering. I telephoned my sister who had gone to live in Pretoria a few weeks before and told her I would not be arriving, as promised, on a tramp steamer in Table Bay.

'There are no ships in Deptford,' I explained, 'only shopping trolleys. And all that romantic stuff about smoky old freighters out of Table Bay is impossible because of the insurance men.'

She ignored the excuse. 'Fly to Durban,' she suggested.

'It's all containerised these days. They don't want passengers.'

'You've been too long in England,' she said, rather archly as I had spent most of the previous fifteen years in Africa and Asia, while she had been gone almost a month. 'They're not so hidebound here: people are hopping on tramp steamers all the time.' This was a transparent lie, but we both wanted to believe it. I suppose all journeys are an act of will, an expression of belief, and implicit in the planning of them is a hope that the ordinary truths of one's life will be overturned.

[16]

'Just go,' said the voice from Pretoria, 'I mean come. Skip Deptford.'

'And the whole of the Atlantic,' I added, warming to the idea. I was a northern European, the Atlantic was a grey and forbidding entity, the Indian Ocean was aquamarine and welcoming. It was a myth to lay alongside the others, despite all the sailing manuals which warn that the Indian Ocean is the most inhospitable and dangerous.

'Get to Africa – it'll start making sense here.'

After putting the telephone down, my hopes were renewed. Perhaps I would do it after all: head out east on slow boats, not religiously following the trails of the pirate hordes, because I would necessarily have to go where my luck took me. But I would find a way up the African coast and across the ocean to the Comoros and finally Madagascar, searching out what was left of those early dreams and the pioneers who followed. They had had their utopian myths of freedom, equality and nudity, while I had blue seas, pirate ancestry and tramp steamers.

PART ONE

MOZAMBIQUE

2

Captain Carvalho

The Portuguese made the breach through which the jackals raced to get their fill . . .
> J.H. Plumb's introduction to Boxer's
> *The Portuguese Seaborne Empire*

At the entry into the channel of Mozambique, we encountered a dreadful storm, with excessive gusts of wind, during which we lost sight of our admiral, and could never hear of him nor his ship more . . . Four days after this unfortunate separation, we had a tremendous clap of thunder at ten o'clock one morning, which slew four of our men outright, without speaking one word, their necks being wrung asunder. Of 94 other men, not one remained untouched, some being struck blind, some bruised in their arms and legs, others in their breasts, so that they voided blood for two days: some were as it were, drawn out in length as if racked. But, God be praised, they all recovered, except the four men who were struck dead.
> Edmund Barker's account of the 1591 English voyage east

Durban is one of the world's great harbours: a broad sweep of optimistic architecture curls around it, all curvaceous art deco lines and a boulevard of palm trees. On the other side, just beyond the railway tracks and the jazzy arts centre, lies the anchorage.

There were at least two dozen ships tied up, but the harbour was vast and getting around them not easy. A less strenuous prospect was to walk purposefully past the security gate, climb the seven floors of the port control tower and ask.

I emerged in a large control room manned by two middle-aged white officers dressed in naval uniforms. On the wall was a large plan of the harbour, phones were ringing, lights flashing on panels, and out the large windows was a stunning view of the entire area.

The harbour is entered between two moles, via a narrow passage which then opens out into a glorious sheet of calm water. As I looked down I could see that on all sides there were wharves and warehouses, cranes were busily unloading, railway wagons being shunted, men driving forklifts and pick-ups, others lounging on broken pallets smoking. A Panamanian freighter had just arrived, its decks stacked impossibly high with containers, the hull and superstructure streaked with rust like the claw marks of some wild animal from which it had narrowly escaped. The ocean out there was dangerous: sudden swells and freak waves up to sixty feet high have been wrecking ships for a long long time – a Sumerian coin was once dug up in the city, probably as a result of an ancient tragedy.

The two men were eyeing me suspiciously.

'Howzit?' said one.

I edged forward. 'I'm not sure if I've got the right place. I'm a writer, from England, and I'm doing a book about the Indian Ocean.'

There was a silence. They exchanged a glance. I pressed on.

'I want to get to Mozambique or Madagascar and I'm looking for a boat.'

There was a longer silence.

'I think you mean a ship,' said one of them.

'Oh, yes, I mean a ship! I'm trying to make my way by ship . . . to Mozambique . . . or Madagascar.'

They grunted. One went back to his control panel, the other drummed his fingers. 'Writer, is it?'

'Yes.'

He nodded, as if to say, we get them in all the time, wanting lifts on boats when they mean ships, to China and God-knows-where, asking about tramp steamers and old sea dog captains who can dish out the vile rum and tall tales. I waited, expecting to hear those dreaded words: insurance men.

He stood up and went to the window. The harbour was a pure, unblemished span of blue as though a hole had been cut right through the earth and we could see the sky beyond. '*Shearwater*'s in.' He pointed out a small beat-up freighter that looked about to drop through the hole. 'But she's not going anywhere for a bit.'

He went to the phone. 'I'll give Ashley a ring at Tallships.'

There was a brief conversation and he put the receiver down. 'Okay, what you do is head out the port to that tall building on the waterfront – see it? With the restaurant on top? Ask for Tallships and then for Ashley. Talk to him about the *Toto* – he might have something for you.'

We chatted for a while about my hope to reach north-east Madagascar by sea and, for the first time, I met someone who was positive. 'Sure, you can do it. May take some time, but you can do it. Try Ashley – say Dick Dawson at Port Control sent you.'

Ashley was not in the Tallships office when I arrived, but his colleague Glynn looked after me.

'It's true we have a ship called the *Toto*. She runs up to Bazurato in Mozambique with supplies for the fishing fleets.'

'Could I go with her?'

'I don't see why not. I'll have to ask the boss, of course.'

My heart leapt. 'What I want to do is get to somewhere like Bazurato and then hop up the coast until I find a ship across to the Comoros.'

He looked confused. 'But the *Toto* doesn't land,' he said. 'She supplies other ships and comes back.'

I returned to earth. 'Doesn't land?'

[23]

He saw my crestfallen expression. 'Look, I'll try and raise Ashley on the radio for you.'

I stood waiting by his desk, wondering what I could do to help my predicament. There was nothing on his computer screen. Next to it, the various lading bills and manifests that were stacked up made no sense. Idly, I moved one aside. Underneath was a fax and one word at the top caught my eye: *SONGO*, destination Beira and Quelimane. But now Glynn was back. 'Ashley's out till one o'clock. Why not come back at three?'

I nodded. 'Okay, fine.' And then, almost as an afterthought, 'I don't suppose you deal with a ship called the *Songo*?'

His eyebrows shot up. 'Of course! The *Songo*. She goes to Mozambique. And Carvalho, the master, he's a great guy. Portuguese but speaks reasonable English.'

'Is she in at the moment?'

'That's the other thing: she's arriving later this morning. Look, come at three and Ashley could take you over to meet Carvalho. I can't promise, of course, she's not a vessel I normally deal with.'

At three o'clock precisely I was there waiting for Ashley, a cheerful young man in a windcheater. 'I've spoken to Carvalho on the radio already,' he said as we drove towards the port. 'And he said he'll see you.'

The *Songo* was tied up next to a freighter from the Seychelles, her twin cranes busy unloading rusty old steam engines. Ashley raised his voice above the noise of the quayside. 'Some English guy buys them for his steam railway in England and Carvalho gets them out from Beira for him.'

There were traction engines too and bits of ancient machinery, all twisted and corroded. We went up the gangway, holding on to the handrail as one crane swung a container out and the boat heeled over. The *Songo* was about 250 feet from stern to bow with a long cargo deck leading back to a block of cabins topped by the bridge. The steps up were at the stern beside the funnel.

'Carvalho's a bit of a character,' said Ashley, opening a heavy rubber-sealed steel door and stepping over the lintel. 'But a good guy.'

The passageway was neat and clean with a print of an Arab dhow on the bulkhead. He pulled the door shut, securing it with two iron levers. The noises of unloading faded and were replaced by the steady hum of generators below. Ashley went to a door and knocked. There was a shout.

Carvalho was sitting on a bench seat presiding over a table of chaotic paper. Smoke curled up from a brimming ashtray that was balanced on a teetering pile of compact discs; in the corner was a case of Johnny Walker and a broken video vomiting wiring over a television set.

'*Boa tarde! Boa tarde!*' He shouted, jumping to his feet. He was slightly built, late forties with greying wiry hair and the grin of a poker-player throwing down aces. 'You are the writer, yes? Come in. Come in, please.'

We shook hands and he bulldozed some paperwork off the bench so we could sit.

'Kevin here is hoping to get up to Mozambique,' Ashley said. 'As part of the book he's doing.'

Carvalho spread his arms and winked. 'So you come to me. Of course you do. I know this coast better than anyone. Who was it sailed into Maputo, Beira, Vilanculos, Quelimane, and Pemba during the war? Who was the only one to do it? Without charts sometimes. Carrying guns in and refugees out!' He tapped his chest, laughing wickedly. 'It was I. José Carvalho.' He leaned forward and taking a packet of Peter Stuyvesant from a half-finished carton tossed it across the desk to me. 'Here. Smoke.' He lit another one himself and puffed contentedly.

I told him a little of my plan: hopping up the coast, stopping in the historical ports, then across to the Comoros and Madagascar in search of pirate haunts. I think I played up the Vasco da Gama angle a little: 1497, the first voyage to India, Portuguese sailor makes history – that sort of thing.

[25]

Ashley gave me a little smile of encouragement. 'So what do you think, Carvalho. Could you take him?'

'No problem! We sign you on as crew, then whenever I want to get rid of you, I sack you for insubordination!' His roar of laughter broke down into a hacking cough. 'Sailor life is very bad, Kevin. I am warning you. Too much cigarettes at sea. Too much stress. Too much going to nightclub on shore.' His grin could have charmed the hubcaps off a Cadillac. 'Last night the crew took me. It was terrible. Maybe in Beira and Quelimane we show you the sailor life. The girls! *Aipa!*'

'Will you stop in Maputo?'

'This voyage, no. We do Durban-Beira-Quelimane.'

'Is Durban your home port then?'

He sat back with a sigh. 'No, no. Our base is Quelimane. The best place in Mozambique – really. It is up a big river – you will see. Zambezi delta. Where Vasco da Gama first stopped.' He pronounced the name in the Portuguese style, with a 'sh' instead of an 's'. 'Very dangerous to sail, but I do without a pilot. Only I know that river good enough. I like to go up at night – twenty kilometres in the moonlight when the river is all silver. Then put down the lifeboat and go home. No bureaucracy, no paperwork – not like this. Hey! Sorry for all this untidiness. I don't like paperwork, you know.'

Ashley was getting restless, thinking of all his own paperwork back at the office. I asked when the ship would sail.

Carvalho sighed. 'Ah! These people. I don't know. Maybe tomorrow. I hope tomorrow. You go to Ashley tomorrow morning for passport stamp – yes? Then come and take your lunch here. Bring your luggage. We will see.'

Able Seaman Rushby was duly signed on next morning but when I reached the *Songo* it was apparent that the ship was not ready. Carvalho was striding up and down in his white overalls, shouting and gesticulating but the stack of containers waiting to be loaded was no smaller. 'Come tonight, Kevin,' he shouted, his hands held

[26]

out in a despairing gesture. 'Maybe we sail. Ten o'clock.' He turned away to let fly a stream of Portuguese invective at a forklift driver who had stopped work. A cigarette changed hands. The forklift began moving.

I spent the day exploring Durban: the Botanic Gardens with its boababs and cycads, the markets with their cheap African carvings – all that skill and effort put into making salad servers – the suburbs of gracious colonial homes, their sides tickled with palm trees, bougainvillea and hibiscus. For lunch I ate a bunny chow – Durban's contribution to world cuisine: a half white loaf scooped out and filled with curry.

At ten o'clock that night I was back at the port, but this time it was a very different place: the shadows seemed threatening, the wharf which had thronged with people during the day was deserted. The *Songo* was quiet, the engines switched off. One of the Mozambican crew was keeping watch, warming his hands under his armpits and stamping his feet. I hadn't thought of it as cold, but this was South African winter and he was obviously feeling it.

I found Carvalho in his cabin with a bottle of whisky on the table. Since my last visit the place had filled up: there were piles of disposable nappies, a mattress, a case of wine, and a further stack of cds. The pile of chaotic paperwork had grown too.

'Kevin! My friend – I am sorry. Maybe tomorrow. But come in and take something. Whisky or beer?'

He lifted a telephone and spoke in Portuguese then got up and put a Bob Dylan disc on. 'My music is old – like me!'

There was a knock at the door and one of the crew came in, a big unsmiling Mozambican carrying a tray of glasses and a bowl of ice.

'This is Machavo, the cook.'

The man turned and went out without smiling.

Carvalho poured a stiff measure of whisky. 'Will you take ice?'

'No, thanks.' But he had a cube held in the tongs.

'I like you to try. This is my ice – from Quelimane. You know

[27]

Quelimane is a very hot place and all the water is brown. The river is brown, the tapwater is brown, but I struggle and struggle and I make ice – clean white ice.' He dropped it in the whisky.

Bob Dylan was singing about driving west across America.

'You have an ice-maker there?'

He began to talk about his dreams for Quelimane, how he had bought some land and would build a big house surrounded by coconut trees and mangoes. His eyes shone. I asked him when he had first come to Africa.

'I was in Angola. That was my first experience. In Luanda they came and told me to beware of enemy frogmen coming to put limpet mines on the ship. So I asked how to catch these enemy frogmen and the soldier took out a hand grenade and threw it down into the water next to the ship. There was a huge explosion. They said: "That is how."'

'And when did you come across to Mozambique?'

'In the 1980s. The war was on and nobody would sail into these small ports, but I saw there was a demand for general cargo. I remember carrying those big guns – Stalin's Organ – for Frelimo. We went right out into the channel, in international waters, then up the river at night. I was afraid, you know, because the rebels might capture the ship and take the cargo, so it was all top secret. When we docked the Frelimo general came on board and sat here drinking vinho verde with me. I told him I had been very careful, but he just laughed, "Carvalho, everyone knows what you are doing: everyone in the town – even the rebels."'

'And you liked the place immediately?'

'As soon as I saw it. You will see. Mozambique is a place where you can build your dreams.'

I thought of all the early Portuguese pioneers: clearing the jungle and building vast ramshackle empires of plantations and slaves. Five hundred years later, men like Carvalho were still sailing in around the Cape, their heads full of crazy notions.

'Tell me about the ice.'

'When I used to sail in Scandinavia there was ice all around.

[28]

We would follow the ice-breaker into Stockholm and it was so cold the ice would be closing up behind the breaker – you had to keep very close to it or you would be trapped.' He laughed. 'So much ice then, and when I came to Quelimane there was nothing – just heat, mud, mosquitoes, and I dreamed of having pure ice, just to have a cold drink. So I bought two ice-making machines here in Durban and took them up there. One day I will supply all of the region. Every petrol station will sell my ice, every bar.' He took another cube and leaning across the table dropped it in my glass. 'But it is very difficult. First you must filter the water, for silt and for bacteria, then it needs electricity and transport which needs petrol, and then places to sell and people with money to buy. Mozambique is a poor country and now is only the beginning of my dream.'

We sipped our drinks thoughtfully. He gestured towards the paperwork. 'Now I have to work – make the cargo plan.'

'Is it complicated?'

He grinned. 'You have many containers of different weights and some trucks and other things – general cargo. Then you have to balance the ship correctly and take into account what will be discharged in Beira, what might be loaded. Then you have to think of the draught: the sandbar at the river mouth is very shallow and if we are low in the stern we may hit it and damage the propeller or the rudder, or run aground. Also there may be a swell and the tide can run at seven knots. When you put more speed on the engine, the stern will dig down a little in the water.' He shrugged. 'So, yes, a little bit complicated.'

I finished my drink. 'I think I'd better let you get back to your calculations. What time shall I come tomorrow?'

'At nine. We will see. At nine I will ask for a pilot, then we wait for him. When he comes we can go.'

At the door I paused. 'One last thing, Captain. Will I . . . er . . . I mean, will you want me to work? It's just that I don't know anything about ships.'

He gave his cheeky grin. 'We'll find some overalls for you. You could wash a deck, couldn't you? Or paint the hull?' I nodded, laughing, unsure if he was joking or not. We said goodnight and I went down to the quayside.

'Go with God,' said the watchman, and I walked briskly back to the town, avoiding the deep shadows.

The following morning at nine I found the quayside clear of containers and Carvalho on the bridge with Eduardo, the Portuguese chief engineer who spoke a little halting English. His skin was pale and sweaty from the engine-room.

'The pilot is coming soon,' said Carvalho, 'then we will go.' He was pacing up and down, chain-smoking, desperately keen to be off.

On either side of the bridge was a door leading out to a wing, an open projection shaded with blue tarpaulin. From there I had a clear view of the well-laden cargo deck where the crew were doing last-minute checks. I waved to a harbour cruise that was going past, pretending to be looking over my ship when all the time I was acutely aware that I was the only person with no duties to perform.

It was a beautiful day: clear blue sky and a moderate breeze. A few sailing skiffs were clipping back and forth across the harbour, but none of the commercial vessels were moving. The hours went by. Carvalho came and went, muttering angrily about 'tea-breaks' and 'paperwork', checking over the figures that the Mozambican chief mate was calculating. The tension grew. I could feel their urgency to get away, to be out at sea, away from the bureaucrats and time-wasters, but still the pilot did not come.

By midday Carvalho was banging his fists on the chart drawers. 'Three and a half days to Beira and if we delay here much longer we will arrive too late to discharge on Sunday and be stuck there till Tuesday! Pah!'

He strode out on to the wing, lighting yet another cigarette. A tugboat had positioned itself off the bow, waiting to pull us out.

But Carvalho waved his hands at them. 'Why I want you? I like to drive my own ship! I am the captain! Grarrrr!'

The tug ignored him which only enraged him further and dashing into the wheelhouse he grabbed the radio and shouted at them to 'Stand off!' The tug, sensing danger, backed away a few metres. Carvalho barrelled out on to the wing and threw his cigarette butt towards them, then lit another and stamped back inside. Catching my eye, he winked. 'Sometimes I am crazy a little bit.'

Fortunately for the safety of the tugboat, the pilot now arrived. The door to the internal companionway was thrown open and he came springing out on to the bridge, a tall bearded man in immaculate whites carrying a life jacket and a walkie-talkie.

He barely had both feet on the bridge before Carvalho had his men casting off. The pilot went out on to the quayside wing, nodding approvingly. 'We don't need the tug; the breeze and the bow thruster will take you out.'

Carvalho gave a little smile. The pilot spoke into his radio, 'Stand off, Jeff, we won't be needing you.' The tug set off across the harbour kicking up an impressively truculent bow wave.

The chief mate was at the controls, not some large old wheel of brass and mahogany but a rather weedy joystick of the sort normally found on children's computer games. I went out on the bridge wing and saw to my surprise that we were already ten metres away from the wall. Suddenly I was underway: I don't think I'd really believed it was happening until that moment. It all seemed too improbable, too sudden and too easy. I had been expecting the engines to die away and Carvalho to shrug and say sorry, Kevin, I've had a call – insurance men, you understand. But there it was: ten metres – no, fifteen – of saltwater between me and Africa. I was definitely moving.

Now I felt that dark moment of anxiety that all big journeys should have as they begin. South Africa had seemed so familiar and undemanding, with its supermarkets, fast cars and English language spoken. Now the great unknown lay ahead: the Africa of land mines and roadblocks, breakdowns and sinkings. In South

Africa you could trust in the things around you, the cars and buses, the telephones and computers; now I was going to places where such objects failed, or had no spares, or were obsolete. I was going where the safety net had a hole in it and you could only trust in the people.

I stepped back inside the wheelhouse. The pilot's radio was crackling. 'MV *Huda*. I'm bringing your pilot out. ETA three minutes.'

'That's my colleague going out,' he said. There was a thunder of rotors and a white helicopter shot over the bow heading out towards the ocean. 'The chopper'll pick me up on his way back.'

We were turning now, moving into the long narrow channel that led out between the two moles to the ocean. I could see white caps out there. Away to the left stretched the Durban seafront: a long yellow strip of sand backed by tall modern buildings. As we moved into the throat of the harbour exit, the pilot pointed out two concrete blocks on either side. 'Those were put there in the war to hold submarine nets. When I was on the ships we used to have a German captain who'd been in the U-boats.' He straightened up into a mock military stance. '"During ze war I was sinking more zan sixty of your ships here!"'

We were now into the passage between the two moles. On the left there was a rough track on top where lovers had parked their cars.

'Is it a dangerous spot? I mean even without U-boats.'

'Oh, yes, one of the worst. We get swells of up to eight metres and lots of dangerous currents. One ship lost some containers here not so long ago – all full of sports shoes. When they hit the beach they burst and all the shoes got mixed up. Half the population of Durban were running up and down the beach shouting at each other – you can imagine: "Size nine Adidas, right foot. Anyone got a size nine right foot?"'

The helicopter now came shooting in from the sea, banked through 180 degrees behind us and came alongside.

'My taxi,' said the pilot, and slipping his life jacket on, he wished

[32]

us a good voyage and went below. A minute later he reappeared on the cargo deck.

The ship was starting to roll as we closed on the harbour mouth. Out there I could see big swells and the white spray as waves hit the wall. The helicopter pilot gently manoeuvred himself between the two cranes, keeping perfect pace with the ship. A line came down with a yellow harness attached. There were only a few seconds now before we hit the swell. The pilot slipped the harness on and waved. At precisely the same moment that I felt the ship shudder with the shock of a swell, the chopper smoothly lifted away, the pilot waving to us as he was winched up.

There was no time to dwell on the professionalism of that manoeuvre: we were biting deep into the seawater and I had to grab on to the handrail. Sheets of spray were being thrown over the bows. Carvalho stood with his feet apart, hands on hips, frowning slightly and moving easily with the rhythm of the ship: the caged tiger who had paced up and down was gone. There were ships anchored out here and we had to choose a course between them that would allow for tide, current and wind. Cigarette smoke curled around him.

I clambered out on to the bridge wing, feeling clumsy and awkward, having to hold on. Astern of us, Durban's tower blocks were diminishing into the haze. Ragged strings of seabirds were stretched across the sky like fragments of broken necklaces and the wind was beginning to sing in the wires. I couldn't believe that the calm of the harbour could be so quickly transformed and for a moment I was seized with a panic: 'What have I done? Why am I here? Five days of this – I'll never survive.'

But this moment passed and was replaced by excitement. When I went in to escape the wind, Carvalho grinned: 'So, Kevin? Your first voyage, hey? Life will never be the same again.' I had no idea then what he might mean. I had been busy with other people's utopias, scouring old books for evidence of utopian yearnings among the misfits and criminal lunatics who manned pirate ships.

[33]

I hadn't thought of the effect this journey would have on me, but it was Carvalho who started me thinking.

My cabin was next to Eduardo's on the deck above the galley. It was, I soon realised, the ship's hospital – and my bunk was the operating table. Despite this, I had a very comfortable billet. There was a desk and chair, a mirror and handbasin. It was certainly a good deal more comfortable than the East India Company ships of the eighteenth century where passengers were expected to furnish their own quarters and often spent the first few hours on their knees hammering cleats into the deck and lashing their possessions down.

I lay on my operating table and was almost asleep when there was a knock at the door. 'Kevin! Come on. Dinner.'

I looked at my watch and saw it was six. Outside it was almost dark and we were rolling heavily. There was a series of internal companionways running up through the entire block of four levels, each flight of steps with an extra wide door at the top and bottom. Moving around was made easier by the handrails on either side, but I staggered down nonetheless, lurching into the walls and missing the doorhandles. There was the outside door and an iron stairway, but I didn't fancy that in this weather.

The galley was at the bottom of the cabin block. Outside there were access doors to the engine-room, all securely hooked back. Looking down the steel ladders, I caught a glimpse of a tangle of machinery and ducting with panels of lights flashing, most of them red. A crewman in oily orange overalls, his ears muffled, glanced up and waved at me.

The dining table was set for six and the other five were waiting. Carvalho beckoned me over to sit next to him. There was a definite hierarchy to the placing: captain on the end of one bench opposite the door, next to him chief mate and then first mate. Opposite the captain were the chief engineer ('Chief' to everyone), first engineer and second mate. Except, of course, that I was there and so someone had been pushed out to the crew dining area.

As I said a cheerful hello to all of them and eased past Carvalho into my place, I wondered if my casual usurpation had caused any resentment.

The table was laid in a way I was to get used to, for it would be the same for every meal: a stainless steel cutlery rack in the centre, bottles of olive oil and vinegar, large container of salt and a plastic tub of white sliced bread. Wine was reluctantly banished, though compensated for on land.

Carvalho was teasing Castro, the first mate. 'Why we get this bad weather? I tell you: Castro does not pay the girls in Durban. Don't you know the curse of the puta brings stormy weather? *Praga de puta.*'

Eduardo grunted and wagged his finger. 'Don't fuck in Durban.'

'What do you mean: don't fuck in Durban. You don't fuck anywhere! I'm beginning to wonder about you.'

Machavo the cook now appeared with a bowl of soup which he placed before the captain who stubbed out his cigarette. The soup was slopping over the side, so he had to use one hand to balance it, automatically lifting one side as the ship rolled.

'One day we will have bacalhau, Kevin. What do you say in English? Salted cod? It is the Portuguese national dish – with boiled potatoes, oil and vinegar.' He began to spoon soup to his mouth, even though we were rolling sufficiently for the condiments to be put on a damp napkin so they would not slide. 'Or Portuguese sardines. There is nothing like that. We have with us – in freezer. Beautiful! We live well, you know.'

There is certainly continuity in Portuguese tastes. On the ships of Vasco da Gama's fleet, the men's daily rations included a third of a gill of vinegar, one sixth of a gill of olive oil, and one and a quarter pints of wine. Salted cod and sardines were regular dishes. If Carvalho had found himself on one of da Gama's four vessels, he would have been quite comfortable with his rations – while stocks lasted.

He waved his spoon. 'When I was young man, I was playboy, you know. In Portugal. I had no money but I had nice clothes and

[35]

nice girls. I used to walk into five star hotels like they were mine – go and find a room with an open door and take a shower, have a siesta, then go out again!'

Machavo came back with soup for Eduardo, who waved it away. He gave it to the chief mate, but Carvalho pointed at my place and, despite my protestations, the bowl was passed across. Machavo glowered. Looking at his back as he stalked away to his galley, I realised that the man most upset at the upsetting of the hierarchy was the one not included in it.

'But even then,' Carvalho continued, warming to his theme, 'even then, I never annoyed Neptune like Castro does, bringing curses down on the ship.' Castro, chuckling good-naturedly, accepted his soup from Machavo. A cockroach scuttled across the table and up the wall. No one took any notice.

'And he is a Jehovah's Witness,' continued the captain. 'He should know better.'

Castro was nodding. '*Essa é a verdade!* That is true.'

Carvalho tapped my arm. I was trying to eat soup and balance the bowl at the same time. The spoon did not seem to want to go in my mouth. 'This is a dangerous ship. I have Jehovah's Witness, Catholic, Protestant . . .' He began interrogating the others.

The second engineer was a Nazarene Christian; the first a Muslim. 'And sure – there is a Communist here somewhere!'

Machavo came in with a bowl of salad. 'Hey, Machavo. What religion are you? *Qual a sua religiao?*'

Machavo frowned. '*Capitão. Não sou religioso.*' He went out. Carvalho leaned forward conspiratorially. 'I'm sure he's a spiritualist! My God, there will be a war.'

So it went on throughout the meal, but with Portuguese slowly taking over. Most of them could speak at least a little English, but the strain soon told. My own Portuguese was rudimentary, though once I'd got used to the peculiar Portuguese pronounciation – something like a Sean Connery speaking Spanish with a mouth full of salted cod – then my knowledge of French and Spanish would prove useful. My mind drifted away from the conversation, too tired to keep up with them.

I thought of the pirate ships and the huge cast iron cauldron of soup, salmagundi, which they kept on deck. This had been the very symbol of their brotherly equality and freedom from superiors. No seating arrangements required, they all dug in, even a great and famous captain like Bartholomew Roberts, 'Black Bart', who was reputedly caught while tucking into his favourite dish. None of that here on the *Songo*: this was the merchant marine where the captain was king and the officers his courtiers. Try and change it over the cook's dead body.

I didn't mind the hierarchy, nor anything else. I was simply pleased to have made it on board a real ship. I had proved the American sea captain wrong. Without pulling strings, or paying money, or sleeping with anyone, or a single argument with an insurance broker, I had got myself signed on as able seaman. Now all I had to do was avoid any task that involved even the most basic seafaring knowledge and find out where I was going. In all the excitement I had forgotten to check where Quelimane was on the map.

Later that evening I climbed up to the bridge and found Carvalho there alone, plotting our course with a pencil and ruler on an Admiralty chart, his hands lit by the low desk lamp. Behind him the bridge windows were black except for the distant bow light. The instrument panels radiated a soft green glow, like the phosphorescence that the sea sometimes gives. The engines had settled to a low steady thrum and the movement of the ship was more regular. If I concentrated I could stand without holding on to anything.

This corner of the bridge would soon be my favourite haunt at night: there was a leather-topped chart desk with drawers below filled with every chart between Cape Town and Cairo. Carvalho was pencilling in our time as we reached a waypoint – a spot off the coast where we had to alter course slightly.

'These days everything is very easy,' he said, tapping in some figures on the Global Positioning System which was mounted above the chart desk. 'Not like before, with sextant and compass.'

'Do you still carry them?'

'Yes, we have them here, but never used.'

The digital readout on the display showed our course altering, but the speed was dropping too. Carvalho went across to the 'wheel' and moved it gently, taking us off the programmed course. 'I drive my ship,' he grinned, 'not the GPS.'

He came back to the chart and stroked his finger down the coast. 'You see, here we have the main current heading south. But between the coast and the current is a counter-current heading north. If we can find that we make better speed.'

'And how do you find it?'

'In the daylight, sometimes you can see the difference in the water; at night, it is only by feeling.'

The early Portuguese explorers had not known about this counter-current and so had struggled northwards against the Agulhas current. The first to round the Cape of Good Hope, Bartholomew Diaz, found the slow progress disheartened his men, so much so that they refused to continue and he was forced to abandon the voyage at the mouth of the Great Fish River.

Vasco da Gama had better luck, reaching this coast on Christmas Day, 1497, and so naming it Natal. Both captains were probably aware of one terrible danger that could strike at any time – the vast freak waves of up to sixty feet in height that came tearing in from the east. Careful research by the navigators had included many Arab and Jewish texts, some of which had been captured when the North African town of Ceuta fell to the Portuguese in 1415. Among the Arab geographers was one Abu al-Fida who stated that the Arabs had not penetrated further south because of huge overwhelming waves. It was probably from these same Arab sources that the Portuguese got their determined belief that a way around the southern tip of Africa did exist.

Carvalho lit yet another cigarette.

'How did you start?' I asked. 'Were your family sailors?'

'No, no. My father did not want it but I joined a sailing ship and went to Brazil. When I came back I did my examinations and got my first ship – a fishing boat.'

'Did you like the life immediately? No seasickness?'

He laughed. 'The first voyage on the fishing boat was very rough and when we returned to Lisbon my family and friends had organised a big party in an expensive restaurant. I got off the ship and my knees were hard – it happens like that. For months I had had no problem, but once I sat in the restaurant and saw all the food, I felt sick. Before I could even get out of my chair I vomited – all over the table!' He laughed. 'I was landsick. It was then that I knew I would be a sailor.'

He had moved on from fishing boats to a cargo ship, working as chief officer on voyages to the Cape Verde Islands, Angola and Mozambique. 'The captain was German and the crew hated him. One day they came to me and said, "We want you to be captain. Let's throw this German overboard." I managed to persuade them not to do it and the next port we reached, I left the ship.'

He had gone back to Oporto, his home town, and left the sea to start a business. 'But it was Mozambique I could not forget. Always I dreamed of Mozambique. I don't know why – there was something between me and Mozambique. One day a shipping company telephoned me and said they had bought a ship to do general cargo out of Quelimane. If I wanted to be the captain, then I should go to Mauretania and collect the ship – in three days. I closed my business and left everything.'

He went across to the wheel and adjusted our course slightly. On the GPS our speed began to inch up towards nine knots. 'Now we find the counter-current.'

'Was that this ship – the *Songo*?'

'No, another one.' He paused, as if weighing up whether to tell me something. I waited.

'It was wartime, of course,' he said eventually, 'and there were many people trying to move by ship because the roads were too dangerous. One day, off Bazurato, we found ten stowaways in the lifeboat and already we had a full list of passengers. I remember it was seven in the morning when we found them and I was very angry. I said to them, "Now we have no lifeboat for you. If this ship goes down, you will go with it."' The GPS gave a little beep and he tapped one of the buttons.

'During the morning we were cleaning the oil tanks in the engine-room and there was a fault in the gas oil purifier. The temperature went up to 600 degrees and there was an explosion.' He shrugged. 'It was a nice ship but very old. There was no fire-fighting system like on modern ships. The chief engineer and myself used up all the extinguishers and then we could do no more: we had to abandon ship.' He stopped for a while, staring out towards the bow navigation light. 'One of the stowaways fought his way on to the lifeboat before all the others – you know they were useless, all . . .' He waved his hands wildly, miming panic. 'I grabbed hold of him and forced him back. "Women and children first!"'

'And did you let the stowaways on?'

'Oh, yes – I only said there were no places to frighten them. Ha!'

'And what happened then?'

'The ship was burnt out and we managed to get ashore near Monto Bello. I had lost everything. All my personal things were on the ship – it was before I had a house in Quelimane. I had only my shirt, shorts and shoes. The communists were in power then – Frelimo – and they made problems at the inquiry saying it was sabotage. I say no, it was bad luck only. I go crazy a bit.'

'You weren't tempted to give up the sea?'

'I was crazy. I went to work on chemical tankers – the most dangerous ships – the highest fire risks. I had to do it. To destroy any fear.'

'Why?'

He grinned. 'Why?! I am Portuguese – Portuguese man – and I have balls!' He roared with laughter and stalked out on to the bridge wing. I could see the red light of the cigarette as he drew on it. The wind was getting up again, making the awning crack like a whip. On the other bridge wing I stood for a while, looking at the stars. When I went back inside, Carvalho was at the computer working on cargo calculations. I slipped open the chart drawer and found the one for Quelimane.

The town was well up the river, a twisting tangled mass of mangrove islands and tidal sand flats, a swampy place and not immediately an obvious choice to build one's dreams. Perhaps the very nature of its location, inhospitable and inaccessible as it seemed, gave the necessary credentials. I dropped the chart back in the drawer and, leaving Carvalho to his mathematics, went down to my bunk.

The operating table had a low rail along one side to prevent anyone rolling out, and it was needed. I jammed myself in with pillows and noticed that one of them had the faint lingering scent of a woman's perfume, the trace, perhaps, of a last-minute assignation for one of the crew before we had left. I got up again and checked my bag: the bottle of whisky I had brought with me was gone.

3

The Scarlet Sinners

There were among them 3 or 4 girls, very young and very
pretty, with very dark hair, long over their shoulders, and
their privy parts so high, so closed and so free from hair that
we felt no shame in looking hard at them . . .
>   Pedro Vaz de Caminha's eyewitness account of
>   the discovery of Brazil by Cabral in 1500

Whale milk is very rich . . . the only sample I have tried was
very palatable, with a nutty, rather than fishy, taste. It would
have gone well with strawberries.
>   W. Nigel Bonner in *Whales*, Blandford Press, 1980

When I woke it was full light and the ship was no longer rolling.
Breakfast was toast and jam with tea from a Thermos flask. There
was no one else around, not even the cook. I wandered outside and
along the ship's side past the cargo hold towards the bows. There
was nothing to be seen but blue sky and water. A companionway
led up to the forecastle and there the sound of the engine was
almost completely muffled. I leaned over the bow, looking down
at the water where the forefoot, the bulbous prong which resembles
an old-fashioned rammer, was clearly visible beneath the water.
Yet there was nothing in the water, no floating vegetation or

[43]

tendrils of spume to judge our speed by: we appeared to be motionless while golden skeins of silk were conjured from the leading edge, unravelling behind us for mile upon mile.

So remote and unvisited are the specks of land beyond the African coast that castaways have rarely had much hope of rescue. In his book *The Indian Ocean*, the sailor Alan Villiers recorded a tragic case that occurred as recently as the 1930s. An albatross caught in Fremantle was found to have a scrap of tin wrapped around its neck. On it had been crudely punched the following message: 'Thirteen men cast away on the Crozet Islands, send help, for the love of God.' When a ship finally did put in at the lonely outcrop, there was no sign of the men. Presumably they had given up hope and set out in a raft, never to be heard of again.

As I gazed into this horizon, I thought I saw a puff of smoke, or was it a small sail? Then another and another. As one faded away another would appear. It was a further ten minutes before I realised what I was observing: whales – lots and lots of them. They were swimming on the surface in pairs, their tails occasionally giving a languid flop. As we approached, one couple seemed oblivious to the oncoming ship and as I leaned over to watch I heard shouting. It was Carvalho on the bridge wing, waving his arms excitedly. I moved across to catch his words: 'Make love! Make love!'

Then I realised.

The whales gave an audible gasp and sank beneath the surface, just seconds before our large bulbous prong added a certain frisson to proceedings. We had gatecrashed a cetaceous orgy.

For the next hour we steamed right through the thick of it. The whale couples happily wallowing together without expending much energy – displays of athleticism are probably neither medically advisable nor wholly necessary when you have a penis that is eight feet long.

During a lull in the love-making, I went up to the bridge and discovered that we were within sight of the coast once more – a low line of treeless dunes. Carvalho was playing with the course again, coaxing extra speed by using the currents. 'If we had a Portuguese with us, he would say, "What are you doing?" He would want only straight lines. But the Mozambicans understand me.'

'I think you would have liked to be a sailing ship captain.'

'You are right!' He began pacing across the bridge, arms held out from his sides like a gunslinger about to draw on the sheriff. 'I am born in the wrong time. Vasco da Gama, d'Albuquerque, d'Almeida – that was the time.' He held his palms upwards, rolled his eyes to the heavens. 'My God! You make big mistake.'

Suddenly he thought of something and went to the chart desk. 'Look! Here da Gama took water – at Inhassaro. And fifteen years ago I came here, like da Gama, no charts, not knowing the place. We waited until the sun was at our backs and then went forward slowly, using only the colour of the water as a guide.'

He was pointing out a shallow bay behind the Bazurato islands. In da Gama's day it had been a famous pearl-fishing area, now it was a treacherous region of shifting sandbars and snags through which a narrow channel led to the small port of Vilanculos. 'When we dropped anchor, we found the tide had gone and we were surrounded by sand! Oh, it was very nice – just like for da Gama.' At that moment more whale couples appeared, spouting lazy jets of spume. Carvalho dashed out on to the wing, bellowing at them, 'Make love! Yes, you can! Make love!' and roaring with laughter.

Life on the *Songo* had soon settled into a steady round of duties and sleeping punctuated by mealtimes: 8 a.m. breakfast, noon lunch, and 6 p.m. for dinner. The crew was small, only a dozen men, but merchant crews have never been huge: three centuries ago the same number might have manned a three-masted cargo vessel, with all the hefty labour that entailed. In those days, one of the attractions in becoming a pirate was an easier work routine as the ships often had crews six or seven times larger than comparable merchantmen.

Our knowledge of what that life may have been like is limited, but some accounts exist. In 1726 a book was published in London entitled *The Four Years Voyages of Capt. George*

[45]

Roberts, written by the captain himself. This account contains a description of Roberts' experiences while a prisoner of the pirate Edward Low off the coast of Africa in 1721. He paints a picture of an easy, carousing existence, drinking and smoking on deck with few duties except to keep a lookout. It must have seemed extraordinarily attractive to an ordinary sailor, toiling as they did under a back-breaking routine. At mealtimes the pirates behaved 'like a kennel of hounds', Roberts reports, fighting over food, and drinking to excess. The captain had a state room, but anyone might enter at any time and make use of the place, the crew being constantly alert to signs of self-aggrandisement. Presented as a first-hand account, Roberts' story is plausible and the use of mariners' jargon convincing. The problem is that he did not exist: Captain George was another creation of that man much practised in the art of plausible fictions – Daniel Defoe.

It is probably worth establishing at this point some basic facts about Defoe's knowledge of pirates, particularly as he is charged with inventing so many of them. All his life Defoe had an interest, almost an obsession, with low-life criminal characters. While writing for *Applebee's Journal* in the 1720s, he met and interviewed many of 'the scarlet sinners of the seas', some of them as they awaited execution. There were also dozens of written reports in news-sheets and pamphlets available to him, plus court proceedings to witness. Quite simply, Defoe had plenty of material and showed that fine journalistic ability to distinguish, not so much fact from fiction, as what the public would believe from what they would not.

The reality of pirate shipboard life was probably far rougher and crueller than the reminiscences of Captain Roberts would suggest. The men were often so drunk as to be unfit to work. When the Englishman Thomas White was captured by French pirates and carried away to Madagascar, he found himself shipwrecked at St Augustine's Bay simply because his captors ran aground in a drunken stupor. (White, incidentally, decided to 'go on account' himself and had an illustrious piratical career based around the very places I was heading to: the Comoros Islands and Madagascar.)

Gambling was another curse: huge amounts of gold and silver could be squandered in days by a single crew. One particularly dissolute lot managed to lose 260,000 pieces of eight at cards and dice in just three weeks. Despite the obvious possibility of disputes, pirates were addicts to a man and rarely agreed to outlaw gaming. Sex was another matter. Bringing a woman on board was seen to be so potentially divisive and dangerous that they often agreed to make it a capital offence. The question of how and when they slaked their thirsts arises, pirates not being an abstemious lot. In one case they bought a shipload of African slave women and renamed their vessel *The Bachelor of Delights*. In another celebrated instance, when Henry Avery plundered a vessel of the Great Mughal, his men became notorious back in England for raping the women on board. In a long open letter Avery hotly denied the charge, and the one that he had taken his pleasure with a princess in the state room. The men, he said, had taken turns with the women, four or five standing in line, but it was always with consent. Unfortunately for him, however, the attack was a matter of record and the denial was a work of fiction – by Daniel Defoe.

The appearance of the whales had had a subtle effect on the ship, because at dinner talk soon turned to girls. While a cockroach strolled around the edge of my soup bowl, I managed to gather that we were set to arrive in Beira on Sunday evening and, with some luck, I would be dragged off to a seedy nightclub as the prize exhibit. Later that night, I sat at the chart desk on the bridge and leafed through the *Admiralty Pilot* for Mozambique. Beira, it informed me, offered ships a number of services including 'de-ratting'.

The following day passed easily. The captain had organised a barbecue on deck and we were all treated to salt cod, Portuguese sardines, boiled potatoes and salads. There was a bottle of wine for me, the rest had Fanta.

[47]

'Machavo,' Carvalho called the cook over and held the open wine bottle under his nose, 'you can sniff it – that's all.' Machavo laughed with the rest of the crew, but not with me.

By eight o'clock that evening we were a couple of miles off Beira and starting our approach in darkness. On the bridge Carvalho and Augusto, the chief officer, were making final preparations. Although they had done this hundreds of times before, no two landings were quite the same, nor ever easy: Beira has a circuitous and narrow approach through hidden sandbanks, and in addition a powerful current.

I went out on to the wing with some binoculars. The Milky Way and Venus glittered on the water, far ahead were some dim lights and the periodic flash of the Maruti lighthouse. A scan with the binoculars revealed no sign of life in the town, just a spectral orange mist where the thick night air lay under the street lamps. A bat flitted around the bow navigation light. Somewhere in the darkness to the west of us lay the ruins of Sofala, the legendary gold port whose reputation had brought the Portuguese here in the first place, little suspecting that the place had been on the decline for years.

From inside the bridge came the reedy warning signal of the GPS; we began to turn to port, rounding a marker buoy. It was pitch black all around us now, but ahead I could see occasional red and green flashes from a handful of other marker buoys, a bewildering sight because it was impossible to gauge which was nearer. The atmosphere on the bridge now was of intense concentration. With the tide hard against us, our speed had dropped to only four knots and we seemed to be making no headway, only drifting closer to the edge of the narrow channel. The headlamps of a car moved slowly along the waterfront and stopped.

We were moving away from the city now and I could see that it was built on the corner of the point where a river entered the sea. The river mouth itself was huge and we were swinging far out in a loop to the west. A turn to starboard now brought us around towards the city and a pilot boat came out to meet us. Ahead were the derricks and warehouses of the quayside with one other ship tied up.

By the time the rope ladder had been dropped and the pilot clambered up to the bridge, the tension was easing: we had passed the main dangers.

'Go to berth five,' he said to Carvalho who shook his head.

'Why five? Three is nearer.'

The man nodded and Carvalho grinned at me.

We edged closer. Gangs of men appeared, waiting for the ropes to be thrown. Beyond them and the stacks of containers I could see the scabby and broken tower blocks of concrete amidst the trees, a scene both mysterious and menacing: Carvalho had told me that Beira was a dangerous town, a place where walking alone at night could be a fatal mistake.

Our final manoeuvres were perfectly judged. The ropes were thrown and we tied up. I went down and not waiting for the gangplank to be positioned, leapt across the gap and stood, for the first time, on Mozambican soil.

A man wearing shorts, tee-shirt and crocodile-skin shoes greeted me.

'*Boa noite!* You English? Welcome to Mozambique. Welcome to Beira.'

Behind me Eduardo in his oil-stained overalls had also jumped across and I heard him mutter, 'Beira is a 3-d town: dirty, dark and dangerous.'

All sorts of characters had gathered now and Carvalho was busy doing the essential work of any captain who wants to be treated well: handing out bottles of wine and sacks of potatoes to all the petty officials whose signature he might need. It was, however, to no avail. By eleven o'clock he was prepared to admit defeat. 'We will not unload tonight,' he said. 'So we go to nightclub.'

Half an hour later a car appeared and Carvalho, Eduardo and I got in. We drove through the silent dark alleyways of the containers and came to a barrier manned by sleepy soldiers. Carvalho spoke to them and we were allowed out.

[49]

The tree-lined streets were an obstacle course of potholes. There were no pleasantly decrepit colonial villas in this area, only rotting stumps of Stalinist concrete blocks surrounded by packs of scavenging pariah dogs. Light came from a few low-wattage bulbs and the reason for this apparent scarcity of electricity was soon revealed: the Club Oceania.

We saw the glow over the mango trees before we got there, then rounding a corner came face to face with a barrage of shimmering fairy lights. Carvalho and Eduardo began to grin.

Leaving the car at the front entrance, we went up a spiral stairway lined with zebra skin to a lobby where three black men in black suits were asleep on a black leather sofa. A sign read, 'The Millionaires Club'.

'Now, Kevin,' said Carvalho, 'we show you the sailor life.'

A bouncer slid open a door and I stepped inside.

There was a second or two in which I took in the freezing cold air, the dance floor covered in dry ice, the mauve walls and the waiters at every pillar – each with arms folded over his gold spangled waistcoat – but it was only a second. Across the leather sofas and low tables was a bar and at the bar a pack of girls. As I stepped inside they turned and, without a moment's hesitation, they leapt from the barstools and began sprinting towards me.

I heard Eduardo growl. '*Girrrrls!*'

Braided hair lashed the air; there were golden limbs, breasts bouncing inside skimpy tops, teeth – especially teeth. Then they were on me. A mouth went over mine and a tongue darted inside like a hot muscular eel. I almost gagged and pushed her away, but another grabbed me around the waist, a third went for my groin. 'Hi, I'm Nina and I like you.'

I could hear my companions' laughter as they expertly tucked a girl under each arm. Then the music stopped and from the dry ice appeared a vision: a blonde-haired black Marilyn wrapped from throat to thigh in pink chiffon. She swayed gently as she prowled forward, insinuating herself between the sofas, spinning round

[50]

twice, reaching out with a single crimson finger nail like a cat's tongue to touch my lip.

'Hey, Americano,' she breathed. 'I luuurve Americano.'

There was a hiss from the other girls. Marilyn ignored them and moved closer. Her parted lips came up to my ear. I tensed.

'I guess you like sweets,' she whispered. 'So why not unwrap one?'

She pressed the end of the chiffon into my hand and, stepping back, began to unwind, spinning herself out like Cleopatra from a carpet. There was not a single man in the place that was not watching.

With a final flick the chiffon was thrown clear to reveal a tiny mini-dress of knitted silver tinsel. It reached to a whisker below the knicker-line. Her eyes were closed in pleasure and reaching down she took hold of the hem with both hands. There was a gasp from some of the men nearby. Those of them slouched over their drinks at the bar now became upright. Surely she wasn't really going to . . . She did. In a single fluid motion, she swept the mini-dress over her head and tossed it aside.

There was a stunned silence as the truth dawned. Somehow, beneath that figure-hugging creation were concealed a strapless yellow lurex bra and hot-pants.

Carvalho was having difficulty breathing, but he managed to clap me on the back and gasp, '*Cerveja!* Come on. Let's get a drink.'

Our group moved, en masse, to the sofas and sank into them.

'Kevin is a writer,' Carvalho shouted at Marilyn who had settled on the arm of my chair. She pouted.

'Oooh, a r-r-riter. I luurve r-r-riters. I can tell you stories, so many stories.' She laughed and took a long drink from the beer bottle which was handed to her. 'There was a man,' she said, then grabbed my ear lobe with her teeth. I managed to pull it free. 'So sorry,' she giggled. 'My lipstick is your ear-stick.' She threw the pink chiffon over me and I felt a hand sliding inside my waistband. I pulled it out.

[51]

'Tell me the story,' I said.

'This man went to Johannesburg on business,' she whispered. 'And he took his wife. They stayed in a beautiful hotel – five stars – on the fifth floor. And the husband found a man to drive his wife around the city. "Take her where she wants to go," he said to him. So every day the husband went out to work and the wife went out in her car with her driver.

'But in the hotel room next door was a man, and he met the wife and they fell in love. Yes, they became lovers.' She licked some of her lipstick from my ear. 'Like me and you, Americano.'

I drank some more cold beer.

'Every day the wife went out with the driver,' Marilyn continued. 'Then the husband would go to work. But as soon as he was gone, she came back and went to the room to meet her lover. You know, the driver was very angry and decided to tell the husband. But when he tried to say anything, the husband refused to listen. "My wife is a good woman – you do what she tells you." Eventually, the driver could stand no more. He said to the husband, "Okay, you don't believe me, but at least come and look."

'So next morning the husband went out as usual and the lover came around. The driver went and fetched the husband. They stood in the hotel car park and looked up at the fifth floor. Then they saw the wife come out on the balcony with her lover, kissing and cuddling.'

An arm wormed its way behind my back. 'The husband saw them and said, "Oh, my God! It's true!" In a rage he ran up the stairs and kicked open the door to the room. But inside he found only his wife – no lover. So he ran out on to the balcony and looked down. Then he sees a man running across the car park. "That is him," he says and goes back in the room and drags the fridge out on to the balcony.'

She began to mime the carrying of a heavy fridge, heaving it up on to the balcony and dropping it. Then threw herself back in the sofa screeching with laughter.

'It landed right on top of that guy and killed him.'

[52]

'Is that it?'

'No! Then he saw what he had done. "Oh, I killed a man! My wife was unfaithful! I will kill myself." He climbed up on the balcony and jumped off. He was killed too.'

This sent her into renewed paroxysms of laughter. 'Then St Peter was waiting at the Gates of Heaven – you know?'

Not a story, then, but a joke.

'And a man comes up. "What did you do?" St Peter says.

' "I was running in a hotel car park and a fridge landed on me," he says. So St Peter says, "Okay, you can go inside."

'Then a second man comes. "I killed my wife's lover," he says. "Then myself too."

'St Peter thinks and says, "Well, you are a murderer but you felt guilty. Okay, go inside."

Then a third man comes.

' "What did you do?" asks St Peter.

' "I was having an affair with a man's wife. One day he came back home unexpectedly, so I hid in the fridge." '

She doubled up in laughter and at that moment I felt arms grab me from behind and a dark chocolate voice in my ear. 'Hi, it's Nina.'

Marilyn turned and delivered a mighty slap to the back of Nina's head. There was a bellow of rage and Nina dived across the sofa and began to lay into Marilyn. They both fell on top of me, a mass of sharp elbows, hair and teeth. I wriggled out from underneath and crawled away on my hands and knees. Carvalho slapped my back and pointed at the dance floor.

I hid in the dry ice where Carvalho and Eduardo joined me with their girls. Eduardo was talking very insistently into the ear of one girl, a beautiful Zimbabwean in a chestnut silk top. She had that look of all the bar girls – not bored but not interested, her eyes dulled with booze or drugs.

A waiter had managed to separate Nina and Marilyn and they joined us. Two hours, several beers and a strip show later, I met Carvalho coming out of the toilets.

'Kevin,' he said conspiratorially. 'Now we go. See you outside.'

I went down with some trepidation, but the two of them were alone and keen to move out quickly.

'Do you ever take them to the ship?' I asked.

'These girls!' They were genuinely shocked. 'Not for fucking, Kevin. Only parties and some drinks.'

Carvalho was in the front seat and he turned. 'You see Marilyn? Beautiful, isn't she? Well, two years ago she was really beautiful. Now she is too thin. Why is that? Drugs? AIDS? I don't know, but I don't think she will be here after two more years.' He shook his head. 'It is big shame – she was really beautiful – like a supermodel. If she was European or American she might earn big money and be famous. I wish that were true, but she is Mozambican, and here beauty is for sale and they make it into a whore.'

We did not talk after that, watching the dark streets as we manoeuvred around the potholes. When we reached the port gate, Carvalho discovered he had been pickpocketed and his wallet was gone.

At breakfast the evening's events were dissected with great enjoyment.

'We only wanted to take you for a beer and you start fighting with prostitutes. Now they will curse the *Songo*!'

Carvalho told tales from his early years: how a stripper and a girl had fought over him with broken beer bottles in Buenos Aires. Then there was the time in Rio when his crew threatened to Molotov the bar over an inflated drinks bill. Someone else mentioned the time they had painted a Kingston brothel in the ship's colours.

Outside the dockers were unloading our Beira cargo and by midday we were ready – except there was a hitch. The port charges were unpaid and no amount of wine and potatoes could put that right. It was sunset before a fax arrived from Maputo and we were cleared for departure.

The tide was now in full flood, the brown water flecked with foam and sucking greedily at the ship. When we reached the sea,

[54]

it was dark and spitting with rain. A heavy swell was smacking into the *Songo* making her stagger and shake. The gauge on the bridge showed twelve degrees of roll, enough to make walking difficult and mugs of tea spill.

At dawn the next day we passed the Zambezi delta and by lunchtime we were anchored off the Rio dos Bon Sinais waiting for the tide to let us go upriver to Quelimane. The coast was a low smudge of mangroves and we could hear the roar of the breakers. At half past three the anchor was raised and we began to nose our way towards the surf. There was a gap of about fifty yards width marked by a tiny buoy, its flag heeled over in the wind.

Up on the bridge Carvalho was enjoying himself. 'We go straight in towards the beach then turn. There's a sandbar there which catches many ships.'

The breakers were now roaring on both sides and we appeared to be almost surfing, the shore closing in fast. Only a few metres out on either side I could see the pale brown fingers of sand spits, reaching towards us. Then we turned hard to starboard, the wind buffeting us and the sea hissing as great sheets of spray were ripped skywards off the sides. Another turn brought us into the river itself and quite abruptly the tumult subsided.

Soon we were winding among islands of vegetation, the river's true size concealed in all the channels and side courses. For most of the time there was no discernible riverbank, only mangroves, but occasionally there would be a wrinkle of earth and settlements of bedraggled thatched shelters crammed on to those few sodden divots of soil. Most were partially flooded by the tide, their inhabitants standing watching, all of them dressed in a few pitiful rags. Naked children dashed about excitedly, leaping into the water or taking to the dugout canoes – each cut from a single tree trunk and up to thirty feet in length.

At sunset Quelimane appeared on the horizon as a scurf of dilapidated concrete above an unkempt mane of green. To the north, vast plantations of coconuts stretched between the town and the coast, while on the southern shore I could see nothing but a couple of dim lamps. The wharf was already half-filled by a huge Chinese ship loading up with logs and we edged carefully into place beside it, barely fifteen feet between our stern and their bow. Almost immediately, swarms of flies and mosquitoes came rushing aboard.

Quelimane was a quite different town to Beira. That first night I walked into the centre with Eduardo, admiring the art deco curves of the waterfront mansions, all long since run to shabbiness, their gardens overgrown with papaya trees and spindly manioc. The broad tree-lined streets were full of weeds and holes, the walls scabbed with dark patches of algae. Strolling couples here moved at half-speed, through the sultry night air, while huge bats glided overhead like manta rays.

The shops were mainly Indian-owned, selling all the cheap necessities that an impoverished country might demand: batteries, soap, children's clothes, pencils. One was less well-stocked, the window display featuring only babies' feeding bottles, dishcloths and sledgehammers. The majority of the people were dressed in rags: clothes so torn and stained that they looked like old floor cloths. To walk down the street in a clean shirt and trousers felt like an act of supreme arrogance. I had never been anywhere with so many people in complete and abject poverty.

Every few yards we stopped to greet people: all the ladies kissed on both cheeks, all the men shaken by the hand. Our first stop was the municipal swimming pool, which had a bar and an empty pool – a waterless watering hole. On the roof we sat and looked out into the darkness where the river lay.

'This mufereira tree next to the swimming pool is Vasco da Gama's tree,' said Eduardo, pointing to a suspiciously youthful-looking specimen to our left. 'They say he tied his caravel there when he landed.'

Da Gama had indeed come up the river in February 1498 and was sufficiently impressed by what he found at Quelimane to name its waterway as the 'River of Good Omens'. He is said to have lingered for a month, careening his ships and resupplying. At that time the town was tiny, with just a few traders who showed little interest in the goods the Portuguese had brought. 'These people are black and well made,' wrote Alvaro Velho, a soldier on the voyage and author of the *Roteiro*, the only chronicle from an expedition member to have survived. 'They go naked, merely wearing a piece of cotton stuff around their loins, that worn by the women being larger than that worn by the men. The young women are good-looking. Their lips are pierced in three places, and they wear in them bits of tin. These people took much delight in us.'

As Eduardo and I walked across to our next bar, we were greeted by some old friends of his, one of whom fastened on to me. Her name was Flesh. Eduardo put the matter succinctly.

'She loves you, Kevin.'

'But why?'

'Because you are *branco* – white.'

Mozambique has been an independent country for twenty-five years, but the cruel truths of colonial economics have not changed: white man equals money. Eduardo at least put a brave face on this, showering money on everyone with the sole proviso that they talked to him and made him laugh.

Ever since da Gama's time the Portuguese had seen Zambezia as a place where a man could make his fortune. The vast fertile lands were carved up into estates and sold off to minor nobility. But the promise of the region had never really been fulfilled: generation upon generation found their hopes frustrated, washed out in the incessant rain, lost in the endless winding rivers and the torpor of afternoon heat. Men and women sickened and died with alarming speed and frequency. Livingstone came here and lost his wife Mary Moffat to fever: 'No man in his senses,' he wrote, 'would have dreamed of placing a village on such a low, muddy, fever-haunted, and mosquito-swarming site, had it not been for the facilties it afforded for slaving.'

'Do you know why it is called Quelimane?' Carvalho asked me. 'It is English – "Kill a Man" – the sun is very terrible, you see.' We went in the afternoon to inspect the place where he had chosen to

[57]

build his own dream: two small plots of land on the road through the coconut plantation. He showed me around very proudly.

'I will plant rice there – in the low-lying area. Up here will be fruit trees and vegetables: pineapples, mangoes and so on. The house will be on the other piece of land: twenty-four metres long and twenty-four wide, with a courtyard twelve metres square in the centre.' He had the measurements for everything in his head and it was all entirely symmetrical. There would be a colonnade around the courtyard, and in the evenings he would walk around it a few times for the exercise, then sit and enjoy a drink, with ice.

There was something dependable and solid about such a vision, one of domestic regularity and order with the jungle kept at bay. It seemed to me to be a dream in keeping with those of the early settlers, like Misson's pirates who only wanted 'some Place to call their own . . . where they might enjoy the Fruits of their Labour, and go to their Graves in Peace'. This was not escapism, a desire to break the mould of everyday routine and become somebody else; more like the opposite, the outsider's desire to be let in.

'How did you decide on those numbers?'

'Because I like them.' He sniffed and raised his chin with Napoleonic defiance. I liked that. I liked the vision of Carvalho on his veranda built to his own whimsical dimensions, sipping cold drinks made with his own ice.

Most utopian writers, from Thomas More onwards, have been keen on dimensions. Cities are relentlessly erected to golden specifications that will guarantee happiness and well-being. In Tommaso Campanella's *City of Sun*, published in 1623, every possible measurement is set out and lots of other details too – right down to button design on clothes and the death penalty for wearing make-up. Of course, obsessions with measurements could lead to hell, not paradise, as Joseph Hall pointed out in his *Another World and Yet the Same* in 1600. There, in the land of Pamphagonia, citizens are not admitted unless their stomach dimensions reached the statutory minimum.

We drove further through the vast coconut groves, finishing up by the ocean where Carvalho drank beer in a thatched shelter and I walked on the broad sands, watching the fragile sails of outrigger canoes beyond the roaring surf. I envied Carvalho at that moment, his dreams so tangibly within reach, his mind so clear as to what those dreams were. My own seemed so distant and opaque. For a few moments I dwelt on the possibility of taking a similar course, using Carvalho's influence to help me find a place; then growing pineapples, rice and coconuts while I wrote books next to the ocean. Slowly, very slowly, perhaps without being entirely conscious of the process, I was drawing alongside and measuring my life against his.

After some beers we went to view the ice factory: a small lock-up in town where Carvalho, eyes gleaming with pride and enthusiasm, showed me the pipes, pumps and filters. A few bags of ice were sitting under sackcloth in a pick-up, waiting to be whisked away to customers.

'Now it is not busy,' he said. 'But one day I will send ice to all the petrol stations and people will come and buy.'

I left him there, discussing production with his worker, and walked around the town. In the centre was a pretty white-painted mosque where one elderly Indian gentleman was praying. I took off my shoes and sat on the green carpet under the sign, '*Lugar Sagrado*'. Islam had arrived on this coast long before the Portuguese and it had been Arab traders who criss-crossed the ocean, tying East Africa, Arabia and Asia into one trading community. They had eaten off Chinese porcelain, drunk wine from Persian glasses and taken local women as concubines. The gold, ivory and slaves they collected went as far as China.

When the Indian gentleman had finished praying, he noticed my presence and we fell into conversation.

'I came here many years ago,' he told me. 'From Veraval in India.'

He was surprised to hear that I knew the town and had been there only a year before.

'Did you come by sea?' I asked, imagining the long voyage

under the stars, the hoary old captain telling tall tales. 'Was it by dhow?'

He frowned at me. 'Dhow?! My God. No. It was Air Portugal.'

My own need to move on, preferably by sea, was not looking very hopeful. Carvalho had tried on a number of occasions to raise a friend of his on the radio, the captain of a ship plying between Nacala and Pemba, but without any reply. There were certainly no dhows around, only the one large timber ship whose Chinese crew I had seen around the town.

When I climbed up on to the ship to ask, I found myself watching the death throes of Mozambican forests: thousands and thousands of logs going inside the vast hold. The work went on twenty hours a day as though they were hurrying, trying to hide the shameful evidence inside the ship. The supercargo was a Hong Kong Chinese pirate who'd cheerfully stripped every poor nation on earth of its hardwood. He'd smuggled gold into India and guns into Saudi Arabia, but he wouldn't take me. 'I got one local girl,' he explained. 'And we can only have one passenger.'

When Carvalho heard, he shrugged expressively. 'Why not stay in Quelimane? It's a good place.'

'Maybe I'll be back.' At the time I said it, I meant it, but Carvalho knew better.

'No, I think not. But you must wait a long time for a ship, or go by road further north.' The thought of someone forced to travel on land obviously distressed him. He listed the ports where I might have some luck: Angoche, Mozambique Island, Nacala, Pemba. 'The first two are very quiet though.'

'What about getting a ship across to the Comoros or Madagascar?'

Carvalho gave a wry smile. 'You are still dreaming of your pirate heaven, hey? But the Comoros are always hard to reach – very hard at the moment. They have some problems with seccessionists, so I heard.' He shrugged. 'You will have to do what all sailors do – trust in God.' What I would have to do, in fact, was trust in Mozambique's decrepit road transport system.

I was wandering through the town wondering what the future held when I heard footsteps running up behind me, then two arms were flung around my shoulders.

'Keviño! Come to my house. Not far. Come.'

It was Flesh. There was a brief wrestling match during which I, wriggling, tried to break her hold and she, giggling, took my efforts to be playful. She was much stronger than she looked. Passers-by eyed us curiously. Flesh's cheek was pressed to my chest, her eyes closed in mock bliss. 'Keviño. We two go travel. I look for you. You look for me.'

It was then I saw the man on the bicycle. He was coming along the street, weaving through the strolling crowds. It was the distinctive orange boiler suit of the *Songo*'s crew that picked him out, that and his impressively muscular physique. It was Machavo.

He spotted us, of course, in that endearing huddle. Suddenly the wobbling wayward bicycle straightened up and began spearing through the throng towards us.

'Machavo is coming!'

Flesh dropped me and jumped back. Machavo crashed into the kerb and, glowering at her, lifted his hand and drew it back slowly across his throat. Flesh's normally ebullient face fell, she pouted and moved further away from both of us. Machavo now pointed down a side street. With a toss of her head, she went. Machavo followed, after fixing me with a final menacing scowl.

This ridiculous scene made my mind up. I would have to leave the *Songo* and Quelimane before Machavo poisoned my food. That night I packed my bags and prepared to leave early.

Breakfast was the least special of all meals on the *Songo*. Toast and jam was the most one could expect, with a cup of tea or coffee from a Thermos flask. I was down in good time that morning, hoping to make a quick getaway unnoticed by the cook.

There was no one else around. I sat in my usual place, poured a mug of tea and put two slices of white bread in the toaster. There was no sound from the kitchen. Only when the toast popped up did I notice the jam jar was empty, cleanly scraped.

The galley door was slightly to one side of the dining area: it was permanently open, but a large aluminium cabinet blocked any view inside. I walked through and turned towards the sink.

Machavo was leaning there. He had a rag in his hands which he was squeezing. It made his biceps bulge alarmingly. He was a big man.

'*Bom dia*,' I said, as brightly as I could. He did not answer.

'*Como está?*' Still no response.

'*Desculpe*,' I went on. '*Não há nenhum jam.*' Not a flicker.

'*Jam*,' I repeated. '*Queria jam.*'

He was looking at me, but there was no reaction. Surely 'jam' was a universal word? Like Coca-Cola or sandwich.

'*Jaaam. Jem. Jim. Djam. Sham.*' He did not answer.

I racked my brains. Was there some obvious equivalent? Often the words of Latin origin in English proved to be almost the same in Portuguese: difficult was dificil, violence was violencia … Machavo shifted, his frown became deeper.

Then I thought of it. I smiled pleasantly. 'Preservative,' I said. 'Give me preservative. I want pre-serv-a-tif.'

The man's face was utterly expressionless, but a growl had started somewhere in his huge chest.

We seemed to stand like that for a long time: his anger boiling inside him, my cheesy smile fading – and then suddenly gone. Preservative. With horror I remembered. My God, what had I done? Preservative is Portuguese for condom.

There was no time for explanations, not with my fatally flawed knowledge. I stepped back. 'Actually. Do you know? I'm not hungry any more. Not at all.'

Then I turned and fled.

In the end, the *Songo* left before I did. The reason no one had been at breakfast was that they had solved their unloading problems and were rushing to grab the tide and follow the timber ship downriver.

Carvalho was frantic to get away with the tide. The ropes were thrown and she pulled away smoothly, the brown water sucking into the widening gap. Nobody waved, they were all busy with their tasks, and suddenly I felt alone, marooned. This had been the worst punishment the pirates ever inflicted on a companion: to abandon them. The hardened toughs had known all along that psychological pain was harder to bear. My first, lucky berth had gone, the second I had hoped for was nothing more than a smokey smudge over a low line of mangroves. I was alone on the quayside watching the quick yellow tide suck at the pilings, knowing that there would be no boat this time; I had to go inland.

4

A Dance to the Music of Chains

Silver padlocks for Blacks or Dogs; collars &c
notice in London Advertiser, 1756

No one can doubt the licitness of the slave trade, who believes
that the Bible is the Word of God.
Reverend Raymond Harris, 1788
He was voted an annuity of £100 by the
grateful Corporation of Liverpool.

The slave trade 'could never be agreeable to the eyes of
divine justice'.
The pirate, Captain Misson, 1681

The unit of transport in Mozambique is the chapas – literally, 'the
battered tin' – generally a pick-up truck into and on to which
passengers scramble until the last one falls off. Then you leave.
Except that invariably just as you do leave someone will say,
'Nampula?! Are you serious? This chapas is for Nampula?' And
get out. At which point you are driven round and around the town
looking for another passenger.

From the driver's point of view, no chapas is ever truly full.

There's always room on top of the old woman who is sitting on top of you. Chickens usually travel free so it is worth carrying a small flock of tough little broilers to get full value. Most Mozambican chickens are veteran chapas travellers and scarcely complain when slipped in a glove compartment or used as cushions. If the chapas breaks down – and it will – the chickens can often be traded for something edible.

My first chapas experience was typical. The driver was a eunuch, the ticket man an albino. We spent two hours collecting passengers and a further hour sorting through cassette tapes and picking up the eunuch's sunglasses from a friend's house. Then we left, surfing across country on a wave of Afrobeat: frothy, neurotic guitars stitched together with a looping loopy bass.

The countryside was as sharp and simple as an independence day flag: brilliant green forest, red road and blue sky. Every village consisted of identical rectangular mud huts with a crude thatched roof surrounded by a few cleared areas of manioc. However, there were few villages to see: the depredations of slavery and colonialism, followed by years of war, have left huge areas of Mozambique relatively underpopulated.

After four hours, we were making excellent progress along a smooth stretch of flat red road when I noticed smoke was pouring from Eunuch's bottom. I stared in amazement, quite expecting to see him spin around and disappear inside the nearest available brass lamp. Instead, there was a sickening intestinal gurgle and what remained of the engine oil was farted from the exhaust pipe on to the road. Eunuch gave a single piercing scream and grabbed his behind in agony. The steam from the boiling radiator had shot up through his seat and finally alerted him to a cooked engine.

We disembarked to find village children scooping up the black residue of the oil from the dusty road and rubbing it into their hair. A cracked hose was found to be the problem. This caused Albino much sadness and bewilderment as he had fixed it himself only the previous day with *'relva forte'*. I had to check this in my dictionary, and then again with him before I understood that he really did mean 'strong grass'.

Eunuch, still rubbing his bottom, declared that his chapas was dead. All the chickens were removed and he sadly began to push it back towards Quelimane, a mere 150 miles away.

I sat for several hours in the sun with the other passengers. A few aid agency LandCruisers whipped past without even a glance at our waving hands. Many had Union Jacks or European Union symbols on the side and were empty of passengers, facts which began to annoy me intensely. My fellow travellers did not even bother to wave at these cars, knowing better than to expect help, but it made me rage at them: 'I pay your bloody wages, you bastards!' I explained the taxpayer system to a mystified audience and after a long thoughtful pause, someone asked why I took the chapas if I owned so many cars?

Eventually two off-duty policemen stopped and I was ceremoniously escorted to the cab rather than the open back. 'Better he has shade,' a voice declared. The truth was, and I knew it, I was 'patrão', a rich foreigner. Even though my compatriots ignored their plight by the roadside, the Mozambicans treated me with studied courtesy. I felt humbled by their good manners and quiet stoicism.

We drove for hour after hour, the landscape puckering into small hills but otherwise unchanging. Night fell while we took a rest in an uninhabited stretch of bush, the noises of the forest rising, as though a giant radio were suddenly tuned to static.

The policemen dropped me at a cheap hotel in the city of Nampula where I took an over-priced and filthy room, then slept soundly. At five o'clock next morning I woke up scratching and decided to pack my bag and leave for the market. I did not have to wait long before I found a chapas heading towards Angoche on the coast. There was another white man on board, a rather serious-looking individual in a peaked cap. People moved so he could sit beside me and I could see he resented this automatic assumption of comradeship through skin colour, but people were so well-meaning and polite he could not refuse.

His name was Jens, I discovered, and he had come from Denmark on a school-building project that had eventually folded.

'I run a fishing business now,' he told me. 'But just starting.'

We set off, bouncing along a rough dirt track, skirting the kapok and cashew trees and admiring huge mountains that jutted from the ground like breaching whales. Jens mournfully listed the problems and setbacks he had faced. There were lots of them, enough to fill several hours of bouncing around in a pick-up truck.

His plans were ambitious: to catch the plentiful fish and seafood off the coast in his own boats, freeze it, transport it to markets in Zimbabwe and Malawi. Then there would be the tourist development, the condiments factory, furniture construction, big game fishing – so far he had a broken freezer and a wrecked boat.

'I try *not* to think that one day everything will be nice,' he said, clutching the side of the pick-up. 'Try to train myself to enjoy life now. Not to expect too much.'

He was a utopianist who had learned to expect the worst. A cyclone had smashed his boats, there were no freezer parts, he could not get bank loans, but his dogged refusal to give up would see him through.

'Where will you stay in Angoche?' he asked.

'Oh, a hotel.'

'There are none. Maybe you can lodge with my girlfriend's father.'

We arrived at sunset in time to note the broad main street, the concrete brutalist blocks and the eerie lack of population. During the civil war which ended in 1992, the South African-backed Renamo rebels had fought the Frelimo government troops in these streets and the pockmarks of bullets still marked the walls. I sat outside an empty bar and waited for Jens who had gone to ask his girlfriend's father if he objected to an extra visitor.

When he came back, he nodded, without much enthusiasm. I had little choice but to accept the offer.

His girlfriend's father, Capatine, proved to be a tall, dignified

Makua gentleman who had come to Angoche in order to manage the half-empty supermarket downstairs. The flat was furnished in severely aristocratic style: high-backed carved dining chairs around a long table where we were served by a white-jacketed servant. The condiments tray in the centre held long-necked bottles of home made mango and lime pickles, a fearsomely hot piri-piri sauce, a half-empty bottle of Benylin and various packets of pills. As the lights flickered and went off, candles were lit and our conversation turned to darker matters.

'The whole coast is addicted to magic,' Capatine told me. 'From Inhambane up to Tanzania, they call the sorcerors for any reason. If you want to keep a girlfriend or kill someone, then magic is used. Even if you buy a new car then protection is needed.'

I liked the idea of mixing ancient arts and new: the sorcerer and the motor car. 'Who does the magic?'

He smiled and shook his head at the question. 'Those who have the power. Some are good people, some are very bad. They may write a name on paper, then burn it and place those ashes in a graveyard.'

The servant came to take away our plates, and Capatine waited until he had gone before continuing.

'Some say there is a type of spider living here in Angoche,' he said, with a sombre frown. 'This creature must be crushed between your palms and rubbed over your body. Doing so will make a man invisible.'

He was sceptical about my ambition to travel up the coast. 'Now there are no ships visiting Angoche, but you will find local boats to take you out to the islands.'

I went to sleep in a curtainless room, wrapped in my sheet against the attack of mosquitoes and dreaming of huge insects climbing the shadowy walls.

Angoche is an intriguing place historically. When the Portuguese seized the coastal trade, Arab merchants began to use ports like Angoche as secret embarkation points. First gold, then ivory enriched the town, but the 'product' most closely associated with the port is slaves.

From soon after their arrival the Portuguese had maintained a fairly steady export of slaves from Mozambique Island, around half of whom generally arrived alive. Regulations insisted that only Portuguese could benefit, but by the late eighteenth century demand from French plantation-owners in Mauritius and Madagascar began to push up the numbers, and the prices.

This was slavery on a vast and bloody scale: in 1787 the Portuguese legalised weapon sales and massive manhunts took place in the north of Mozambique. One set of statistics for Mozambique Island in the year 1819 give some idea of the savagery involved: 1,200 slaves dead before sale, 1,804 dead before embarkation, 2,196 dead during the voyage. Descriptions of life on the slave decks make gruesome reading with bodies dragged out of the narrow stinking confines, sometimes alive, and thrown overboard. Slave voyage logbooks of the time are often little more than body counts, sometimes with a terse comment about the vexing propensity of blacks to die for no apparent reason. Of those captured, less than half ever reached the plantations and those that did were scarcely more fortunate. Brazilian owners, in particular, simply worked the slaves to death and bought fresh ones.

This industrial-scale boom in human traffic soon aroused anti-slavery opinion, especially in the English Quaker communities, but some pirates had long since shown themselves opposed to it. No doubt many saw their own hard-won liberty as being a freedom from slavery in itself: in Bermuda and Barbados the black slaves and poor white servants made common cause and revolted throughout the 1650s, uprisings which were savagely repressed. If the pirates were to pick up any egalitarian and utopian ideals, then it was in those same islands, home to the radicals and revolutionaries of England. Quakers, preachers of the Everlasting Gospel, Muggletonians, Levellers and Ranters, they were all exported along with the gaol-birds, highwaymen, strumpets and sodomists. One can well imagine that such a strange brew of humanity would eventually spawn that most dangerous of subversives: the pirate utopian with anti-slavery opinions.

Pirate ships were certainly manned by mixed-race crews: Bartholomew Roberts had seventy-five black men among his crew at the time of his death in 1722, Edward England and others were widely reported to have black sailors aboard. Captain Misson, typically, saw the common cause of slaves and the oppressed: 'Men who were born and bred in Slavery,' he railed, '. . . dance to the Musick of their Chains.'

Whatever small blows were struck by the pirates, true abolition was far off and out at sea, at least, would be won by Royal Navy firepower. Three years after the British parliament passed the Act of Abolition in 1807, the Royal Navy frigate *Nisus* was despatched from Cape Town to Mozambique and Johanna with the novel mission of suppressing slave raids on those places by Madagascan war canoes. The problem had come to light when a well-groomed and courteous emissary of the Sultan of Johanna had arrived in the colony, begging for assistance. Johanna, he claimed, was being ravaged by blood-thirsty savages who arrived in vast fleets of war canoes and carried off anyone they could catch.

As Britain was newly installed as world power, a chance to flex muscle was discerned, and perhaps for the first time in British history, gunboat diplomacy adopted.

The surgeon on board, James Prior, left a garrulous and enter-taining account of the voyage which I had put in my bag with some trepidation. Too often an 'original' account can prove so dull a travelling companion that it has to be ditched. Prior proved otherwise. Mercifully free of the Victorian niceties which would plague later memoirs, he observes the 'fine forms' of the ladies at Cape Town country dances and appears almost laddish in his pursuit. Yet the aim of the voyage is not forgotten, as the ship sails north along the Mozambican coast, he records that 10,000 slaves per year are passing out of the Portuguese possessions and that the officials are quietly amassing fortunes.

Such Royal Navy activity succeeded in chasing the slavers to the margins – towns like Angoche. Various treaties followed, each further limiting slavery and empowering the policemen, but Angoche flourished. British officers were wined and dined at Quelimane, Mozambique Island and Ibo. Meanwhile, barges full of slaves slipped out of remote river mouths under cover of darkness, meeting ships disguised as 'whalers'. In Angoche, Cuban and American vessels began to risk the shallow waters during the 1830s, a practice the British became aware of and ordered a bombardment. Still the independent sultanate thrived, its armies swelled by unsold slaves. Attacks by the private armies of Portuguese slave warlords could not shift them and the net result was that northern Mozambique became the realm of bandit chiefs, armed by the profits of slaving and able to dominate the unarmed Makua people of the interior.

Few accounts from this time give any indication of how the trade was conducted. What we do know seems mysterious and bizarre: one quarter of all slaves were people accused of witchcraft, many were sold by deception, unwittingly haggled over as they passed through the market. In one case the 'slave' refused to accept the right of the vendor to sell and it was the vendor who ended up in chains as a slave.

In this bizarre atmosphere of intrigue and suspicion, Angoche had survived.

On my first morning in Angoche, Jens took me to meet an old lady who he thought might give me some of the flavour of what the town had once been like. The apartment was up a flight of concrete steps where we were met by the lady's daughter, Elsa, a large jovial woman. She took us into the living room where Kenny Rogers was singing on the cd player below a rug of Jesus and a turtle shell. An elderly gentleman in a skullcap was watching a James Bond film on television with the sound turned down.

'My mother is not here at the moment,' said Elsa in Portuguese. 'This is my uncle – Assani.'

Tea and biscuits were brought out and Uncle Assani took an interest in my questions.

'Some of the outlying islands have almost disappeared,' he said as James Bond wandered into a Turkish hammam somewhere in Russia. 'This is because the first Arab sultan who came here was robbed of his money belt and cursed the place.'

'How many islands are there?'

'Eight.'

A dark-haired super vixen had pounced on James Bond and was squeezing him between her voluptuous thighs. 'Oh, good,' said Elsa, turning the sound up. 'Sex.'

'There is a seven-headed cobra,' said Uncle Assani, eyes riveted on Bond's assailant who had been thrown clear, loosening what little garments she was wearing. 'He comes along the coast and eats people sometimes.'

There was the shuffle of footsteps in the passage and the old lady appeared. 'Ah!' she said, seeing the tv. 'Sex!'

Elsa smiled apologetically. '*Desculpe*. My mother only speaks Coti.'

The old lady sat down and we all regarded the screen. Jens took another biscuit. He was impatient to get away, but I needed him to translate Elsa's Portuguese translation of her mother's Coti.

'The original inhabitants of the islands were giants,' said the old lady. 'The Bonimawiya. But before the Arabs came they were turned to stone or they disappeared.'

Bond was now definitely on top, meting out some tough love to the misguided wench who was pretending to hate every minute of it.

'My own uncle disappeared,' said the old lady, matter-of-factly. 'He was a small boy at the time and one day he was gone. Nobody knew where. Actually an Indian boat was here in Angoche at that time and they had taken him as a slave. He went to India and worked hard. After many years he became free and started to be a merchant himself.'

Bond's sex scene was over so the sound was put off to allow

[73]

Kenny Rogers back in, grumbling about his wife abandoning him.

'When he was old,' the old lady continued, 'he returned here to Angoche and the first shop he walked into was his own brother's. That is how we came to know what had happened to him.'

'So many disappearances,' I said. 'Angoche is full of ghosts.'

The old lady laughed. 'Oh, my father was able to make himself invisible very easily. Sometimes we would see his things floating around the room and then we would know he was invisible again.'

Bond had effected a miraculous escape from a doomed helicopter with a half-naked girl strapped to his immaculate Jermyn Street suit. Jens was fidgeting, he had bureaucrats to meet. No one took any notice: impatience is an invisible emotion in Mozambique, especially during Bond movies.

'In those days people would sell their children to the slavers,' said the old lady brightly. 'Or if someone annoyed them, they sold them.'

Jens's translations were getting shorter and shorter.

'And do boats go north up the coast?'

'My father was a trader,' said the old lady. 'He used to take a big sailing ship up to Tanzania and then to Jeddah.'

Jens was standing by the door as he finished this. 'I have to go now.'

'And do boats still go?'

He sighed.

The old lady and the others shook their heads. 'It is finished. Angoche is finished. All quiet now.'

Despite the commonly held belief that Angoche was moribund as a port, there was a regular traffic in small dhows. I spent a few days hanging around the beach hoping one might declare an interest in sailing northwards to Mozambique Island but none did. Instead I visited the islands off shore, surviving a stormy outward journey in which a madwoman tried to drown herself and the dhow became temporarily entangled with a mangrove forest.

The islands are all encircled by mangroves and many of the villages of thatched palm leaves and mud walls are accessible only by narrow winding creeks. There were no roads, cars, electricity, running water, restaurants, shops, or telephones to serve the population of almost 25,000.

'We are poor,' said one youth. 'There are only five bicycles on all twelve islands.'

Everyone agreed that there were five bicycles but not everyone agreed that there were twelve islands. Some said fifteen, others eight, a small but vocal minority insisted there were just five. I decided that it depended on the time of day: at high tide the number was high as the islands were all separated. Then as the day wore on and the waters fell, so did the number of islands. Far from being ignorant of their own geography, the islanders were clearly able to keep an up-to-the-minute account.

Walking between the islands as the sun set, I encountered a small office which was registering voters for the upcoming national elections, the forms all beautifully printed with individual computer barcodes that could be read by candlelight.

Scepticism and bemusement about the elections were rife: many political parties were no more than Maputo based outfits unknown in the countryside. Renamo were the main opposition, a party sprung from the bandit ragtag army who had been paid by the CIA and apartheid South Africa to harass and disrupt the socialist administration of Frelimo. As many people around Angoche had had their homes destroyed and their animals stolen by this group, it seemed utterly bizarre to expect any votes. Democracy, however, required it.

Perhaps any paradox was possible in that place: I certainly managed to walk to another island without getting my feet wet. There, with night falling, I found three youths who were willing to take me back to Angoche. We paddled down a muddy creek and sailed out into the bay. Once we were far out on the waters, the breeze died and we sat, unmoving, watching the stars twinkle. After a few brief attempts at paddling, one sighed in exasperation and climbed out. The sea was waist-deep. It was that moment all sailors must dread: time to push. We made it back to Angoche several hours later.

Only when I lay down to sleep that night did it occur to me that I had never considered the islands as utopian tropical paradises. From the moment of arrival I had solely been concerned with escaping.

Having waited a few days in the hope of a boat going north, I finally gave it up. Angoche intrigued me: its whispered stories of missing people and invisible men like the echoed voices of the people who had simply disappeared across the ocean; a place as scarred by slavery as any American ghetto. But after so many had been forced against their will to go to sea, I found there was no hope of disappearing in that direction for me; the harbour was full of ghosts too – big, rusty ones that were full of holes.

Saying goodbye to Capatine and Jens, I took a chapas back to Nampula. From there I caught a bus to Ilha da Mozambique.

The once-great island is connected to the mainland by a long causeway and from a distance presents a magnificent sight, its shores fringed with palm trees and stone buildings. Close up the prospect is less inspiring: the houses in a state of complete dilapidation, ceilings fallen, walls long since unpainted. Compared to the Portuguese town on the Indian island of Diu, a place I had visited a year before, it was architecturally ruined. In the face of the inhabitants' poverty, the hopes of various international agencies that the island could be restored to colonial splendour seemed ridiculous and extravagant.

The hotel was closed, but I found a room in the government resthouse and walked along the lanes, keeping to the shade. Swallows dived along at knee-height, weaving expertly between the women carrying baskets of shopping on their heads, their faces masked against the sun with white paste. At the end of every street was the sea, a perfect shimmering blue broken only by the occasional triangular sail.

[76]

I was sorry not to have arrived by dhow myself. Once upon a time Arab ships would have sailed on up the Swahili coast to Arabia, carrying mangrove poles and slaves, some continuing to India where they could buy spices and silks; now they did no more than ferry passengers across the narrow straits to the village of Caboceira. Ilha as a port, the great Portuguese base which gave its name to the country, was dead.

Vasco da Gama had reached here a week after sailing from Quelimane, several days faster than I had managed. The locals had come rushing out to greet the newcomers in dugout canoes, playing anafils, a Moorish trumpet. The atmosphere soured, however, when the Portuguese were found not to be Muslims. A confrontation became inevitable, and equally inevitable was a Portuguese victory: they had guns. The islanders threw up wooden palisades along the beaches, but it was no defence against the Portuguese bombardment. Two men were killed and a mass exodus to the mainland triggered. As for da Gama's men, 'When we were weary of this work we retired to our ships to dine.' The casual brutality in the face of resistance had started; the justification always being that they were unbelievers and consequently damned souls to be ruthlessly slaughtered. Da Gama favoured stringing prisoners up from the yard arm and allowing his crossbowmen some target practice; children, if they were lucky, might be reprieved and handed over to the priests for conversion.

That first night I spent on the island, I wandered the quiet lanes, hearing the soft voices of the men sitting in doorways and the sound of mass from the sixteenth-century Church of the Misericord. Climbing the stone steps, I looked in on the candle-lit scene and saw a Portuguese priest in sunglasses and surplice performing the ritual for a handful of believers.

Life on the island now is often as short and painful as in colonial times: outbreaks of cholera are frequent, malaria endemic, the graveyards threaten to take over the island.

Despite the early hopes of its Portuguese conquerors, the island never became much more than a way-station, a point of safety for

[77]

the fleets crossing the Indian Ocean from Goa. After the initial flurry of activity to build a fort, churches and slave market, the island began to slide inexorably into indolence and languor.

In 1812 the frigate *Nisus* arrived, its indefatigable chronicler James Prior on board, ready to note triumphantly the decay of Portuguese rule and the sharp contrast with well-scrubbed British vigour. As the youthful British officers sprang ashore, the governor, Don Antonio Manuel de Mello Castro e Mendoza, extended a languid greeting from a supine position in his palanquin. It was, Prior reports, one of those rare occasions when the man left his house, 'lest he should endanger his invaluable health'.

It is possible, perhaps, to see a moment of history in this fleeting encounter. The young Britishers, full of brash confidence and energy, exactly as da Gama had been two centuries before, were now sneering at the hopeless indolence of the tottering Portuguese empire.

Don Antonio shocked his visitors with his lack of interest in the fate of Portugal or European affairs, nor did he show much concern over the activities of illegal slavers and Madagascan raiders. Nothing could be done.

Strangely, the slave trade was in full swing at that time, yet Prior seems unconcerned: presumably that was 'legitimate' trade, as yet not outlawed. His concern is the savages of Madagascar who are enslaving the rather civilised and amusing Johannese.

Relieved to escape the ennui of the island, the *Nisus* sets out for the Comoros, intent on its mission of putting a stop to this nonsense of savages becoming slave traders.

I envied them that ease of departure, and in the very direction I wished to take. There were no boats to be had in the island except dhows back to the mainland, nor did I have any luck when I took a chapas a few miles north to the port of Nacala. There I found Carvalho's agent friend, only to hear that a ship bound for Pemba had left the previous day and none was now expected for at least three weeks. It would have to be another chapas ride.

We sat in his front room watching his collection of tropical fish go round and round the tank. He was British but had long since abandoned the home country. While he chain-smoked and reminisced about the sea, I ate matapa, the local staple of leaves, coconut milk and ground peanuts, waited on by his beautiful Mozambican girlfriend. His tales were of the hopelessness and failure of trying to achieve something. Bureaucracy and corruption stifled any attempts: 168 signatures to release one cargo from the port. What could anyone do? I couldn't help but think, a little unfairly, of Don Antonio lying in his palanquin.

PART TWO

THE QUERRIMBAS

5

A Hard Heaven

Without the utopians of other times, men would still live in caves, miserable and naked; . . . Utopia is the principle of all progress, and the essay into a better world.

Anatole France

An acre of Middlesex is worth a province of Utopia.

Thomas Babington Macaulay

Pemba is at the tip of a promontory with the ocean on one side and a huge sheltered bay on the other. In atmosphere it is like a shabby colonial town: large villas on shady boulevards of cracked concrete, dilapidated stores selling all kinds of cheap goods, and then huge areas of thatched huts beyond the tarmac. Many of the old villas are ruins with families camped out in them. On the hill a cemetery holds a small Allied war cemetery, one of the graves marked, 'Sacrificed for monarchial ambition'.

Three kilometres south on the Indian Ocean, past an ocean boulevard of massive baobab trees and a ruined social club, lies the town beach, a short shallow bay of yellow sand lined with coconut palms and the beach houses of the wealthy, or once-wealthy. Some are elegant colonial structures, most are brutal quick-build 1960s concrete.

[83]

I found a place to stay there and settled in. There were three bars: one at each end of the kilometre-long beach, and one in the middle. During the week it was quiet: mostly the beach catered for wealthy Nampula families who would motor down on a Friday night and open up their beach houses. Then the place came to life. A servant would arrive first, start sweeping and throw back the shutters. Chairs appeared on verandas, sheets were aired and taken in. At sunset, as the lights came on, the families would arrive. They were largely of Indian or Portuguese origin – few Africans were rich enough to use or own beach houses.

On the sand, however, any social differences were forgotten. Anyone could go to the beach. Anyone could light a fire and cook fish, or turn cartwheels, or sit eating peanuts sold by the ragged little girls with their measuring tins, or strike up a conversation.

On Sunday afternoon, I was talking to an Indian merchant who had been born on the island of Ibo which had been the provincial capital before Pemba. It is part of an archipelago of small atolls and islands, the Querrimbas, which run for almost 200 miles all the way from Pemba to the Tanzanian border. The chain was reputedly beautiful but also the haunt of smugglers, its mangrove-clad creeks perfect for hiding contraband. I was to hear plenty of stories: ivory and hashish going out while other drugs came in – cocaine and heroin mostly, for the South African market. If I could not find a passage to the Comoros, then I was determined to cover this archipelago in the small dhows, or galowas.

The merchant frowned. 'No boats to the Comoros,' he said. 'But you can get galowas to Ibo. There is no other way. You take a chapas to a village called Tandanhangue, then wait on the beach.'

'And then further north?'

'All the way to Zanzibar, if you like.' He grinned. 'And have the time.'

We talked about Ibo for a while. He told me that it had once been the major port and town of the north, but when everyone moved to Pemba shortly before the First World War, it had become a ghost island.

'Take food,' he said. 'And bottled water.'

Keen to move on, I was at the chapas stop next morning an hour before dawn to find a group of locals wrapped in blankets and a young European woman sitting on a large pink rucksack studying a sheet of paper.

'I think today is a good day to go to Ibo,' she said when I introduced myself. 'The planets are lining up nicely for me on the eleventh, so travelling is okay.' Her name was Theresa and she had a Swedish accent, but her complexion was dark, with bright black eyes and shoulder-length black hair. She squinted at the paper. 'My problem is I can't see very well.'

I read it for her, and we agreed that it was an auspicious day to travel. My tone of voice, however, gave me away.

'Don't you believe in it? I'll bet you're a Virgo and you don't go astral travelling either,' she said which was correct on both counts. She stood up. 'I'd better find my specs.'

The contents of the vast pink rucksack spilled out: designer dresses, a vast pot of homemade face lotion – she dabbed some on her face – jars of essential oils, bottles of wine, a tape recorder, her Leonard Cohen collection, several rolls of toilet paper ('I didn't know if they had it in Mozambique'), even a bottle of champagne ('Don't you always take one – I do!'). Unfortunately, there were no spectacles, and then the whole lot had to be stuffed quickly back as the chapas had arrived.

We were early and got the best position in the driver's cab, me sandwiched between Theresa and the Muslim driver for reasons of religious decorum, but the warmest position on a chilly dawn.

Our route was around the bay and then north through the open bushland, stopping in every village by the red dirt track. The sun was up now and the women and children were out sweeping the area in front of their huts.

'Where is your country?' asked the driver, sharing a bunch of bananas with us.

'London.' I had got used to the city being more widely known than the country.

'Is that in Ethiopia?'

'No.'

'It's a rich place, isn't it? Ethiopia.'

'I'm not from Ethiopia.'

'Where are you from?'

'London.'

'In Ethiopia?'

We abandoned this conversation and rolled on gently through the forest and grasslands. I asked him about religion: were most people Muslims? He nodded. 'But there are some Christians – they hate us.'

'Why?'

He thought about it. 'Because we take our shoes off in the mosque.' I waited but there appeared to be no other reason for this communal hatred.

After several hours the trees thinned out and we entered an area of grassland. On a low hill ahead of us stood a radio mast and a few dilapidated concrete buildings. From there we were able to see the ocean again and a beach backed by a strip of palms. Out across the blue water were several low islands, all covered in mangroves and coconuts. We drove down as far as we could, then the driver showed us the beach where some men were repairing a boat. It was about nine in the morning and already very hot.

'Somebody will go to Ibo,' he said airily, and left us there.

We found some shade. Beyond the sand was a small creek through a line of mangroves. The water was obviously too low for any of the small dhows to set out, so we had to wait for the tide. A few white egrets and a purple heron watched.

'I need the bathroom,' Theresa said. 'Can you ask them where it is?'

'I don't think they have things like that.'

'I need to go. There must be someone who has a bathroom.'

I slouched over to the boat-repairers.

'*Bom dia! Amigos. Er . . . onde fica a casa de banho?*'

They looked mystified. There was a discussion in Kimwane, the local language. I recognised the occasional word of Swahili: Kimwane is a coastal trade language similar to Coti in Angoche and Naharra on Mozambique Island, a lingua franca born of Swahili, Arabic, Makua, Portuguese and Indian influences. The people here could build languages almost as easily as they built boats: fashioning something useful from the materials at hand. Probably the tales of Captain Misson's universal language had their origins in this simple communication of the coastal peoples.

There were, however, some things more easily communicated by actions. I tried again, adopting a suggestive crouching position. This did the trick. The men pointed at the beach.

We spent the next half hour watching Theresa striding up and down with a large white roll of toilet tissue, trying to find a hiding place on the open beach and in the mangroves. Eventually she gave up. 'It is too disgusting! Piles of it! I haf never seen anything like it. Urgh!' She sat down. 'And I have scratched my finger. Now I will catch cholera.'

'You can't catch cholera through a scratch on your finger.'

It was the wrong thing to say apparently. She went and sat in the sun.

'Are you going to Shaytani?' asked one man who was shaping a plank with a small hand adze, the only tool they used. 'It is nearer to here than Ibo. There is a branco there.'

'A branco? Portuguese?'

'No, not Portuguese. I don't know what he is, but he is a branco. He lived here all his life.'

'Is he alone?'

'No. He has his woman.'

'Is there a place to stay?'

'I think so.' He made a face. 'But nobody goes to it.'

A youth appeared on the beach carrying a long pole around which a filthy sail was wrapped.

'He goes to Shaytani,' said the boat-repairer.

'And Ibo?'

He shook his head. 'You go with him. Tomorrow you find a galowa to Ibo.'

I looked across at Theresa and translated what he'd said. I could see she was thinking: white man on an island – maybe with a bathroom.

She stood up and picked up her massive rucksack; the men cast appreciative looks at her. 'Strong, too,' said one.

We went down to the water's edge and hailed the youth who was busy fixing the pole to the top of the mast. This was the boom, the lateen rig, an Arab invention which the Portuguese borrowed.

Other passengers had appeared now: an old lady smoking a cigarette with the burning end inside her mouth and a youth carrying a single piece of luggage – a pumpkin. They waved us to follow. We waded out to the boat and, throwing our things into the bottom, climbed on to the small poop deck. A price was agreed and two more sailors appeared. The minimum crew for a small dhow is three, largely because the clumsy lateen rig must be hoisted over the top of the mast each time the boat turns.

These sailors were clearly experienced men: they wore only dirty shorts with a neat hole worn out in each buttock, the result of sitting for long hours at the rudder on a rough wooden deck. Two golden buttocks on display, you might say, is a badge of office for the Mozambican sailor.

The dhows have no keel, so apart from fixing the lateen, the second big task before sailing is to fill sacks with sand and dump them around the base of the mast. While they did this I clambered forward, admiring the boat. She was around forty feet long, which is about as big as these little coasters can get, given the need to travel through narrow creeks and shallow waters. Made from hardwood that was sun-bleached to a silver grey, each plank and fitting was handcut with an adze, often making ingenious use of the natural shape of the original tree.

Once the ballast was on board, the anchor was lifted – an old differential from a truck – and we were gently poled out into the sea. There was scarcely any breeze and I was doubtful that we would move at all. I was wrong. One of the great advantages of the dhow is that it makes use of tiny breezes, filling up the huge sail and smoothly easing forwards. The sail on the Mozambican dhows is not triangular: the leading corner is squared off, allowing a significantly larger sail area.

When we were out of the lee of a mangrove island, the wind picked up and immediately the vessel responded, putting its shoulder into the water which curled away like liquid glass.

The captain began to sing in Swahili then switched to Kimwane. The old lady smoked her cigarettes inside her mouth, 'to stop the wind stealing it'. When another dhow passed at two hundred yards distance, she leaned out and held a conversation with a passenger in a devastating bellow. The others shouted greetings: 'Salama sana. Habarini? Al-hamdu lillah!'

These were Arabic words via Swahili, another coastal trade language. I felt myself here at the end of a long and ancient linguistic rope which led north up the East African coast all the way to Arabia and on into Asia. These people were Muslims with Africanised Muslim names – Mamodi, Ibraimo, Iza and Abduli – and though their version of Islam occasionally apppeared as tenuously connected to Mecca as their language was to Arabic, it was a link that four centuries of Portuguese rule had done nothing to change.

I asked the captain about the branco on Shaytani.

'He is German,' he said. 'Senhor Schwarz. He was born here – on the island. It is his island and he is old now.'

'Is he a good man?'

He looked at me as if mulling over the meaning of the question. 'Yes. He is a strong man.' He squinted ahead and pointed. 'Look. This is Shaytani and there is the German's boat.'

It was a long emerald line of mangroves with taller trees, coconuts and casuarinas, behind. To the extreme left it ended in white sand, the sea growing paler and paler as it approached, a scene of utter tranquillity and beauty. The German's boat lay on its side, marooned by the tide a quarter of a mile off shore. It did not look like a vessel that had much usage. 'The engine is broken,' confirmed the captain.

I wondered if we were being watched. When Robinson Crusoe had seen strangers approaching his island, he had prepared for war. But the captain dismissed the suggestion. 'His place is on the far side, on its own. He looks to the ocean not to the land.'

There were other residents too, he said, a large village some of whom worked on Senhor Schwarz's farm.

'When did they come here – these Germans?'

He smiled. 'You must ask him and maybe he will tell you. I only know that it was before I was born.'

'And he runs a guesthouse?' It seemed unlikely somehow.

'Yes, they have a place – some rooms. But I don't know if it is working. Few people visit the island now.'

I was saved from translating this unsatisfactory answer for Theresa by the sound of the hull scraping along the sandy bottom. Very gently we came to a halt in thigh-deep water. Everyone got out, including the crew, and we waded for ten minutes, our bags on our shoulders, to reach the beach.

There was a welcoming party of children who had come out from the neat square huts under the coconut trees.

'Take them to the brancos,' ordered the sailors, and we set off, our shoes in hand and feet burning from the sandy ground.

The village was beautifully swept and tidy: neat thatched huts with cotton curtains at the windows and occasional attempts to grow flowers at the front. It was after one o'clock now and we were tired and thirsty, but there was no sign of anything like a shop – I had not heeded the Indian merchant's advice on food and drink. At the end of the village we came to a long line of old casuarina trees, their gentle needles softening the ground and the breeze whispering in the tops. The children stopped and would go no further. I could see a pink house at the far end of the long avenue and they pointed. 'Go there!'

'Show us.'

But at this request they took fright and bolted.

We trudged on and came to the pink house which was clearly locked up and empty. Beyond was a large pleasant bungalow, the long eaves covering a broad stoop. A few chickens scampered away across the yard. No sound came from the house. We opened a low picket gate and went on to the stoop.

There were racks of carefully tended plants here, huge cabacete shells like the helmets of conquistadores, sturdy weather-worn chairs with brass ashtrays. The house faced out across some roughly trimmed grass, past a cashew tree to a long brilliant sweep of white sand and a blue ocean cut into lighter and darker by the surf of the reef. The only sounds were the distant roar of the waves and the breeze in the casuarinas.

We stood gazing at this for some time. I was thinking: I want to stay here for a long long time, eat the fish I catch and the coconuts that fall. I thought of the Indian gentleman on the foreshore at Deptford: 'For you English, paradise is a beautiful beach and good weather.' Others, he seemed to be saying, have worthier, deeper ambitions. I wished I could show him this elemental paradise: sun, sea, air. Surely if the basics are right, the rest will follow. I turned back to the house and noticed the placement of each chair and side table, how it all fitted together: a place to put a cold drink next to a seat to catch a cooling breeze and watch the reef. Nothing was new, but nothing was broken, simply smoothed by years of use, like the mechanism of a fine old clock.

A sound from inside the house put a stop to my reveries.

'Hello?' I went and peered in through the mosquito mesh window. It was dark inside, but I could make out a sofa and armchair, some bookcases, and a gun.

I went to the fly door. 'Hello-o? Anyone at home?'

The sound was like the clink of cutlery on pot, but there was no reply. With what I intended to be a reassuring smile at Theresa, I took hold of the fly door and, pulling it open, poked my head inside. 'Hello?'

I had a second to take in the comfortable spacious lounge with its sturdy furniture and well-thumbed treasures: books, models, some silver coasters, a cigarette box and a hunting rifle. Then I looked to the left and took in the dining table, the two figures, one hunched over his soup, spoon halted in mid-air, the other a woman of formidable visage, glowering. Her voice came like whipcrack.

'VE ARE HAFFING OUR LUNCH!!'

I should not have leaped backwards. My bag was directly behind me. I stumbled. Neither should I have attempted to grab the fly door, which was swinging slowly. I hit it, slamming it against the frame with a resounding crack. Regaining my balance, I stood frozen in horror at what I had done, then the whip cracked again.

'SIT ON ZE VERANDA – AND WAIT!'

I pulled a face and pointed to the chairs. We both sat down. I whispered to Theresa what I had seen.

'Do they have rooms?'

'I didn't really get a chance to ask.'

What seemed like a very long time passed. We heard the clink of cutlery and pots, but not one word passed between the diners.

At length, the fly door creaked and a man came out. He was about seventy years old, wearing a bush shirt, shorts, socks and boots. He stooped slightly and his face was sketched with lines of sunshine and tobacco. Lighting a cigarette, he gazed out at the ocean for a moment, then turned, as if noticing us for the first time.

'So,' he said in English. 'You came on the dhow?'

'Yes.'

He nodded. 'Want a beer?'

Not waiting for an answer, he went back in the house and reappeared moments later with two South African-brewed beers. They were cold.

'You have a lovely place here,' said Theresa.

He nodded, glancing around. 'Yes. My father built it. 1949.

[92]

I've lived here since then. Fifty years.' There was a hint of pride in his voice, as if to say, there were others, but they did not last the course.

'Were you born here?'

But he had switched off. He flicked the cigarette stub away. 'So. How can I help you?'

'We heard you have rooms to let – a guesthouse.'

'How many nights?'

We glanced at each other.

'One,' said Theresa firmly.

I shrugged. 'Yes, one or two.'

He nodded affably. The crashing of plates had ended inside the house and now the fly door creaked again. A sour-faced woman glowered out at us.

'Vat do you vant?'

I hesitated, expecting her husband to explain, but he did not.

'We heard you have a guesthouse.'

She reached back in the house, grabbed something and handed me a card.

'Price list.'

We studied it carefully, trying not to catch one another's eye.

'We'll have dinner, bed and no breakfast.'

She snatched the card back.

Theresa added, meekly. 'But no meat for me at dinner, please.' The broad Germanic face turned and glared. Theresa struggled on. 'I . . . er . . . I don't eat meat – red meat, that is. I eat fish and chicken and eggs.'

She was cut short by an exasperated hiss. 'Zat is going to cause some difficulty. You don't eat meat!' There was no disguising the utter contempt in her voice. 'Vy not!?'

'I just don't like it,' said Theresa with a disarming smile. 'I mean, I don't feel sorry for the cows or anything, not at all.' Our hostess waited and Theresa hurried to renounce any signs of pity for condemned animals. 'If we didn't kill them, there would be too many of them, wouldn't there? Cows must be killed and

[93]

somebody has to eat them. I want them to be eaten. Really. But I don't like the taste.'

The hiss was mollified slightly. She turned on me. 'And you? Vat about you? You don't eat ze meat also?'

'Oh, I love red meat. No problem.'

She scowled. 'I vill see what I can do.'

Her husband had disappeared during this exchange, now he reappeared with two more beers and his wife left us.

'It's good you can get beer here,' I said.

He shrugged. 'The launch is kaput, but we get anything we need shipped from Pemba. Otherwise we're pretty self-sufficient.'

'So your father came after the war?'

'No. He came in the 'twenties. Fifty German families came out to settle in Mozambique and he and my mother were one of them. Now there's just myself and my wife left here. I think there is one other German on the mainland.'

'They left because of the civil war?'

'Some, but we didn't get bothered here too much.'

'It must have been difficult here years ago?'

He lit a cigarette. 'It was better in many ways. We'd have dances and things – social events. And then the big dhows would come in from India with their spices and cloth. There were merchants here then, selling copra and cashews every year to the dhows. They'd run up to Arabia and across to India.'

'When did that finish?'

'I suppose the 1960s was the last time we saw them.'

'And there's no shop now?'

'No. The last Indian with a place gave it up a few years back.'

His wife appeared with a clutch of neat white sheets. 'Come!' She set off across the grass towards the beach. It was then that I noticed the little hut with its own veranda, standing a hundred yards away. We hurried to keep up. Two doors were thrown open: the first held a large bathroom with two hard towels, some white enamel bowls and a jug.

'At sunset two buckets of hot water will come,' she said. We

[94]

went through to the other room, two single beds with hard grey blankets, a table and a stack of a magazines called *Fair Lady*. It had a kind of scrubbed comfort about it, the old-fashioned simple elegance of a pioneer homestead.

'You vill eat in the house at seven,' she said. 'Wiz us.'

She strode away.

'Some welcome,' I said.

Theresa claimed one of the beds. 'I know people like this in Sweden,' she said. 'Farmers in isolated places who are just like this. They don't mean to be rude. It is their way. A welcome for them doesn't mean lots of conversation: it's a cold beer.'

I went and sat down in a battered leather chair on the veranda. I sensed a little north European pride here. 'They'll charge us a fortune for them.'

'No.' She was perfectly confident, rightly as it turned out. 'They will charge nothing.'

A warm breeze played across the veranda and I watched the line of surf wriggling. On an empty stomach, the beer had made me drowsy. I heard the bathroom door bang as Theresa went in, then I was asleep.

I had a sudden, vivid dream that I was standing by the sea waiting for a boat when a fat Chinese Buddha appeared, his earlobes long with heavy brass rings and his eyelids sewn down. His manner was vaguely threatening.

'You want a boat?'

'Yes.'

'Does anyone know you are here?'

I began to back away. 'Yes, lots and lots.'

I woke up. Seconds seemed to have passed, but in fact I had slept for over an hour, during which time Theresa had washed and changed. The afternoon light had ripened to a deeper, more golden hue, but the line of surf seemed just as far away.

We went and walked across the sand which proved to be a hardened salty crust, featureless except at the high tide mark where there were piles of turtle bones and cowries as big as a man's fist. Delighted by these treasures, we began picking them up as we walked along, behaviour that soon attracted a following of local children. They sang in high reedy voices and turned cartwheels and watched us. It intrigued them: this hunt of ours among the rubbish that the ocean throws out every day. Useless shells and bits of bone. They tried to help, bringing smaller ones that would be easier to carry, or bits of wood that might at least burn on our fire. There was nothing to interest them here: no plastic bottles or tins, nothing but the usual rubbish. And two crazy foreigners picking it up.

In Voltaire's classic, *Candide*, the hero wanders through Eldorado, picking up useless gemstones and nuggets to the astonishment of the locals who howl with laughter when he tries to pay for his dinner with them. It is a favourite device of the utopian writer, the over-turning of values, and travel can achieve the same ends, hence the beach-booty shells we were clutching. But the effects are temporary, the Schwarzes' collection of objets trouvés looked as though it might not have been added to for many a year. Gradually the wondrous becomes familiar, our shells were destined to be workaday soap dispensers in someone's bathroom, or ashtrays. I wanted the Schwarzes to tell me that it need not be that way; I wanted them to be there at dinner, relaxed after the day's heat, telling me that they had found happiness and contentment in a perfect tropical island where the locals were soft-spoken and smiling, the sea full of fish and the trees full of fruit. But I feared they would not.

It was totally dark by the time we set off back and neither of us had a watch. 'I have a feeling that punctuality will be required,' I said, and in hurrying, walked into a prickly pear bush. Several of the tiny spines went deep into my little toe and broke off. The island idyll was not shaping up terribly well and I had just realised how much I wanted it to be true: a man and a woman loving each other, a homestead, a wild tropical island, the simple pleasures of life and cold beer too. Somehow the Schwarzes were undermining all that. Like a perfect apple saved for last and when bitten into, full of worm holes.

I hobbled in to the bungalow at five past seven. The old man was sitting in the living room smoking and writing in a small black notebook. A generator was thumping in the distance and the room was lit with table lamps, one made out of a huge shell.

'Have a beer?' He fetched two for us. We sat in silence, listening to the sounds of his wife in the kitchen. After a few minutes, she appeared.

'Come!'

We walked through and found the table laid with food. 'You – sit here. You – there.'

We each had different bowls. I had a delicious beef stew, beans, pickles and pasta. Theresa had tomato sauce and pasta. Our hosts appeared to be eating cornflakes. The old man put his head down and ate, he clearly was in no mood for talk.

'So you are fairly self-sufficient,' I said to his wife.

'Yes.'

'The beef is your own?'

'Yes.' I waited, but she did not elaborate.

'You grow vegetables and fruit?'

'Yes.'

'What kinds?'

'All kinds.'

'And for cheese and butter?'

'Yes.'

Theresa tried to help me. 'It sounds wonderful. I wish I ate red meat sometimes – home-grown, mmmm.'

The woman stirred her cornflakes very slowly, then dropped the spoon with an ominous clank.

'You think we live in paradise, don't you? You city people. You think it is so much paradise.'

Theresa smiled winningly. 'You do have things we miss. I mean there's no pollution here or anything like that. Not a scrap of paper or plastic on the beach.'

Suddenly the woman's face became animated. 'City people come here and think it is paradise. Well, I tell you it is hard life – very hard. We work hard all ze time and there is much stress, maybe not like with pollutions in cities but it is big stress. It is hard life.'

The attack was over as quickly as it had begun. The cornflakes crackled once again.

'I am from Lapland in Sweden,' said Theresa. 'And we have farms there which are very remote – where the people don't see strangers for a long time.'

There was no answer.

'Do you get lonely?' I asked.

'No – we are too busy.'

We ate on in silence. I had the feeling that if I could only devour every last morsel of the stew, I might redeem myself just a little bit. If I could lick the spoon and ask for seconds, it would be better. But there was at least one cow in the bowl, plus sufficient pasta to supply an Italian country wedding, plus beans for a Mel Brooks movie. By the time I was full, the pile of food had barely been scratched. My hostess saw this and gave me a contemptuous stare.

'Don't you eat? You are on a diet?' She made it sound like a perversion she had read of, with some disbelief, in a *Fair Lady* magazine.

'It's very good – but I've eaten so much.'

Her gaze rested briefly and significantly on the unconsumed cow. I tried to force a little more down. It was obvious that I had eaten several kilos of red meat, but still she fixed me with that disparaging look.

'It must be difficult here if you get a health problem,' said Theresa, casting me a look. 'What do you do for a doctor?'

'Zere is no doctor.'

I knew what was coming.

'I scratched my finger this morning,' Theresa went on sweetly, 'and I thought I might have caught cholera in it.' She glared at me and added, 'You can catch cholera that way, can't you?'

There was a long pause. The last of the cornflakes crackled. 'Our main meal is lunch,' said Frau Schwarz with an air of finality. 'Haf

[98]

you finished?' She cast a final withering glance over the results of our city-bred appetites. 'Go and sit.'

We rose and followed her husband through. He had fished two more beers out of the fridge. I sat down.

'Not there,' came a shout. 'Zat is my chair.'

I moved – quickly. The old man lit a cigarette. He looked tired. 'You will leave tomorrow?'

'I have some friends in Ibo,' said Theresa.

'I will arrange a boat for you,' he said. 'High tide is at ten, so come for coffee at eight and we will go to the beach.'

He lapsed into silence again, rolling the cigarette in his finger-tips. When we finished our beers, we said goodnight and left. As we strolled back the only sound was the distant surf. When I reached the veranda of the hut and looked back at the bungalow, I saw the lights were already off.

Next morning my little toe was a brilliant shade of scarlet and extremely painful. I hobbled after Theresa to the promised coffee. Frau Schwarz was in her chair, sorting out the wages of her staff with a man who stood outside at the window. She counted in German and pointed to a Thermos flask and two cups. We sat down.

I noticed that there were some family photographs on a book-case. When she finished with her staff, I paid what we owed and asked if they were her children. Her face softened.

'Yes.' After a pause, she added, 'They are the only thing that I miss here.'

'Where are they?'

'In South Africa. Our son works in Johannesburg in the fast food industry.'

'He's not a farmer then?'

'No. He lives in the city.'

City people, I thought: so the farmstead, built up over two generations, a place hand-carved from a wilderness, would have no inheritor to carry it on. Perhaps the bitter taste of this defeat was what had soured the atmosphere.

[99]

She leaned across and opening a drawer took out a magnifying glass.

'Now,' she said. 'Show me your toe.'

I was surprised. She had noticed me hobbling. The toe was examined closely and her verdict delivered. 'The spines have gone inside. All you can do is wait for zem to come out. It is pain,' she added. 'I know.'

There was a single moment then when I felt we connected: shared suffering of prickly pears. All she wanted was the understanding that this was not paradise – it was a home, it was hard work, it was not easy, and it was suffering. Paradise didn't just fall in your lap, it needed years of labour and even then it could be snatched away from you at the last minute on the whim of a child.

Her husband stumped along the veranda without coming in. 'Are you ready?' he asked through the netted window.

His wife was following my gaze down to where a bright, colourful picture lay in the open drawer. It showed two small children in a garden, the garden outside the window. For the first time, she volunteered something. 'When they were small, they liked it here.' She put her hand tenderly on the drawer handle. 'It was good in those days.'

Then she dropped the glass inside and pushed the drawer shut. The colours disappeared like the maw of a clam as it closes. 'There is work,' she said, and standing up went out without saying goodbye.

6

Of Piss and Eggshells

What else are all your terms,
Whereon no one of your writers 'grees with other?
Of your elixir, your *lac virginis*,
Your stone, your med'cine, and your chrysosperme,
Your sal, your sulphur, and your mercury,
Your oil of height, your tree of life, your blood,
Your marchesite, your tutie, your magnesia,
Your toad, your crow, your dragon, and your panther;
Your sun, your moon, your firmament, your adrop,
Your lato, azoch, zernich, chibrit, heautarit,
And then your red man, and your white woman,
With all your broths, your menstrues, your materials,
Of piss and egg-shells, women's terms, man's blood,
Hair o'the head, burnt clouts, chalk, merds, and clay,
Powder of bones, scalings of iron, glass,
And worlds of other strange ingredients,
Would burst a man to name?
                                     Ben Jonson, *The Alchemist*

The day was cloudy, and by the time we got out on the dhow and moving, the sea had gone from pale green to black and liver-like, the surface smooth as if covered with a thin membrane. We skirted flooded mangroves watched by egrets and herons. Then with a brief exhalation the rain arrived, hissing on the swell.

[101]

After a couple of hours we managed to pole our way through a narrow gap in the mangroves and emerged on the edge of a mile-wide channel. On the far side was Ibo town: the red of the pantiles running across the horizon like a glimpse of sunrise between the choppy grey water and a leaden sky. We were 'contra-vento', as the sailors pointed out, and it took an hour to tack across the bay. Slowly we saw more detail of the town: the shingly beach dotted with broken boats, then the cracked and stained walls of houses, buttressed against the attack of storms and high tides. There was a church with a campanile, a couple of small forts and what appeared to be a promenade. On closer inspection, only the church appeared in reasonable upkeep, the rest were in the clutches of strangling figs. The seeds of this parasitic tree are spread by fruit-eating bats, then gutters and cracks are colonised, aerial roots sent down which thicken and multiply and finally destroy what first supported them.

We waded ashore rather gingerly: what had appeared to be shingle turned out to be the broken shards of years and years of accumulated broken pot, broken bottles, and broken pantiles. There were little pieces of old blue and white porcelain, the Chinese porcelain that had once been the staple of the Indian Ocean dinner service and a convenient ballast for Portuguese ships. Also there were the sturdy glass necks of Portuguese demijohns in which the cheap wine from the Douro still comes.

Our dhow was heading back to Tandanhangue, so we found ourselves alone with the rain apparently finished and the sun trying to appear. Next to us was the church which faced a large open space, the paths neatly marked with coral blocks and the spaces dotted with flowering trees. Around this were colonial Portuguese buildings, some clearly in use, others abandoned. To our right was a long street of single-storey houses, each with a neat veranda at the front; the once lovely pale blue and pink walls were now patched and peeling, as weather-beaten and sun-bleached as the shells that were scattered all around.

[102]

Leaving our bags by the church, we went up to the first building. The ornate carved door was open and inside, among the goat droppings, lay an elephant's skull, one huge molar tooth remaining. Further along the street we found ancient ivory-inlaid doors hanging from their hinges, trees poking through roofs, and wooden balconies leaning towards collapse. The clouds had parted and the sun come out, lending a golden glow to the faded beauty of the ruins, but it could not disguise the fact that this was a ghost town. The merchants whose signs were fading with the years had gone: Chinese, English, French and Portuguese. And with them had gone the life too, leaving a skeleton staff of those too old or too poor to shift across to Pemba.

I sat on a wall and watched an old man, stooping and stick-like come walking up the street. He stopped and smiled at me, his eyes bright and intelligent.

'Are you British?'

'Yes.'

'Ah! Now we had an English merchant here. That was his place.' He pointed to an abandoned and roofless house. 'William Phillipi. Long gone, of course, like the rest.'

'Do you remember those times?'

He laughed. 'When I was a boy, these streets were full of people: Portuguese soldiers in uniform, white hunters loading up their trophies, Arab and Indian merchants, horses and carts, even cars – yes, they were brought on two galowas tied together.' His eyes shone as he spoke and he gazed around, seeing the street as it was, not with the dessicated leaves rustled by the breeze, or the packs of goats trotting in and out of the abandoned rooms, their walls hostage to the strangling cords of fig roots.

'Did you work here?'

'I am an Iboan,' he answered proudly. 'And I worked here in the Portuguese administration. I saw forty-two different governors come and go.'

This was a tribute to the island's infernal ability to kill people like flies. A British visitor in the 1820s, one Captain William

Fitzwilliam Wentworth Owen, noted in disbelief that the governor on Ibo had survived thirty-six years, contrary to all expectations. This Hercules poured scorn on the dangers of the 'sickly season', but four weeks later he was dead too.

Theresa and I belatedly introduced ourselves to the old resident and shook hands. His name was João Baptista.

'Now this place,' he said, patting the square columns that stood on the low wall where I sat. 'This was a store for an Indian merchant. He brought castanha – the fruit of the cashew – and took it to Goa every year. Over there was Suki, a Chinese, his sons are old, but they still keep a shop in the village of Pangane up the coast. Come.'

We walked further up the street. 'See here. JFS – that is now a big company in Portugal and Mozambique. The founder started here as a poor boy selling papaya.'

He pointed across to a tumbledown colonial house, its once elegant shady veranda and columned entrance being slowly dismembered by the giant fig trees. 'That house belonged to two Mozambican sisters – very fat women – and they were slave traders.'

'And you can remember them?' I asked in surprise.

'Oh, they were too old for work when I was a boy, but still alive, yes.' The slave trade had certainly continued long after it was officially outlawed, well into the twentieth century.

We walked back to the church and collected our bags.

'Where will you stay?' he asked. 'Let us go and see Dona Eliza – she has the key for the bishop's old residence.'

Dona Eliza was sitting in her yard reading, the last Portuguese resident of Ibo. She had been born on the island and lived all her life there but, now she was getting old, planned to leave for Portugal.

'I can let you stay in the bishop's house,' she said. 'Do you want dinner tonight?'

One of her workers took us across to the Casa Obispo, a huge rambling mansion set behind a high wall and surrounded by tall gloomy trees. Out in the garden stood the rotting skeleton of a light aeroplane.

'A Frenchman came in it,' said the caretaker. 'But he left it here and never returned.'

The house was set up on a stone plinth with broad shady verandas. The rooms were huge and almost bare, except for some single iron beds and one or two antique wardrobes labelled 'obispo'. The caretaker showed us the bathroom.

'*Amanhã de manhã*,' he said. 'Tomorrow. You want matabicho?'

I was nonplussed: mata, I knew, meant kill; bicho meant beast. '*Desculpe*,' I apologised. '*Eu nãu falo bem Português*.'

'*Matabicho*,' he repeated, miming eating. I suddenly realised what he was getting at: kill the beast – breakfast!

'*Sim, quero*.'

That night we ate a scrawny chicken by lamplight in the bishop's dining room, the dark corners of the room rustling and scratching with unseen creatures. Several small boys despatched in various directions to locate a drink came back with two tiny lemons. Theresa raided her rucksack and we drank the red wine. It was then that she revealed the news her horoscope had given her: the next day was the only favourable sailing day before Christmas. She would have to return to Pemba where her friends were waiting. It was a great shame as we were getting along well.

'He's a missionary,' she explained while popping the champagne. 'He spent four years in prison for invading the Seychelles.'

It was only after she had gone the following day that I realised she had mixed up missionary with mercenary.

After Theresa's departure, Ibo's essentially melancholic atmosphere came down hard on me. I walked along the foreshore picking up shards of Chinese porcelain and visited the gloomy fort where the Portuguese had kept their slaves after capture on the mainland.

As fortresses these coastal bastions had attracted the attention of pirates eager for a base, but Ibo and the other Querrimbas were always rejected on account of the shallow waters surrounding. The only recorded attempt to establish a pirate base on the East African coast seems to have been the assault on Zanzibar in about 1701 by George Booth, John Bowen and Nathaniel North. Booth died in the attempt and the others fled east to Madagascar. (Bowen had been with Thomas White when their drunken captors' pirate vessel was shipwrecked at St Augustine's Bay in south-west Madagascar. Nathaniel North would inherit Bowen's command when he died of 'the dry Belly Ach' while in Mauritius.)

Finally, I resolved to cheer myself up with a trip to the last remaining site of interest that I had not visited: the cemetery. For this I enlisted the help of João Baptiste, finding him in his ancient reclining chair on the shady veranda of his house.

'*O cemitério? Aipa!*' He jumped up at my suggestion like an old puppet whose strings have suddenly been jerked aloft. '*Vem! Vem!*' he cried. 'Let's go.'

I could see that I was not the only one wondering how to kill time on Ibo.

The cemetery was on the far side of the town and João Baptiste gave me a running commentary on all the services that the town had once possessed. 'This was our power station. Here was a cafe where we sat and looked out at the sea.'

We passed along the old promenade, stopped to shake our heads at the ruined tennis court and the lone nineteenth-century grave where the deceased was described as 'the legitimate son of . . .'.

The graveyard itself was behind a high white wall and a wooden palisade to keep goats out. We pushed it open. Inside was a broad square ground dotted with tombs in varying stages of ruin.

'Look,' said João Baptiste, pointing to one of the better-kept plots. 'This one is for Dona Eliza's mother.'

Most of the stones dated back to the period between 1880 and 1920, Ibo's heyday. Some were for soldiers who had guarded the island, others were sea captains, merchants or administrators. I wandered across to the chapel which was teetering on the edge of complete disintegration. Next to it was a small mausoleum, the steps covered in spiny seed burrs and the peeling pale blue door slightly ajar but stuck fast.

I forced it back a few inches and managed to get my head inside. There was a stone table in the centre of a small room and on it a lidless coffin containing a corpse wrapped in filthy bandages. One leg had been moved and a skeletal foot, some tendrils of dried flesh still attached, was resting on the rim of the box, as though the occupant had made a last minute bid for freedom.

I retreated quickly and rejoined João Baptiste. 'Somebody in Angoche told me that witchcraft is a big problem along this coast,' I said.

He nodded, eyes brightening with interest at this new topic for discussion. '*Sim, sim!* There are too many witches – especially here on Ibo. They even have a school.'

'Really! Could I visit it?' I imagined some little rural self-help project, run with the assistance of one of Europe's more progressive NGOs and an earnest young aid worker called Harry Potter.

He laughed. 'No, you cannot. Nobody knows where it is, or who runs it. But we know it exists.'

'And these witches,' I said, bringing the subject around to what had triggered my enquiry, 'sometimes they use dead things?'

He nodded enthusiastically. '*Sim!* Always, they are using dead things.'

'So grave-robbing is a problem here on Ibo?'

He looked pained. 'It is. There is too much of grave-robbing.'

'By these witches?'

Now he looked puzzled. 'Witches?'

'Yes,' I used the two relevant words I knew in Portuguese. '*Feiticeiros e curandeiros.*' The former are sorcerers, the latter more like medicine men.

But João Baptiste looked like a man who had lost the thread of the conversation. He repeated, '*Feiticeiros?*'

'Do they rob the graves?'

'No, not the feiticeiros – they do not rob the graves. Feiticeiros are often good people, you know.' He shuddered a little. 'No,

[107]

the grave-robbing, that is something truly evil – it is the work of carpenters.'

Silence fell upon us. We continued walking around the graves until we came to the gate.

'*Carpinteiros?*' I asked, a little weakly. 'You mean men who cut wood and make doors and windows.'

He smiled with the pleasure of one who is finally getting his message across. 'Yes, they steal the wood from the coffin to make furniture. It is a very evil thing.'

We pushed the gate shut behind us and set off along the track towards the town. Despite the setback concerning the pernicious evil of cabinetmakers, the germ of an idea was forming in my mind.

'So you don't actually know who the witches are on Ibo?' I asked.

João Baptiste gave me a sidelong glance and answered in similar, oblique fashion. 'It is better not to know such people,' he said.

'But sometimes it must be necessary to consult them?'

He gave me a rather cagey nod. '*Talvez* – maybe.'

'For example, if someone was going on a long journey?'

'*Sim.*'

'Like a journey on small boats to the Comoros Islands and Madagascar?'

He drew his breath in sharply. '*Aipa!*'

'Then you would need some insurance, wouldn't you?'

'That is true. It would be foolish not to do that.'

We stopped to look out from the end of the promenade. On the muddy flats several small children were gathered in happy little bands of squatters, their underwear around their knees.

'And do you know of such a person – an expert who could supply me with that insurance?'

He thought for a while before answering. 'There is such a man. We can go now to see him.'

I readily agreed and we set off inland, passing along winding tracks that led through long dry grass and groves of cashew nut trees. Eventually we came to a white-walled hut with a palm thatch roof. João Baptiste called out and a large tubby gentleman in his mid-thirties appeared. He was dressed in a white shirt, black trousers and a red chequered Arab headscarf. They greeted each other warmly and I was introduced.

'Come,' said the man, moving us aside into the shade of a thorn tree. João Baptiste gave a long explanation in Kimwane, the man nodding seriously at each point and making some observations of his own while delicately fingering a set of prayer beads. Their voices, I noticed, had dropped from the loud bonhomie of greetings to a low conspiratorial whisper.

'You must understand,' said the man, at last. 'That this is a secret matter and no one should know about it, except you and I.'

'*Compreendo*,' I agreed, nodding earnestly.

The sorcerer came closer. 'I can prepare for you an intatibu,' he said. 'An insurance. It has great force: if a man attacks you with a knife, he will not be able to cut you. The intatibu will even prevent him thinking thoughts of attacking you. The same for a gun: if a man shoots at you, the bullet will not strike your body.'

I had to get him to repeat this three times before I was sure I had understood correctly, but there was no doubt. As far as practical protection for travellers went, the intatibu was clearly a cut above the usual insurance schemes. 'That is a very powerful thing.' There was much nodding and agreement. 'But you see,' I added. 'I will travel by ship to Madagascar and I was thinking more about storms and shipwrecks and pirates.'

He smiled self-confidently. 'This intatibu will cover those things. It will give you dreams where you will predict the future.'

'I do have bad dreams sometimes,' I admitted and he smiled as though he had already been proved right.

'You must place the intatibu under your pillow at night, then you will no longer be troubled.'

[109]

There was a lull in the conversation and I sensed that perhaps this was the moment when I was expected to enquire about remuneration.

'Such a powerful charm might be too expensive for me,' I declared. 'Certainly it cannot be cheap.'

The man nodded sagely. 'By God, you are right!'

'I was hoping to purchase something of less power, not the top of the range model, you know, just the basic cover – and pay only, say, 20,000 metacais.'

There was a stunned silence. Such an amount was sufficient to buy almost two cans of beer on Ibo, assuming they could be found.

'You might think,' said the sorcerer at length, 'that we live in the arsehole of Judas, but I can tell you: it is very dangerous to joke about such matters.' There was more than a hint of menace in the way he said this. 'I am offering to prepare a life insurance for you. Something that will protect you for the rest of your days – from bullets, knives, storms, shipwrecks, bicycle punctures – almost anything.'

'So what does it cost?'

There was a brief discussion between João Baptiste and the sorcerer in Kimwane. I wondered if I should ask about the talisman's power against salesmen, sharks and cheats.

'Five hundred thousand,' said the sorcerer with some finality. This was absurd – probably enough for me to splash out and buy every goat on the island and still have change for half a dozen houses.

There was a flurry of negotiating and we settled on a middle figure: 40,000. An hour later I emerged, rather shell-shocked, from the sorcerer's house, having been subjected to an endless round of droned chants: incantations that had been rubbed and rounded in African mouths for so long since leaving their desert homeland, they had become something strange and different, not like Arabic at all. These were abracadabras – the esoteric knowledge of lands far away which could not be understood, only borrowed. And who is to say that knowledge, just like people, does not broaden and grow as it travels.

I was clutching a small white package about the size of a rabbit's paw which would protect me at all times.

'Keep it hidden and close to your skin, otherwise it won't keep bullets away,' the sorcerer said, speaking as if he had received exasperating complaints on this score.

'Oh, and one last thing,' he added. 'When you . . . you know . . .'

'What?'

He brought his open palm down on to his fist, creating a popping noise. 'Understand?'

I shook my head. He did the popping thing several times and raised his eyebrows furiously.

I suddenly realised this was an Iboan nudge-nudge wink-wink. 'Ah! I understand. With women.'

'Take it off before and put it on after, when you have washed yourself.'

'What if the woman attacks me – I'll be naked and without protection.'

He smiled mysteriously. 'God is merciful.'

At the bishop's house I discovered that two new visitors to the island had arrived: Jan and Tamara, a young couple who were on their way, they told me, from Switzerland to Brazil. The apparent wrong turning they must have taken along this route was due to Tamara's brother who lived in Maputo and had recommended a few weeks in the north of Mozambique. Tamara was rather regretting this advice, having had to walk several miles that morning before they could find a dhow for Ibo. Her arrival, however, had revived the bishop's residence. Suddenly, as with Theresa, there were large numbers of young men, eager to be sent on errands: beer-finding missions, chicken-location reconnaissaince, fish-landing reports from the beach, seafood availability, liaison with Dona Eliza. Tamara, needless to say perhaps, was good-natured, vivacious, a fluent Portuguese speaker and rather pretty.

[111]

Once I had mentioned my attempts to sail north, she called on several young admirers and sent them spinning out into the late afternoon sunshine in search of sea captains with sturdy boats – 'Without holes!'

'If you don't mind,' said Jan. 'We could come along too. Maybe we could even charter a boat – between three it might be reasonable.'

So it was agreed that we would travel onward together. However, word soon came back that Chico, the owner of the best boats on Ibo – 'guaranteed no holes' – was in Pemba. The same messenger also confided that there was not a single can of beer to be had on Ibo and the supply of chickens had dried up; all he could offer was some small fish – he indicated with his hands – something of approximately herring size.

At sunset we set out to find another boat-owner. Ibo is at its best then, as night approaches and the last rays touch the scarred walls and broken pantiles; the barefoot children of families who camp inside the fallen ruins scamper through the dust, and old men lean on their sticks and grin toothlessly. Outside the abandoned electricity generating station, a man pushing a bicycle stopped to speak to us. He was very tall, dressed in a cellular basketball vest and reeked of pineapple aguadiente.

'Good evening,' he declared grandly. 'My name is Alawi and I am the Sheriff of the Ocean.' He swayed gently, his hands firmly gripping the bicycle.

We told him of our search for a boat.

'Chico has the best boats,' he said immediately.

'But Chico is in Pemba.'

'Then you should want Salimu.'

'Yes, yes, we want Salimu.'

He began laboriously to turn his bicycle around to point in the other direction. It took quite some time as the pedals kept biting his ankles.

'You stay where?'

'At Casa Obispo.'

[112]

'I will send a man. You want Pangane? Okay. You wait there.'
And off he wobbled into the growing darkness.

Back at the bishop's house we felt our way on to the veranda
in the darkness and lit an oil lamp. Our dinner arrived, having
been carried on a tray through the streets from Dona Eliza's house.
There was only a little bread, but plenty of sticky rice had been
provided and several small, bony fish.

While we were eating a man arrived bearing a note. Tamara
read it out, translating from the Portuguese. ' "There comes the
man that is in charge of the embarkation that same. You have
the authorisation to travel to your travel to Pangane. Everything
is okay. Signed: The Ocean Sheriff of Ibo, Aulawe Sangage." '

We now took interest in the bearer of the note, a wiry and
weather-beaten old man who said he was a nakhoda of a dhow
and was called Nhenhe. I noticed with approval that the buttocks
of his shorts had been completely worn out to expose his muscular
bottom. This man was definitely a hardened sailor. He was also
cheerful and friendly. We agreed a price and he promised faithfully
to come and collect us an hour before the dawn.

After he had gone and Jan and Tamara were asleep, I went
and sat on the veranda. The garden beyond was like a dark
void, utterly featureless and black. Overhead, however, the true
void was full of light: the stars were cast in a vast vault of soft
luminescence in which the shapes of the mango trees scooped deep
caverns.

7

Shani's Dream

I am as free as nature first made man,
Ere the base laws of servitude began,
When wild in woods the noble savage ran.
John Dryden, *The Conquest of Granada*

To come to the point at once, I beg to say that I have
not the least belief in the Noble Savage. I consider him a
prodigious nuisance, and an enormous superstition ... he is
a savage – cruel, false, thievish, murderous; addicted more or
less to grease, entrails, and beastly customs; a wild animal
with the questionable gift of boasting; a conceited, tiresome,
bloodthirsty, monotonous humbug ... My position is that, if
we have anything to learn from the noble savage, it is what
to avoid. His virtues are a fable; his happiness is a delusion;
his nobility, nonsense.
Charles Dickens, June 1853

A thinking man is a depraved animal.
Jean Jacques Rousseau, *Discourse on the
Origin of Inequality*, 1754

At five there was a knock at my door. It was Jan and Tamara,
already dressed and ready to go, wondering if I had had any bad
dreams, particularly those involving storms or shipwreck.

[115]

I had to admit that I had had a vivid dream in which I was chased by a mad elephant around a small wood whose trees were steadily being depleted by evil carpenters. At the end a tourist minibus arrived and the elephant simply stomped it flat, tourists and all. When I looked around, all the trees had gone and I had to run and run until I woke up.

Nhenhe came for us when the sky was just beginning to pale in the east. We walked through the silent town and on to the beach. The only other person around was an aged fisherman who was repairing a wooden pulley wheel by filing it down with a sting ray's tail. On land there seemed to be not a breath of wind, but when we waded out and climbed aboard I could feel a very gentle breeze coming from the south.

It was a good boat, the timbers long since smoothed to a fine-grained grey by the sun and sea. Nhenhe and his two crew fitted the rudder, then carried the lateen pole out with the sail furled around it. One of the crew was a tall morose individual, the other a short athletic-looking man in his late twenties who shot withering looks at our luggage and our wobbly attempts to porter it out to the boat.

The anchor was lifted – the rusty block of an old car gearbox – then we were propelled by long mangrove poles out towards the point. We watched the sun touch the tip of the church belltower and begin to climb down. It seemed all the colder for having that golden warmth so near but yet to arrive, especially when we emerged from the lee of the point and felt the breeze strengthen. The sea had a smooth oily texture, as though the night had flattenend it. The mangrove poles made soft dull thuds as they touched the hull. I felt a great pleasure to be moving, to watch the water slipping by the hull and the sail unfurl and then fill as the men hoisted the lateen. They walked easily along the gunwale, toes gripping like fingers and even the morose sailor let a grin slip through. It was only a job and Pangane only a day's sailing, but there was a simple, primitive pleasure in feeling the wind take us there.

[116]

Nhenhe sat, like all the nakhodas do, on the small poop deck at the stern, one leg stretched out in front of him, the other crooked so his heel rested against his knee, and his hand on the rudder. He was smiling.

'Kusi is blowing,' he said, 'and I am happy.'

The lateen began to creak and we were surfing down the sides of waves that had come through a gap in the reef. This was where the big merchant vessels of old would have dropped anchor, safe inside the reef but unable to approach Ibo's shallow shores. Nhenhe gave an order and the sail was tightened so that we heeled right over to the gunwale, creaming through the water. A few shifted sandbags helped right the boat a little. Jan lay on the prow smoking, while Tamara and I chatted to Nhenhe.

'What does it take to be a sailor?' asked Tamara.

Nhenhe answered very seriously. 'To be a sailor you must study swimming,' he said, 'and hunger.'

'Is it dangerous?'

The boat was crashing into some big rollers now, though nothing so bad as to disturb Jan.

'You must know when to run and hide from the sea,' said Nhenhe. 'Sometimes you have to throw ballast overboard, even the cargo – even the president's bag to save life.'

'And dangerous sea animals?'

'There is nkunga, the sea cobra. When you are fishing he comes and looks to see if you have fish. If you have, then you must give to him or he will take your legs! Aieeee!' He brought his hand down with a slap on his thigh. 'You can choose. Your fish or your legs.'

To our right, we could see the reef now. A roaring white line cutting across the horizon. Tamara gave me a crafty look and touched Nhenhe's arm. 'You say it is dangerous, but what about going beyond the reef – out in the channel to the Comoros and Madagascar?'

Nhenhe drew his breath in sharply. 'Oh, boy! The Devil is in that sea! Waves so big they take your breath away and then the

[117]

amlani jumps up, right over the ship and swallows you up in his stomach and that is when you die.'

He tried to explain what the amlani was, but he ran out of Portuguese words trying to convey just how horrible it was.

'I think I've heard enough,' I said, but Tamara was persistent. 'So you must be very prepared?'

'You don't even put a foot over the side because a shark will take it off you.'

'How long is the voyage?'

'Forever, because you will go down in the deep and never reach the other side.'

Tamara was loving this.

'So you need protection?'

'Yes. Fortunately there are those curandeiros and feiticeiros who will protect you.'

'Who is the best?'

'The best is on Matemo island.'

'And on Ibo – who is the best curandeiro?'

'There are none. They are all big thieves – the biggest of thieves!'

I was regretting ever telling Tamara about my visit to the witch doctor, but her teasing was stopped by the smaller of the crew. He had been sitting next to Nhenhe, listening thoughtfully to our conversation. Now he leaned forward.

'That is not so,' he said. 'The biggest thieves are politicians and brancos.'

There was an awkward silence, then he added, 'And Tanzanians.'

There was more silence while we digested this before Tamara coolly asked, 'Why Tanzanians?'

He began to talk rapidly, his face animated and hands chopping the air. 'I had a galowa like this one. A good boat which I kept at Pemba. Four days ago I went down to the beach in the morning and it was gone. I heard that some Tanzanian pirates had stolen it. Now they are running for the border, hoping I will not catch up with them. But I will never give up,

I will chase them even into their own land and take back what is mine.'

Nhenhe and the other sailor looked away, as though a little embarrassed by the outburst.

'You are alone?' I asked.

'I set off walking from Pemba along the beach. I walked all night and came to Tandanhangue. There I talked with the people and sailed to Ibo. They said the pirates had been seen passing in my boat, but it was already painted a different colour.'

This seemed an unlikely tactic to me: the galowas are almost always sunburnt grey with vague patches of worn paint. Fresh colour would have been a dead giveaway.

'So you are chasing the pirates now. How many of them are there?'

'Some people say five, others seven, but they came in a galowa so I think there are more of them – in at least two boats.'

'Don't all the boats look alike?'

He laughed. 'To you, a branco. What do you know about the sea? Or our lives? White men are weak and know nothing of such matters. Can you pass the day here without drinking something? I have seen the whites, always complaining, always needing water, or a soft chair, or food, or sleep. We blacks are tougher: I can walk all night without food or drink and still work on the boat next day. I don't drink alcohol, I don't smoke cigarros. I can wait.'

Tamara frowned. 'Wait? What do you mean?'

'You brancos cannot wait one hour without grumbling, but we blacks can wait for days without complaining.'

There was a silence while his attack sank in and he took this as further proof of white weakness.

'You can't even argue! And I've seen your football on television – all the best players are black.'

'True,' I said, thinking I'd like to provoke more of this. 'But why is it that black Mozambicans are poor, while white men are rich?'

'Isn't it true that the brancos have the world's money factory

[119]

in Switzerland?' he demanded. 'All the money is made there so they choose the best for themselves. They give us weak money and keep strong money.'

I liked this theory, imagining a mint somewhere in the Bernese Oberland churning out first-rate money and defective shop-soiled stuff to palm off on the Africans.

'What about these elections?' asked Tamara. 'What do you think of them?'

He narrowed his eyes. 'At the last election,' he said in a low voice, as if government snoops might be listening, 'the forms were blue, this time they are red.'

He leaned back, his point proven. But we were slow-witted.

'So what?'

'Don't you see? Red is the colour of blood. And also the Frelimo slogan this time is "The Fight Must Go On!" That is how I know war will come again.'

'You believe so?'

'It is certain.'

'Aren't you afraid?'

'No. It is good. I like war. In war you can make money. In war the black man makes money. Last war, I travelled many times with eggs from the interior to Pemba and sold them. It was dangerous, carrying them through the bush, through Renamo territory and minefields. No rich man would do that! I made 38 million metacais and bought my boat.' His face clouded at the memory of his lost boat. 'You see in wartime the brancos cannot control everything through the politicians; their licences and permits and contracts and agencies – that is all meaningless. So the black man can benefit. Even a poor boy can take a few eggs, walk some days in the bush, then sell at great profit. In peace that is not possible, the branco or the Indian will carry the eggs in his car and the policemen are paid to prevent others doing likewise. All the money runs to the politician, the Indians and the brancos.'

Suddenly his apparently hare-brained opinions began to make

more sense. I wondered how many other poor Mozambicans had learned such a lesson from the chaos of the previous years.

'So what do you want for Mozambique?'

'If I could choose, I would choose war.'

The normally good-humoured Tamara was beginning to show signs of impatience with him. 'But in war your children cannot go to school. They might die. Do you have a family?'

'*Sim!* I have a wife and two children.'

'So what will you do? What is your ideal life?'

'If we cannot have war, then let them bring a government of brancos.'

At this we began to laugh. 'Two minutes ago,' said Tamara, 'you said brancos were all thieves and weak!'

There was obviously no contradiction in his mind. 'Brancos are rich,' he declared. 'Weak but rich.' He rounded on Jan who had come back from dozing on the prow to hear the argument. 'How is it you can afford to do this? To come here. Why? Only for looking? You are not even working. But I work hard and I cannot go there to your country. Here the blacks have no money – except politicians. They make money selling our lands to foreigners. Tell me why are you here? What do you want?'

Jan shrugged good-naturedly. 'I don't want anything,' he said. 'To see the countryside and talk to people, find out about their lives.'

The sailor waved his hand contemptuously. '*Aipa!* Only for that? You spend so much money, enough to feed a village for ten years maybe, only for that?'

Here was our moment of supreme discomfort: to be suddenly unmasked as rich dilettantes masquerading as hoboes by this devil of an autodidact. But he spoiled his chance to twist the knife in our liberal consciences by rushing onwards. 'Right now you have more money in your pockets than I could earn in my whole life, but you are weak. We could kill you now. Ha! We could just kill you like that! And throw the bodies to the sharks!'

His face had become wild with his words, his eyes brilliant with

[121]

the madness of his own notion. I suddenly saw a little Idi Amin, or a Bokassa next to me, a street tough with a golden tongue and streak of insanity.

'What could you do? Brancos cannot fight. I take my knife and kill you right here! Then we three are rich for life.'

For a moment, we all hung there awestruck by the terrible abyss he had opened, a glimpse of the madness in Mozambique's bloodsoaked and hopeless history. In that brief moment of time, as the dhow slid onwards under the taut sail in shallow seas of perfect blue, it was as if he had shown us the chasm beyond the reef where the seabed plunged to 3,000 metres. In that instant, we too were aware of our fragility; we believed he might do it.

A few seconds passed before Jan said drily, 'I only carry credit cards.'

Tamara leaned forward. 'He is joking, isn't he?'

And I smiled. 'Of course.' And the others saw the smiles and relaxed. Our bloodthirsty tyrant relaxed, grinning. And we were no longer sure if we had quite got that right. Perhaps it had been all a joke. Yes! It was all a joke, a damn good joke. And we all laughed.

Jan retired to the sun-baked deck at the prow, his cap pulled down over his eyes. The breeze was dropping now and our progress was slow. An hour passed in silence.

We had left behind the island of Matemo while talking, one of the larger inhabited islands of the Querrimbas. Away to the east on the mainland, a long white beach lined with coconuts could be seen stretching for miles and miles then curving out to a point. 'At that point is Pangane,' said Nhenhe. Our course, however, was out near the islands, too far to see signs of life on that long idyllic stretch of sand, apart from a few dugout canoes drawn up. By midday we were approaching Pangane, a string of thatched huts under the coconut trees. Depending on the wind, the boats would head for the north or south side of the point, passing through a narrow strait between the rocky point and the island of Makelowa. As we were sailing with the kusi, the south wind, we went to the north beach for shelter, skimming in towards several canoes and dhows anchored in the shimmering pale blue waters. When I jumped out and waded ashore, I found the sand littered with beautiful shells: whole giant clams horny with corals and worms, finger-sized olives with tiger-back striations, sheep's-eye cowries and many more, all strung out along the beach as though the ocean had flung aside its necklace.

The three of us stood there for some time, scarcely able to believe we had discovered such a place. For Nhenhe, though, it was just another village by the sea, with its own problems. 'See that boat over there? It belongs to some Nacala men. Don't sail north with them, will you? They are not good people.'

He and the crew led us up the sand and under the trees. The village proved to be several hundred houses, almost all identical mud and palm thatch huts built under an old coconut plantation. The people were thin and wiry and walked with a strong, short-stepping gait, the result, no doubt, of spending their lives wading through soft sand. All the streets were simply sand. People lay in the gentle shade of high palms: women in bright sarongs of gold, orange and black, heads resting on hands, gossiping, as if waiting for an unseen Gauguin to finish. Old men raising hands from their rope beds.

'*Salaama sana. Uku kandepi?*' Where are you going?

'*Chez Suki.*'

Nhenhe pointed out the racks of drying octopus and the goat coops: cages of sticks up on stilts. 'They put them inside every night because of the lions.'

'Lions!'

He was very insistent that it was true. The lions came down from the forest to the west where elephants and buffalo also roamed. He became a little vague, however, when pressed to date the last attack. Nevertheless, I discovered later that he was quite right about the forest and I saw elephant tracks.

On the south side of the village we came to the walled compound of the Chinese man, Suki, and went inside. Unfortunately, Suki

[123]

himself was away but there were some rooms to rent and we settled in.

Suki's workers were friendly, and fascinated by Jan's family photos: his father's ski bar in the Swiss Oberland and his brother's guesthouse on a beach in Brazil.

'It is just like Pangane, but Pangane is better,' Jan said to them. But the cook was not convinced. He scrutinised the photo closely and at length stood up.

'No, it is not the same,' he said. 'Your brother's place is better.' He tapped the photo emphatically. 'There you have straight hair and here we have curly.'

After a lunch of fried fish, I set off alone up the beach to the north but I had not gone more than half a mile when I met Shani, victim of piracy and our would-be murderer.

'Is there any news about your boat?' I asked.

He shrugged. 'Nothing is certain, but I believe those pirates have passed this place. I will try to continue to Mocimboa da Praia as soon as I can get work on a boat.'

Mocimboa was effectively the last stop before Tanzania. 'What will you do if you find them?'

'Call for help – people I know. These pirates may be armed.'

'And if they have reached Tanzania?'

He scowled. 'I will follow and steal it back.' But I could see that this possibility worried him. It seemed likely that his bravado would end at Mocimboa and the border. The others I had spoken to gave me a palpable sense that the Tanzanians were seen as more sophisticated, more ruthless, and stronger. Tackling them was not something to be taken lightly. In this they had created a psychological advantage, something pirates of previous centuries would have recognised.

For three days we waited in the hope of a dhow going north. One day I visited a nearby island where I found a well-preserved Portuguese fort all overgrown with trees, abandoned and unused since the day the Portuguese had left.

Back in Pangane, Jan and I entered negotiations to charter a boat. A price was agreed and before dawn one morning a sailor came to call for us. We heard him hammering on the gate and then his face appeared at the window. It was Shani.

He led us through the village which was waking up with the first light: men already mending nets, women lighting fires and children running errands. The sea was calm and in the east the sun cut a narrow gash in the haze and began to rise through it, driving the blue back with a golden flush of orange and pink.

Shani walked next to me, speaking quietly. 'I heard that those pirates passed through here at night,' he said. 'Today I will watch for them.'

I watched his face in profile, a crafty and quick-witted face that I did not trust. And yet the plan was forming in my mind even then, that I would go with him and find these pirates. The real-life thing! It was too good to miss.

As usual, there were three sailors. They helped us load our baggage, then the anchor was raised, the sail set, and we were moving.

It was a perfect day: a light breeze in from the south-east, the sun warm but not yet hot, and ahead of us slivers of islands – green on white in a cobalt sea. We sat enjoying the ride: the gurgling water under the hull, the creaking hemp ropes and murmur of wind on canvas. But the peace was not to last, not with Shani on board. After an hour he spoke up.

He pointed out one island further out to sea. 'That place was sold to an American who will not allow us to go within five kilometres of the shore.' The other sailors nodded. 'What is he doing there? Our people have fished around that island since before the Portuguese came. Now we cannot. And why? Because he wants to bring rich friends from Johannesburg by plane so they can lie on the beach and drink cold beer. On other islands, people say the whites are smuggling drugs, or ivory, or leopard skins.' He leaned forward towards me. 'Hey, amigo! If you want to buy some, let me know.'

[125]

'How can he do that?' asked Tamara. 'Surely, he cannot behave like that – this American?'

'Listen. His friends are politicians and every politician is a thief,' Shani declared loudly. 'He goes and fetches money, then eats alone.'

The sun was getting up and the breeze had dropped. There was just sufficient room on the forward deck to lie down. I dozed for an hour, and when I woke, found that we had barely moved.

There was a small island less than half a mile ahead which we began to inspect with interest. Could we row there, I asked.

Shani liked the idea. 'There are fishermen there who may have fish to sell in Mocimboa,' he said. 'And they may have some news.'

Now I realised that the hump of white sand was not topped with burnt vegetation, as I had thought, but with crude shelters and fish-drying racks. As we paddled closer, we could see people sitting on the ground and their boats tucked away on the far side of the island. We paddled around and dropped anchor twenty yards off shore, then dived overboard and swam to the beach.

The ideal of a tropical island is fairly well ingrained in western consciousness. Right from the beginning of Spanish and Portuguese exploration, the accounts of adventurers had begun to inspire tales of island paradises. Shakespeare incorporated them into *The Tempest*, drawing on Spanish accounts of island castaways and the New World. One work, *De Orbo Novo* by Peter the Martyr, was particularly influential. First published in 1504 (in English in 1555), it observed that the naked Indian of 'Hispaniola' is happier for the absence of 'weights or measures . . . deadly money . . . slanderous judges or books, satisfied with the goods of nature, and without worries for the future'. In classical antiquity the idea of a lost golden age had existed, but this book turned that on its head: the golden age was here and now, and to be found in the tropics.

In Peter the Martyr's account, the Europeans descend like a plague on to this paradise. Spanish conquistadores compete to see who can hack the head from an innocent Indian in one blow. Cities are razed. Genocide takes place. The limits of utopia retreat before the ferocious advance. And this was not something written with the benefits of hindsight: this was a contemporary report from the frontline, directly accusing the Spanish of destroying the paradise they had discovered. Under Charles V, the Spanish did try to reform as a result of the criticisms, but to little effect.

Montaigne took up the thesis in 1580, asserting that for the Indians 'the very words which mean lie, treason, simulation, avarice, envy, slander, forgiveness, are unknown.' The Indians, it was said, had no known words for 'mine' and 'yours' – private property did not exist. The ideal of a noble savage in his savage paradise was born.

As we stumbled out of the surf, wondering what kind of savage paradise to expect, there was a welcoming party of naked children who danced around in excitement, doing cartwheels in the sand. In fact there must have been more than 300 people on this tiny atoll and their ramshackle village occupied almost all the available land area, the rest being taken up by huge cairns of discarded shells and the racks where sea cucumbers were drying. A great delicacy in the Far East, the creature looks like the forgotten banana at the back of the cupboard, but I knew from personal experience that well-prepared and marinaded, it can be as delicious as a car tyre.

Shani was not interested in sea cucumbers, neither did he take up the offer of hashish. I saw him wander off in search of a familiar face, hoping to glean information about his boat.

The fishermen were not unfriendly, but appeared stunned by the arrival of strangers. I managed to glean that they had come from all over northern Mozambique and southern Tanzania, one even from the shores of Lake Malawi. But the promise of riches from sea cucumbers had not fully materialised. There were simply not sufficient stocks to catch for the Tanzanian merchant who came to collect them. The children were happy, however, bursting with joie de vivre and chasing each other with screams of laughter.

[127]

One of the young men I spoke to had learnt some English while in Tanzania.

'Is that a good island?' I asked, pointing south towards the horizon where the American's island could just be seen.

He nodded. 'Very good place. The man make it very nice with houses and gardens – like a paradise. But only for his people.'

'Do you fish there?'

'No, we are here.' He gestured to show me his island. The crowded and flimsy shelters of twigs; a sick girl lying in the sand, her hair tangled and flies on her shiny face. 'You see how we live,' he said. 'When one man digs the earth to build a high place for himself, he also digs a hole. So he there, we here.'

'It's very crowded here,' I said. 'Do people fight?' I was thinking of Henry Neville's utopian tract, *Isle of Pines*, written in 1668 and set in these waters.

But the man moved his chin sideways in a gesture of disagreement. 'No. We are all poor men and we try to help each other. If we need something, one of us will go to the mainland. It is okay, we have fish to eat.'

I looked around us. It was a scene of utter destitution and hopelessness but, apart from the sickly child, no one appeared to be actually miserable, almost the opposite. A quick tour of the entire island revealed a man selling a few essentials – soap, combs and plastic shoes – from beneath a thatched shade. Otherwise there was nothing but people, shells and dried fish. After only an hour it was oppressive and I joined Jan and Tamara who had spent their time lazing in the clear waters.

Even the most optimistic utopian occasionally had to admit that sheer force of numbers could mitigate all the love and joy that eternally fluttered around their remote island paradises. Henry Neville was a member of Cromwell's Council of State and his *Isle of Pines* proved immensely popular, not least because most readers thought it to be a factual account and, by the standards of the time, it was pornography.

The story details the life of one George Pine who had the

misfortune to be shipwrecked with four young and lusty women on an island well blessed with fruits and tame animals. Having eaten and drunk his fill, George's thoughts turn to other matters and he persuades two 'maids' to bed. Just to add a little extra zest, one of them happens to be his master's daughter whose sense of propriety, amongst other things, has been loosened by the shipwreck.

As time goes on and 'Custom taking away shame (there being none but us) we did it more openly, as our lusts gave us liberty.' Soon the other two, including a handsome negress, want a bit of it and George is rutting night and day, getting them all pregnant. As the years go by, George produces prodigious quantities of children – 'having nothing else to do'. The children mate with their brothers and sisters and carry on much like Dad who dies aged eighty with 1,589 living descendants.

But the idyll sours. The overcrowded community splits into descendants of the negress and the rest. Laws and religion appear. A rape is committed and civil war breaks out which outsiders eventually have to subdue. The book went to several editions and was translated into numerous languages. Henry Neville himself died at the age of seventy-four. Sadly, however, he left no children.

Ironically, the little community on the atoll, happily free of utopian dreams, expecting no more than a few sea cucumbers, appeared to be reasonably content. But I refused to believe it. I found Shani on the beach and put it to him that it was a terrible place. He was shocked.

'This island? But they have everything. Lots of fish to eat. They get some money from the dried squid and sea cucumbers, and they spend almost nothing. They have hashish – you want some? There are no thieves, no politicians, no brancos to make laws, no policemen.' An island utopia, I thought, and founded on such traditional values for utopianists, particularly piratical ones – all they had wanted was freedom from the law-makers.

I wondered how close Montaigne's idealised conception of the

New World (he never got closer than the quayside at Bordeaux) would have fitted with Shani's opinions of the gruesomely crowded atoll. Perhaps Shani was the late twentieth-century noble savage: sufficiently wise in his ignorance to see that the best he could hope for was a tiny world blissfully free of politicians, thieves, brancos and Tanzanian pirates.

'What about doctors for the sick, schools for the children?' I asked him.

'Everyone must die one day and what do they need to know that their fathers cannot teach them?'

The mention of policemen had reminded me of his problem.

'There is some news,' he said glumly. 'A boat was seen in the night, heading north. It could be mine, but no one here knows my boat well.'

'Last night? We're only hours behind them.'

He frowned. 'They could cross into Tanzania tonight.' I could see the big question of whether to follow across the border was on his mind. It crossed mine that I might be going with him.

By late afternoon the wind had got up again and we re-embarked, sailing northwards as the sun sank behind the distant forests of the mainland. The sea was an amarinthine wine with a glittering trail of phosphorescent polyps rolling from the bow. Shani pointed out the stars used for navigation. 'That one is for Mocimboa, that one for the Comoros.' He had sailed there once, many years before. 'The people are Arabs,' he said. 'And can understand our language.' I asked why he had gone.

'It was when the brancos came to our village,' he said. 'My father believed that they would eat him.'

'Really?' It was impossible to tell when he was joking.

'Even now you can find old people who believe that.'

'Do you?'

He laughed. 'No. The brancos eat only money.'

By midnight we were surging forward with an island to starboard and the sound of the reefs roaring somewhere in the darkness. One of the sailors went and lay on the prow, staring intently down into the water.

'What's wrong?'

'Rocks.'

'Where?'

'Under the boat.'

He explained that there was a rock wall between the island and the mainland with only a narrow gap through which to sail.

'What happens if we hit?'

'An accident.'

'What kind of accident?'

'Usually the boats do not go down.'

Almost as he spoke, there came a new sound: the rasping sigh of the keel touching a sandbar, but then silence, we moved on. Suddenly, there was a crunch, the boat shuddered, then again.

'Danger!' cried the helmsman belatedly.

The mangrove poles were quickly pulled out of the hold and we eased away to port. The roar of the water was now very loud, but I could see nothing. Another rock butted the hull, unleashing a tirade of abuse for the watchman on the bow. The island was now almost behind us and the lights of Mocimboa da Praia appeared across the bay. Slowly the tension eased and eventually the lookout returned to the stern: the danger was past.

We could hear drumming as we approached the town. There were a few lights around a radio mast and some oil lamps glinting through the coconut and baobab trees.

Once the hull scraped ashore, we waded on to the sand. There was no one around, only the dark shapes of many dhows drawn up; everyone was in the village, watching the communal television or drinking. We had come from the darkness of the ocean like a raiding party and now climbed up the sandy bank into the streets, an Indian file of barefoot people with bags on our shoulders lit by the yellow glow of oil lamps in doorways. A few lounging men stared or called out. Arrival by night has a magic: the clatter of railway wheels on a bridge, then the rotten seedy station at the

[131]

heart of the city, or even the road – I'd felt it as a twelve-year-old boy listening to 'Yellow Brick Road' on the transistor radio as we drove into London at 3 a.m. But nothing quite matches a beach-landing from the ocean on to an African shore. And the strutting walk of the sailors told me they had the same feeling: they had come from the ocean, they were not of this place, they were something better than the townspeople, they dealt with the elemental forces of wind, wave and water, not unpaid bills and rowdy neighbours.

Shani led the way to a small hotel where the owner said proudly, 'This is the road to Tanzania. I can arrange transport for you.'

Jan and Tamara took up the offer, wanting to speed their journey to Dar-as-Salaam, but I had arranged to see Shani on the beach next day.

In the morning I woke late to find it pouring with rain and Jan and Tamara already departed. When the downpour had ended, I walked down the muddy road to the telephone office and rang the shipyard in Pemba. I had been there and met the manager, Charles Gornal-Jones, someone who would be most likely to hear of vessels heading east. It was fortunate I did so, because he had some interesting news.

'There's a Norwegian guy here who is sailing to Mayotte in the Comoros and then to Madagascar. I asked him already and he says he can take you as crew.'

This was wonderful news: Mayotte, I already knew, was a separate, French-administered island, but it would bring me to within fifty miles of Anjouan, the Johanna of the early voyages.

'What type of boat is it?' I asked.

'It's an old yacht – quite big. You'll like it.'

'And the captain? What's he like?'

There was a pause. 'He's a good sailor.'

'Okay, tell him . . .' Then I thought of Shani and the pirates. Surely there would be other vessels going? The chance to hunt some real pirates was too good to miss. 'Tell him I am very interested. I've just got to see someone here in Mocimboa. Tell him . . . I'll let him know.'

'No need,' said Charles. 'Just be here by next Friday, then you can be stamped out of Mozambique. He sails on the Saturday.'

I wandered back down to the beach via the old wharf, deserted except for one elderly Swahili gentleman with a large white beard. 'Yes, we still get ships,' he said. 'There was one came about a year ago.'

The beach was alive with people. In places streams poured off the high bank and made natural showers where naked boys were washing. I greeted one group of youths who answered in English. 'We came from Tanzania,' said one. 'It was a British colony.' He smiled. We were both strangers here.

'Why did you come?'

He made a face. 'There is no work there. We are heading for South Africa. Those two men have a cousin there – they are Somalis.'

'Do you have a passport?'

'Oh, sure.' Clearly, he did not. I imagined him crossing the Kruger National Park where the lions regularly dine on the desperate migrants. If he survived that, he might get a job picking fruit, like the Joads in *The Grapes of Wrath*. And there were millions more like him, all heading for the economic hotspots: Johannesburg, London, California, anywhere they could lay their hands on some hope of a future better than cucumber fishing.

'Do you know what to expect?' I asked him. 'In South Africa.'

He affected nonchalance. 'There's money there. You can even find gold.'

El Dorado. He'd be picking nuggets off the ground. We were crossing paths en route to our own El Doradoes: they just happened to be in each other's back yard.

His friends were calling him back and I left them to look for Shani. I found him in a small market under a baobab tree halfway down the beach. We sat on a log and ate bananas.

'Any news of your boat?'

'Nobody has seen it. I asked these men who take passengers out to the islands here. Nobody saw my boat.'

'Maybe it is in Tanzania already?'

He nodded. 'Maybe.'

'Will you go after them? Do you have a passport?'

He banged his fist on his chest. 'Me? I don't have.' His eyes were bright and it occured to me that he might be drunk. 'What is this border but a creation of the brancos? They make this border and they make the passports and they say I cannot go when I am chasing those who have wronged me.' He was waving his arms and people began to gather, grinning stupidly at me as if to say, madmen are always a good show.

Shani ignored them. 'No, I do not have a passport, but there is no need for it. The pirates have not passed this way. I asked everybody and they have not been seen. I will go back now. For sure, they are between here and Pangane.'

At dawn the following day I was on the beach, watching lines of people with luggage on their heads thread through the shallows to the dhows. Shani called me and we went down to the same boat. There was only one other passenger, a silent man wrapped in a blanket who chain-smoked Sportsman cigarettes from Tanzania.

Despite the clouds and the stormy look of the sky, the breeze died when we got out to sea. We were becalmed. As the sun rose, the clouds cleared and the heat became intense. We passed the rock wall with ease this time, simply poling our way along, but then we drifted. I fell asleep, waking periodically as one leg or an arm cried out for circulation. Each time I saw Shani, still alert, at the helm and the others dozing.

At noon the sailors gathered around an iron pot containing two handfuls of uncooked rice thrown in cold water. They called me over and we ate, all crouched on the deck in a circle. It reminded me of the pirate rule: all pirates eat the same food. They carried this to the extreme, putting a huge iron cauldron on deck and cooking up the common soup named salmagundi. In times of plenty that might mean a stew containing fish, pork, chicken, anchovies, cabbage, corned beef, pickled herrings, pigeons, palm hearts, turtle – the meat and the eggs – onions, olives, oil, mangoes, mustard and several good measures of vinegar and spiced wine. The resultant dish was, of course, disgusting, but they were usually too drunk to care.

I forced down what I could of the rice, doing my bit for egalité and wishing I had a cigarette instead. Then I went back to dozing in the shade of the sail. Once I woke to hear singing and watched in astonishment as a dhow approached. The crew were paddling and chanting a lovely melody, oblivious to our presence.

I wondered how we would settle the issue with the pirates. Would they be armed? Were they just sneak thieves, opportunists, who would run at the first shout?

More often than not, a classic pirate attack in the golden age resulted in complete capitulation before anyone was hurt. Such was the mystique fostered that few captains dared risk the wrath of their attackers. And the symbol which cowed all was the Jolly Roger.

It is difficult to conceive of the dread in which this flag was held by honest mariners. *Peter Pan* and a million Christmas pantomimes have worn away the menace. No one knows how or why it came into existence: the earliest record of the skull and crossbones being flown is in 1700, after which it seems to have caught on very quickly. The origin may have been the gateposts of St Nicholas's Church in Deptford, as likely a place as any, though it was a commonly used device on graves at the time. Other recurring elements in pirate flags were symbols of blood or violence, such as daggers or bleeding hearts, and an hourglass to denote time running out. One fact, often forgotten, is that the flag varied from ship to ship: Blackbeard, for example, had a devilish skeleton spearing a red heart, while the Welshman Bartholomew Roberts, arguably the most successful pirate of all time with over 400 ships captured, had himself depicted trampling on skulls or drinking a toast to death.

[135]

Once their emblem was hoisted, the pirates expected complete and instant surrender or 'no quarter' would be given. It intrigued me to know if their modern day counterparts might be so bold, but Shani was reluctant to discuss it. 'They will not give up their stolen goods without a fight,' was all he would say.

When nightfall came, we had still not reached the island of the fishermen. I lay on my back on the prow and watched the stars swing. The wind was picking up now: the rhythm of the mast as it swayed across the sky becoming deeper and stronger. I must have slept again, hypnotised by the regular movement and I experienced strange fractured dreams, random pictures and memories cascading through my head.

I woke with a start. The roar of the reef was loud. Stiffly, I lifted myself on to my elbow. When there is no moon at night on the sea, the phosphorescence of the waves can be intense. Now I saw the reef as a slash of roaring white, cutting across the horizon. It disoriented me: we seemed to be sailing towards it, then I could make out the dark mass of an island ahead and the boat was turning to the wind. I sat up. Something was wrong.

The three crew and the other passenger were huddled together talking in low voices on the stern deck. When they saw me clambering awkwardly towards them, they stopped and watched me. The boat was rocking wildly now and I grabbed for the rope stay which held the mast. I had stopped too. The four men watched me.

Only then did I remember Shani's outburst: 'We could kill you now! We could just kill you like that! And throw the bodies to the sharks!' It was dark and I was alone. I had no weapon to save my skin, the very thing that made me valuable in their eyes. It suddenly hit me with appalling clarity that Shani was every bit a pirate himself. Hadn't he offered me leopard skins, hashish and ivory? Why had I ever got back in this boat when I did not trust him?

'Hey, Keviño,' Shani called softly. 'You sleep long time.'

I wanted to step forward, sit down with them, act normally.

The body language of the others was that they were undecided. Shani was the leader.

'Why have we stopped?'

They exchanged a glance. There was a long silence, then Shani rose and stepping around the crouched passenger came to the edge of the poop deck. I could not see both of his hands. I instinctively stepped back and glanced to the side. The reef was roaring loudly now and in the darkness I could scarcely tell where the mainland lay. If I dived over the side, where would I swim? My pockets were empty too: in the heat of noon I had stuffed my money belt in my bag. The sea had appeared so warm and friendly during the day, but now it was menacing. I could see myself thrown against sharp corals, disoriented and bloodied. At best there would be a long walk back to Mocimboa along the beach. The interminable formalities flashed through my mind. I would miss my passage to the Comoros. I would have no money or passport. I might drown on the reef.

Then I saw the fire. It was on the island and barely a hundred yards off the port side. 'Shani. There's a fire there.'

'I know.'

We stood silently: me gripping the stay, he balanced easily with the movement of the boat. I was unsure if I could even get over the side before he reached me. *White men are weak and know nothing.*

One of the others spoke in Kimwane. Shani grunted. The man spoke again. Shani shrugged and turned away from me, then he squatted down and rummaged in the locker under the stern deck. When he stood up, I could see he was empty-handed. He took off his shirt. 'I will go now.'

'Go? In this sea at night. Are you crazy?' I was relaxing. I sat down into the hull, back against the ribs of the boat. They were not going to kill me. 'Who is there, Shani? Is it the pirates? On that island?'

'That is not an island.'

I squinted across, but the fire had passed out of sight. I could

[137]

see nothing. I wished I had knowledge of the stars, enough to orientate myself: but the Southern Cross was not to be found and I recognised none of the others.

'Is it a village?'

'No. There is no village. There is nothing – only a stupid branco, three small birds and a lion.'

Quickly Shani dived over the side into the choppy waters. To my surprise the silent passenger then followed him. For a few seconds we could follow them, but then the darkness and the reef's roar hid them.

We waited. The anchor had been dropped, but we were pulling it. The two men braced the mangrove poles against the shallow bottom and tried to push us. An hour passed like this. Then the passenger appeared suddenly, hauling himself up and on to the side with a grin. He spoke to the others in Kimwane and they began to raise the anchor, then the sail.

'What about Shani?'

They all looked at me and laughed. The boat heeled with the wind and we moved forward. I tried again. 'Who were those men with the fire? Were they the Tanzanians? Did they have his boat?'

They laughed again. 'That one is Shani business. You know Shani have a lot of business.'

We must have pulled well back from the invisible shore, because they eased the boat around to a new course. 'Which way is Pangane?' I asked.

They waved directly ahead. I went and lay on the prow, my favourite spot, feeling the gentle cushioning effect of the waves as we cut through the water. I did not understand what had happened, except that Shani must have lied. Perhaps that was his village and he did not live in Pemba at all. It had been an elaborate joke. I had lied to him too, saying that I was interested in seeing the leopard skins and ivory. As I watched the stars reel drunkenly across the heavens, I decided that the Tanzanian pirates were disgruntled business partners in those illicit trade

[138]

goods. Perhaps they really had taken his boat, as payment for some outstanding debt.

The wind carried us quickly that night. The boat rocked from side to side and swung the mast hypnotically across the stars, but for all its efforts, I did not sleep again.

PART THREE

COMOROS

8

Per's Dream

Roll on, thou deep, and dark blue Ocean – roll!

Lord Byron

Take one ounce of Sirupe of Clove-gilliflowers, one drachm of
Confectio Alchemes, one ounce and a half of Borrage-water,
and the like of Mint-water, one ounce of Mr. Mountford's
water, and as much of Cinnamon-water; temper all these
together in a Cordiall, and take a spoonful at a time when
you are at sea.'

seventeenth-century cure for seasickness

Two days later I was in Pemba again, noting with some alarm that
there were no large yachts anchored at the usual place off Wimbi
Beach. I telephoned Charles who reassured me that the yacht had
not departed.

'Everything is fine,' he reassured me. 'The yacht is around at the
shipyard in the bay because the wind has changed.'

That was not so welcome. The men on Ibo who had warned
me the seasons were changing early had obviously been right: the
weather in the Mozambique Channel would be far rougher than
I had expected.

'It can be choppy,' admitted Charles. 'But you're writing a book,
aren't you? You'll want some action.'

[143]

Action was something that held no terrors for Charles and his partner Vera, both of whom seemed to devour life with an enviable zest and enthusiasm. Their house was a former Swedish aid workers' cabin, with neat beechwood surfaces, scrubbed floors and low modern furniture. Into this restrained sliver of Scandinavia they had piled their own more tropical style: warthogs' tusks on the coffee table, fossilised fish teeth from Lake Turkana, skulls and baskets from all over Africa, then some more lively additions to the house: two crusty old hunting dogs, four cats, two vervet monkeys and a baboon called Flora.

Charles was shockingly proficient at everything: he had built the thatched gazebo in the garden, could speak several languages fluently, and was a qualified geneticist, game ranger and Zulu witch doctor; he could hunt, cook, build boats, tell stories and make flutes from papaya stems. The only blind spot seemed to be snakes which liked to bite him when he picked them up.

The following day when he took me down to Wimbi Beach in the hope of catching Per Willy, the captain of the yacht. We found him sitting in a little beachside restaurant. He was a thin, sharp-eyed man with weathered features and a strong Scandinavian accent. Charles introduced us, made his excuses and left. I sat down.

'Yes, Charles mentioned that you may like to sail with me to Mayotte and Madagascar,' he said. 'I will stop in Mayotte some two or three weeks to pick up some parts, then go to Nosy Bé. If that is too long for you, there may be other boats to Madagascar.'

I nodded.

'Have you sailed before?'

I knew he would ask this and I knew lies would soon be uncovered. On the other hand, the truth was painful. 'Well, I . . . er . . . bit rusty . . .'

I was saved by a passing acquaintance of Per who called out and waved.

'Yes,' said Per, coming back to the conversation, 'where were we? Do you ever get seasick?'

[144]

'No,' I stated firmly, and truthfully. 'I have never been seasick.'

'Good,' he said, 'because you know if there is one man who is seasick and can do nothing on the boat – well, he is useless.'

I made some sympathetic noises, as though I too had been troubled by such soft-stomached timewasters.

'On one previous voyage,' he said, 'I took two Israelis and they complained all the way. It was terrible. They wanted me to use the motor when we had no wind for five days.'

I shook my head in disbelief: use the motor!

'What type of boat is she?' I asked.

'A Swedish yawl. Built in 1943 by Tore Holm, a famous yacht-builder. Nice boat.' He took a sip of his beer. 'My terms are that you pay for your own food and drink: five to ten dollars per day should be enough.'

I nodded.

'Give me your passport now.' I handed it over. 'I think we will sail Sunday morning but there are some things for me to sort. I am selling an island.'

'You own an island?'

'Yes, one of the Querrimba group. Only small but nice place. The buyer is there now and he is supposed to come back so we exchange papers. We will go there before crossing to the Comores.' He stood up and held out his hand. His manner was friendly, but strangely formal. He is the captain, I reasoned, and I'm just the swab. We agreed to meet at the shipyard on Monday morning.

The weekend passed quickly in a blur of parties and dinners. On Sunday, the governor of the province came to lunch at Charles and Vera's place: a youthful, very composed man who was said to have stunned the population of one island, not only by taking the trouble to visit, but because he carried his wife through the shallows to the beach. Before going into politics he had been a research botanist and had studied in England.

'I liked the organisation of the place,' he said. 'And the chance to be self-reliant – cook your own food, that sort of thing. But you know, although people were friendly, it is hard to make friends.'

[145]

On Monday I received a message from Per that he was delaying until Tuesday. This was a blessing as I had discovered a book on Charles's shelf entitled *The Sailors' Handbook*, and I was desperately trying to learn about halyards, sheets and stays. It had occurred to me that if Per fell overboard, I did not know how to turn the boat around. The language of the book was reassuringly firm and muscular. It was almost Elizabethan with its thwarts, and midships and gunnels and all sorts of sturdy words that spoke of solid timber steeped in saltwater and handled with practised assurance by men who understood words like thwarts, midships and gunnels. Unfortunately, I was not one of them.

I found myself drifting down the bookshelf towards the 'wrecks' section. Charles liked wreck stories almost as much as he liked man-eating lion stories and his bookshelves were a treasure-trove of such tales of heroic disaster and death. When I had worked my way through them, I was mightily impressed that any ship got across the Mozambique Channel at all.

My first view of my own berth came next morning at eight. She was lying at anchor fifty yards offshore next to the small Pemba shipyard: an elegant white-hulled yacht with cutaway stern and varnished wood cockpit. To my unseasoned eye she looked rather too pretty for battling against the ocean.

Per was rushing around in his Land Rover making last minute purchases and fuming about bureaucracy and unreliable people. His island-buyers had not returned, but he had to get out of Pemba to avoid harbour charges. There was something else too.

'We haf another crew member,' he said to me. 'An Australian girl – nice one too – yes.'

I smiled thinly, Per's English gave every impression of having been learned from a Scandinavian voice mail service and its range did not extend to laddish suggestiveness.

An hour later, Per reappeared with Lucy, the Australian, who was tall, blonde, beautiful and looked suspiciously competent when it came to boats. 'I've done a bit of sailing off Sydney,' she said. 'Just small competitions and stuff.' She cast a knowledgeable eye over the *Maribel*. 'Nice boat, Per. Does she sail well? Isn't that the Royal Norwegian Yacht Club flag?'

'Ha! I can tell you a story about that flag . . .'

I began to shrivel up inside. I just knew that before long I would be curled up in the cockpit in a pool of vomit, watching this Amazon stride up and down the deck nonchalantly splicing mainbraces with her teeth.

There were still various jobs for Per to do which he said would take an hour, so I took the chance to do the last important thing I had been putting off: I went to find Shani.

The directions he had given to his house were quite simple: from the fruit and vegetable market in town, go down the hill, turn right at the bottom and walk for one kilometre. Then look to the right and you will see a mud hut with white-painted walls. And there it was. I walked up to it and greeted a woman sitting outside.

'Is Shani here?'

'Shani?'

'Yes. The one who had his boat stolen.'

She made a face. 'I don't know anyone called Shani.' She called across to two men lounging against a wall. 'Hey! You know Shani?'

They shook their heads.

I persisted. 'My Portuguese is very bad,' I said. 'Maybe his name is different: Zani, Shami, Djani – I don't know. He is a small man with a wife and two daughters. In the war he carried eggs to Pemba.'

The woman was staring at me. 'I told you. I never heard of him.'

I tried everywhere along that road. Two mechanics thought they might know him and took me on a long detour into the village to a hut. When we got inside, the man was not Shani. A schoolteacher took me to the big baobab by the sea where the fishermen sold their catch. None had heard of a boat being stolen within the past month, though I had the feeling I might not have been told anyway. I was photographing the beautiful baobab

[147]

when a youth in Nike tee-shirt came across. 'Hey, man! You speak English?'

I nodded.

'You want Shani right? Well, he ain't here. But I can give a message.'

'Was his boat stolen? The men here say no boat has been stolen recently.'

He grinned. 'Sure they say that. Maybe they don't know everything. Maybe they like to say they don't know. You got business with Shani – talk to me.'

I put the camera away. I didn't trust this man. 'No, not business. Look, if you see Shani, tell him Keviño came to say hello, okay?'

He made a circle with his forefinger and thumb, already drifting away from me. 'No problem.' I watched him go and decided to give Shani the benefit of the doubt. It was his real name, or real nickname, and he had had his boat stolen. More than that I would never know.

Back at the shipyard, we loaded our bags on to the little dinghy and Per rowed us quickly over to the *Maribel*. The stern was five feet above the tender and undercut. Lucy swung herself up, the baggage followed, then with much difficulty, I followed. The trick, I realised afterwards, is not to push off with your trailing foot because that sends the skiff skimming away. I pushed off with my trailing foot.

There was a guffaw of Norwegian outrage and Per disappeared along with the tender under the stern. An almighty clunk followed, the vibration of which was transmitted through the timbers to my feet, then he reappeared, tight-lipped.

I smiled apologetically. 'Sorry.'

'No shoes on board!'

'Sorry.'

'You are dripping seawater on the boat.'

I had got wet in launching the tender.

'Sorry.'

'I go now to bring more things. You stow your bags forward.'

He rowed away, the sunlight flashing off his spectacles.

Lucy was already exploring down below. 'Hey! Great boat?' She had that infectious Australian habit of turning statements into questions. 'It's beautiful down here?'

The cockpit had two benches either side of a table with a blue tarp sheet thrown over the boom for shade. Astern of the table were a large old compass and a fine brass and mahogany wheel. I stepped down the four steps into the galley. On the port side was a gas cooker on gimbals with a worktop on either side and a small sink. Brass handles on the worktop gave access to a fridge and a freezer. A few dozen spindly cockroaches skittered across the formica.

Opposite the cooking area was a baize-covered chart table with various clocks, radios and gadgets above it. Stepping further down the boat, I followed Lucy into the main cabin which had two cots on one side and a dining table and bench seats on the other. Light came from a large double skylight which also featured a small dried barracuda hanging by a thread. Everything was beautifully done in tropical hardwood with brass. Lucy was sitting at the table grinning, and with good reason – it was a fine yacht.

'So you're fairly experienced at yachting?'

Her grin broadened. 'I done a bit. Ocean racing, but in racing yachts, nothing as grand as this?'

Beyond the main cabin there was a second cot, the largest and most comfortable, with a small bathroom opposite. Squeezing around the main mast brought me to a steel bulkhead door and through that was the forward stowage with two bunks, both tight under the deck and narrowing to only a few inches in width at the bow. It was possible to get on deck from this small cabin via some climbing notches in the woodwork and a hatch. I emerged in front of the mast in time to see Per rowing quickly back towards us.

Keen to make amends for my earlier gaffes, I went to the stern and took the rope from him to tie the dinghy on.

'No, leave it,' he said sharply. 'I will do something.'

He shinned up on deck with an admirable show of athleticism, then led the dinghy around the side towards the bow. A rope was loosed from the mainmast and he slipped down once again into the dinghy and tied it up ready to be lifted. Lucy and I stood watching.

The following hour was spent readying the boat. Per cleared and stowed and lashed and tied; if we were allowed to help, our knots and folds and lashings were quickly undone and redone with a brisk efficiency.

Down in the cabins, he assigned places: myself in the bows, Lucy next to the bathroom, himself in the main saloon. In the galley he dropped foodstuffs into the fridge and freezer, cockroaches skittering away in profusion.

'Ach! These roaches should not be here,' he complained. 'I have put down powder to make them change sex.'

The roaches waved their feelers at him. 'But how does that get rid of them?'

He looked puzzled.

Lucy grinned. 'It confuses them.'

Per had no time for aimless banter on the subject of transexual cockroaches, he had ropes to coil and knots to get knotted. Although his actions were always precise and exact, there was something feverish about it: he was almost desperate to get underway.

'If we are lucky we can sail out without using the motor. That is better.'

'Let me get the sail covers off,' said Lucy, taking charge of that task with a natural ease that I envied.

The sail covers came off and were stowed. The mainsail was raised and the genoa, the triangular foresail, was winched out. Then he and I hauled up the anchor and Per went to the wheel.

Very gently and silently the big yacht turned away from the shore, the boom swung slowly over the cockpit, ropes slapping the mast. The sail filled. Per braced a bare foot against the wheel housing and hauled the mainsail in. The ribbons on the sail's surface now stopped wriggling and stretched out straight. 'They tell you if the sail is using the wind efficiently,' he explained.

[150]

We coasted around the point, watching the men working on the dhows drawn up under a baobab tree. The old Arab slave market was further round, its white walls gleaming in the sun.

Per was noticeably more relaxed now we were at sea. He pointed out the huge jellyfish floating around us and claimed to have seen dolphins playing a variety of basketball with them. I asked him about the island we were heading for.

'It is called Quipaco. I think the buyer lives in Botswana, but I haf no idea why he wants it.'

'Why are you selling?' asked Lucy. 'Did you get a good price?'

But he didn't want to answer that and a boat appeared on the horizon to distract our attention.

'That is him,' said Per. 'Coming from the island.'

It was a game fishing launch moving fast through the gentle seas. When they recognised Per's yacht, they made a circle and kept pace with us, ten yards off. There was a black Mozambican crew and a white man with his wife and son.

'I've left the papers for you to sign at the office,' Per shouted across the gap. 'I'll be back in a couple of months.'

They waved and nodded, then turned and headed for Pemba.

'Why do they want the island?' I asked.

Per shrugged. 'I don't ask.'

Or you're not saying, I thought.

Another hour of sailing brought us to Devil's Point, a barren rocky promontory where the winds and currents picked the sea up into sharp choppy little waves. Beyond here we steered north, the low wooded island of Quipaco directly ahead and the sun sinking over the mainland.

'I tried to buy that area of mainland too,' said Per. 'No one lives there and it has many wild animals. It would have been like a nature reserve. There is a leopard who swims the straits to hunt on the island.'

As darkness fell, we anchored on the sheltered side of the island. There was a single lamp glowing from the watchman's hut, but apart from that nothing to be seen.

[151]

We sat for a while in the cockpit under the dim light of a torch bulb that dangled from a wire thrown over the boom. Per and I were drinking Malagasy rum, a truly vile distillation which, Per declared, had melted several of the plastic bottles he had decanted it into. We talked about sailing.

'I started when I was small boy in Tromso,' he said. 'Building boats, painting boats, stitching sails: I remember my brother used my mother's sewing machine to make the sail once and the needle went through his thumb. How we larfed!'

He had gone into boat design and eventually harbours, working for many years in the Seychelles and Tanzania. Other projects had come and gone too: a bush aeroplane service, a gold mine that never produced gold, and a gemstone mine. From his account none seemed to have worked out, although he had clearly never lost his shirt. Now here we were at the island, everyone's tropical dream: a private domain to govern like some latter-day Prospero, and he was giving up on that too.

'There are complications,' he said. 'Essential papers were stolen from my car and other things left behind.' He suspected a conspiracy; people were out to get him; the country was sinking into a pit of corruption and decay; he was getting out – once again. Per, I guessed, was probably never truly happy unless he was heading out to sea in his own yacht, preferably alone.

At dawn the deck was soaked with dew and the island much closer than I had thought. It was really a madreporic coral outcrop: a flat-topped plug of ancient reddish coral standing a few metres above the waves and covered in stunted woodland.

'Is there a beach?' asked Lucy.

'Not really.'

'Y'planned tourism without a beach?'

'There is a place where they could haf swam.'

The supposed tropical utopia was fast-diminishing, but when we rowed across I began to appreciate that there was more to this tiny atoll than was first apparent. We rowed through a narrow gap into a dark green lagoon, surrounded by giant mushrooms of coral, each standing three of four metres tall above the water, heavily undercut by centuries of erosion and topped with bushes and trees. It was a landscape both fantastic and grotesque.

'I wanted a drinks bar on one of these,' said Per. 'Clients would row out to it.'

A shoal of sardines suddenly exploded from the water around us and below the boat in the clear water there were living corals, looking like strange specimens glimpsed through bottle glass and formaldehyde. As we drifted silently under the overhanging trees to a landing point, a man appeared, dressed in only a pair of ragged grubby shorts. He helped us clamber out across the vicious jagged rocks on to a narrow path. I noticed that he greeted myself and Lucy warmly, but with Per he was more distant. Per spoke to him in Portuguese, telling him to go and kill a chicken so we could take it with us.

We followed the man to a clearing in the centre of the island where a small camp had been built: there were some half-finished thatched shelters and a few transplanted coconut trees on the verge of a spotty yellow death. These had been Per's landscaping plan, designed to please the tourists who were going to flock here.

He pointed out what he had done on the island. He had gone to the trouble of preventing local people from fishing with spearguns or micro-mesh nets – basically a mosquito net – around the shores and was proud to have seen fish stocks rise. But when I asked if the new owners planned to continue, he shrugged. 'That is not my business.'

I could see that Shani would have had words to say about Per – another outsider coming in, buying up islands and making spurious laws and unfeasible plans before throwing it all up on a whim. I recalled the Schwarzes' steely will to succeed and her dictum that hard work was needed, lots of it.

'This is my place,' Per said, taking us across to a tent which had been erected under a thatched shade. Next to it was a thorn tree and a line of crudely cut stones.

'Are they graves?' I asked.

He nodded. 'When Vasco da Gama came north by this way the local pilot told him that this island was the mainland. When they discovered his error, da Gama had him and his party killed.' He waved his hand toward the stones, grinning. 'I tell people that these are their graves.'

In fact, the surviving contemporary report of da Gama's expedition says only that the Muslim pilot was flogged for his mistake. Quite likely the twelve graves were the victims of disease during some later voyage.

Per now disappeared into his tent to sort out which things he would be taking with him. Lucy and I wandered off around the island. It was a strange place: the forest stunted but dense and full of spines and thorns. Underfoot sudden potholes in the rock would gape, ready to trap the unwary. A whipsnake moved nonchalantly out of my way as I passed a cross chestnut, a mutant tree whose leafless branches are pale and patched with green, skin peeling from them like a hideous disease. The path had been cut some time before and was now disappearing as the forest reclaimed it. Eventually it stopped at the shore where the sea boiled and scratched under a viciously scabby coral overhang. There was a baobab here, the bark rippling and folded around its base like the petrified remains of drooping bloomers. Around it lay fallen flowers, thick rubbery florescences with a frizz of pollen-bearing anthers. I thought of the people in Angoche and their cemeteries beneath the sleep-inducing baobabs and slipped one dried specimen in my pocket as a souvenir.

Per had given me little indication as to why he had bought this place: perhaps he thought it self-evident that a civilised man would wish to tame a wild tropical paradise. Indeed, such dreams have been a powerful motivating force ever since the early eighteenth century, and the book that first voiced those dreams proved to be one of the most influential ever written.

The origins of the story lie in a familiar maritime situation: a falling out at sea. In 1705 a certain Captain Stradling, making his way across the Pacific, lost patience with a tiresome Scotsman aboard his ship and marooned him on a desert island. The Captain can have had no idea what consequences his action would have. Alexander Selkirk survived for four years on the island of Juan Fernández before he was rescued by Captain Woodes Rogers on his round-the-world expedition. 'Our pinnace,' wrote Woodes Rogers, 'returned from the shore, and brought abundance of craw-fish, with a man clothed in goat-skins, who looked wilder than the first owners of them.'

Fortunately, the pilot on this voyage was one William Dampier, rather down on his luck after earlier triumphs; he recognised Selkirk and recommended him to the captain who promptly made him second mate.

When the expedition made it home in 1711, Woodes Rogers wrote an account of the voyage which contained a short description of Selkirk's adventures. It was seized upon by Daniel Defoe: Selkirk became a castaway rather than a maroonee and Robinson Crusoe was born. Appearing in 1719, *Crusoe* was an instant triumph. Reprinted over 700 times, it is arguably the most successful book of all time, excepting the Bible. Indeed it is often claimed to be the first novel in English, Defoe creating an illusion of reality in a way never before achieved.

Here was a story of civilised man thrown into a savage paradise which cleverly melded the recurring themes thrown up by European expansion and exploration: What is a civilised human? What can he learn, if anything, from savages? With it, several ideas became fixed in the English mind: the resourceful solitary survivor, the white man benignly supervising the black with the wisdom of white civilisation, and the tropical island paradise. Defoe's triumph was to paint the Christian into the picture, a man not at odds with his new world, but working with it. When Crusoe rescues Friday from the horrors of cannibalism, he introduces him to the joys of a well-prepared steak (animal, of course) and shows him to wear clothes, eat salt and pray to God. The civilised man had at last found a place to work his dreams: he had found his place in paradise. With him Defoe had created a myth that would sustain many a lonely district officer, far from civilisation, administering justice to the heathen.

As a schoolboy, rushing home on a Thursday evening to hear that familiar tune of the children's television series, I could think of no finer fate than to be shipwrecked in the tropics. *Robinson Crusoe* might have inspired more tree-houses than essays, but the myth had seized my imagination and become part of my ideals of the perfect life. To own and live on a tropical island was a dream: now here was Per, throwing it up because he had had some paperwork stolen from his car. It did not seem credible. I would have said he had given up on life, except that he had given up so many times before.

At the end of the island I stopped. I could not sit down because the coral was so jagged; anything like a fallen log was alive with biting ants. Per's island had just about finished the island idyll myth for me, completing the work begun by the Schwarzes, Ibo and the fisherfolk. I suppose I wanted to believe that perfection is possible in the right circumstances, and the tropical island had always seemed like the right circumstances.

I wandered back across the island alone: Lucy had disappeared up a different path, but an hour later we met up outside Per's tent. He had selected a few severely practical items to take along: useful bits of rope, a torch and some tools. It was as though he were grabbing a few essentials from a wreck before swimming ashore, except this was the other way around. There were no souvenirs among them and he showed no emotion as he led us back to the boat. A disinterested observer would never have guessed that this was goodbye to a dream, the end of something. He delivered a final lecture to his abandoned worker who took it with equanimity: the new boss had taken him on as caretaker and though the pay was meagre it was better than a life of rural destitution. So he stayed, marooned like Selkirk, but by economics.

We clambered over the rocks and into the little boat. I offered to row, but Per was insistent. I waited for him to express something: disappointment, sadness, maybe even joy to be rid of the place, but if he had any thoughts on the subject, he kept them to himself. Back on the *Maribel* we prepared the boat, then set sail east.

No one really ever knows how they will react to the ocean. You can mess about on rivers and lakes, do some coasting behind a coral reef, learn a few useful bits of jargon from the sailing handbooks, but nothing can prepare you for that moment when the wind-driven craft hits the big swell.

Per was an experienced mariner and knew what was coming: as we approached the reef he showed us how to put on a harness and clip to the running wires that went right around the deck. 'You never, never, leave this cockpit without the harness attached,' he warned. 'If I fall overboard, then you hit this red button,' he pointed to the autopilot – an innocuous plastic box attached to the bulkhead in the cockpit. 'That will free the rudder and the boat will turn into the wind. You drop the mainsail and wait for me to swim up.'

There were two life belts: 'This one you throw over at night; this one in day. If you forget then the person will die. Even if we are only one hundred metres from a person in the water – in these conditions, we cannot see them.'

I looked ahead. We were starting through the gap in the reef now, the bows began to rise and fall sending great slow sneezes of spume out across the darkening waters. The *Maribel* seemed to be getting smaller and smaller: suddenly she was tiny and fragile and the swell was bigger and stronger.

The wind was up to twenty-five knots, blowing steadily in from the south. 'Good sailing conditions,' Per assured us. The digital pilot showed we were making seven knots. 'We must decide which watch to take,' he said. I offered to do 2 until 6, rather heroically I thought, but secretly liking the idea of being alone at the helm under the stars. Africa was soon barely a dark smudge on the horizon.

Per became a different person as the land fell away. He so clearly loved the open sea and being in command of his own vessel. He

[157]

kept popping in and out of the galley, preparing the lobsters he had bought from two fishermen just as we left Quipaco. In between that he was teasing an extra knot from the boat, tightening the genoa or mainsail a touch. Lucy and I watched him with mingled admiration and horror. Neither of us was able to go down below for more than a few seconds: the effect of entering the galley was like drinking a bottle of Malagasy rum in a single gulp. Suddenly the world came spinning down, the timbers were hard and unyielding and seemed to punch back when touched, yet the sea was soft out there.

Per sat in the cockpit eating with gusto, his plate piled high with lobsters and potato salad, a tumbler full of foul red wine. 'There is dry bread down there,' he said cheerfully. 'Very good for the stomach.'

I debated what to throw overboard first: the contents of my stomach or Per. We were heeled right over with three-metre swells coming in from the south-east, other metre-high ones cutting in from the north. Every few seconds we would rise up on a swell, then the bow would dip and plummet and we skidded down the side only to rise again. When a counter-swell hit us, a sheet of spray came sizzling back along the deck and we would roll, as if the boat wanted to corkscrew its way through the ocean.

'When the old trade wind ships reached the Far East,' said Per, starting on a second healthy plate of pink lobster meat with lashings of mayonnaise, 'their masts and rigging would all be leaning over to port because it had been stretched that way for so long.'

As the sun was extinguished, the wind became chilly, a lone brown bird, a noddy, glided along the furrows of the waves, disappearing and reappearing as we rolled. It was the only sign of life we saw.

Per put on the navigation lights and fetched a light snack of chicken drumsticks and salad washed down with a glass of rum. Lucy and I nibbled at the dry crusts that I had steeled myself to fetch. Secretly I was glad she was finding the weather rough too, not showing me up as I'd expected.

[158]

As the stars appeared I decided to head for my bunk and try to rest. Lucy wished me luck. She had decided to stay on deck for the entire voyage.

Passing through the darkened boat was a horrible experience. Cupboards and bunks and hard edges rose up and smacked me. I had to cling to the mast to get around it and then the door to the cabin hit me on the head. I struggled up on to the bunk and lay down holding on to the mattress. This was not like drunkenness; this was not like lying down on the ground and clinging on for fear of falling off. This was worse. It was the world that was drunk, reeling and retching until there was nothing to hold on to, nothing secure or solid. I could feel my stomach lifting as the bows came slamming down, falling through space to hit the bottom of the swells, then the water was roaring and gurgling down the sides and we would be lifting up to do it again and again and again. Jammed in the corner, eyes shut, elbow tucked under the anti-roll bar on the side, I forced myself to think of something else, of anything but the boat and my digestive system. After some time I slipped into a strange half-wakeful dream where I could hear voices whispering in the water as it raced down the sides, inches from my head. Then I found myself on a rocky ledge above an azure blue Mediterranean Sea. Below in the water was a Cretan temple and standing on one of the broken columns, Richard Branson, who was beckoning to me. 'Come on, jump!' But when I jumped the sea began to drop too and I was falling faster and further than I ever wanted into a deep black hole of water. I had been lured to my watery doom by an adventurous entrepreneur – perhaps my Iboan intatibu was belatedly warning me.

I was awake then and could hear Per shouting. 'Kevin! Your watch.'

Staggering out into the cockpit I found the stars out and Lucy wrapped in an oilskin fast asleep in a corner. The wind was stronger now and we were clipping along, touching nine knots at some times. Per went below and fell asleep instantly. I could see his face from my position at the helm, blissfully at peace.

It took half an hour for my stomach to settle from the journey through the boat. When it did, I began to enjoy the situation. The ocean was streaked with dim phosphorescent trails that stretched like a fragile rippling skin over the black void below two miles of saltwater, domain of the coelocanth, the living fossil fish whose existence was only discovered to science in 1952 when a Comoran fisherman caught one. When I lay back on the bench I could see meteorites scratching at the earth's atmosphere and satellites drifting over Orion's Belt. Human navigation still relies on celestial bodies, even if they are man-made.

As the sun stole gently up Per reappeared to check our course and position, marking the line on his chart. He was very pleased with the speed we were making: on course for a record run, in *Maribel* terms at least.

To celebrate he devoured a bowl of lobster legs with red wine, salad, and bread. 'Ach! We are getting low on mayonnaise,' he complained, larding the remainder on to his bread.

I had no desire at all even to see food, but I did need the loo – not to pee, I had managed that over the taffrail in the night, crawling on hands and knees to the edge and only remembering afterwards that I should have hooked myself on to the safety wire. I could not manage in the way the dhow sailors did: sticking their bum overboard while continuing with the conversation. No, this one meant a visit downstairs and I was frankly dreading it. Eventually, however, I could wait no longer.

The toilet was a tiny cubicle filled with oilskins and canisters and bottles and ropes. Being in there was rather like going over the Niagara Falls in a barrel, but I managed the business pretty quickly. When I stood up again, however, we hit a bad patch of ocean. For several seconds I was thrown around, banging my head and elbows, unable to even get a hold on the doorhandle. When I did, I knew I was going to vomit.

With a lurch I bowled outside, hit the galley, bounced off, took the steps in a reckless bound, landed on my knees in the cockpit and managed to thrust my head between the gunwale and rail.

At that very moment, the meagre contents of my stomach came hurtling up.

Almost instantly I felt better. I turned and slumped on the bench. Lucy looked on sympathetically: she had already been sick several times. 'Are you okay?'

I nodded. 'Much better.'

Per was standing at the wheel, legs braced against the compass housing, eyeing me as if I were a pariah dog on a priceless carpet.

'It is all psychology,' he announced.

'Like many brutal murders,' I muttered.

The ocean too was not sympathetic, redoubling its efforts: we were blasting along like a crazed corkscrew for hour upon hour. After sunset I went to my bunk again and lay down. Soon I was dreaming that I was in an underground room, desperate to escape, but then an old man appeared and told me that the only way out was a narrow tunnel that emerged in Prince Charles's house. The talisman, I decided when I woke up, was telling me to rely on my elders and betters.

The second night watch was a little easier: the wind was stronger, but the swells were more regular and gentler. Lucy managed to sleep below for a few hours and I was left to contemplate the stars alone.

At dawn Per pointed out the island of Anjouan, a faint but dramatic presence: its steep sides rising almost vertically from the horizon and the summits enveloped in cloud. It was a thrilling moment for me: Johanna, as the Indiamen and pirates knew it, had been a pivotal point in the seventeenth and eighteenth centuries, a bizarre and wonderful island that captured the imaginations of the great pirate captains as readily as they caught galleons in its waters.

A glance at the catalogue of East India Company ships in the British Library reveals how regular and frequent visits were from the legitimate side of the mercantile fleet too. It was partly for this reason that the frigate *Nisus* was given its slave-raider suppression mission in 1812, showing the flag and delivering cannons to the sultan.

[161]

Further back in history, long before written records began, this remote island was said to have been reached by Javanese invaders. These were joined in the tenth century by Shirazi Muslims and Hadhramis from the Yemen. Slave-raiding on the African coast added to the mixture, some Indians, the occasional eccentric with madcap notions of empire-building: it was a blend of races spanning the entire Indian Ocean coast.

And yet, from this human melting pot little had emerged: I could find no famous names, no great works of architecture or literature, no poets or painters, not even a tradition of sailing or maritime achievements. Anjouan absorbed people, but gave little back. Old history books claim it does at least exude a rich, heady aroma – the result of the cultivation of plants for essential oil production, notably ylang-ylang and cloves. The isolation had increased with recent years: while the rest of the world talked of the global village, Anjouan was taking care to remove itself, fighting a war of independence with the rest of the Comoros two years before. Since then, unrecognised by any government on earth, it had gently erased itself from the map, as though all along it had been a mirage, a Niamh-Niamh, mistakenly put there and now quietly removed. It had become lost to all those cornerstones of modern international society such as the United Nations, the World Bank, the Arab League (it is Muslim) and the IMF. It was the little island of friendly fisherfolk writ large – Shani would have loved it. A place beyond the reach of Interpol. No one went there any more, not officially: it was a black hole in the ocean into which unwary dreamers might disappear, never to emerge. And the only sign of their passing would be the faint aromatic scent of a perfumed oil on an offshore breeze.

Per had visited Anjouan years before when it was still a member of the Comoros Islands. But there was precious little news of what was happening there now, except that internal fighting had been reported. When I suggested we might stop there, Per laughed at the suggestion.

[162]

'Am I crazy? No yacht would go there now. We go to Mayotte. I am not ready to be killed. Ha!'

Mayotte itself, most easterly of the Comoran group, appeared on the horizon an hour after Anjouan disappeared. Its rocky slopes soon showing some detail: little coastal settlements and patches of green.

Although it is the most barren of the four islands, Mayotte is now the richest. For this it must thank its lagoon which gives the island the safest anchorage in the Comoros, a factor which encouraged the French to occupy in 1843. When the four main islands voted on independence in 1974, the Mahorais stood firm against the fashion for self-determination and voted to stay with their colonial masters. It was a pragmatic choice, and one the French have been paying for ever since.

Given the political instability on Anjouan, I would have to establish some contacts in Mayotte before I attempted to cross. Such future plans, however, were soon put aside as we aimed for a narrow gap in the northern end of the reef. From there we would be able to round the point and head south to the main east coast settlements. As we passed through the divide and reached the calm waters, life became wonderful and I swore a solemn oath never again to travel by yacht as long as I lived, so help me God.

By contrast, Per was obviously a bit sorry that the voyage had finished and on top of that he had noticed that the strong winds had broken one of the wire mast stays. He cheered himself up by raising the Royal Norwegian flag and shouting, 'Haha! The Vikings are coming.' We also had a bite on our fishing line and jubilantly hauled in a large yellowfin tuna. Once we were safely cruising the lagoon Per trimmed the sails and set about gutting his prize ready for the pot, cheerfully reminiscing about drinking glass after glass of cod liver oil as a child.

Around us boats were moving: other yachts, some launches and fishing boats. We tacked gently all afternoon, Lucy and I operating winches and ropes with renewed enthusiasm, waving to other boats and soaking up some sunshine. We could even bear to watch Per devour the tuna and joined him in a glass of red wine.

The sea was a deep lapis lazuli blue and away to the west, Mayotte rose up through rolls and rills of lime green vegetation to the peak of Mount Sapere at 570 metres. There were few beaches to be seen: the Comoros are volcanic outcrops and stretches of sand are rare, something which has restricted their popularity as a potential tourist destination.

By sunset we were closing on Dzaoudzi, the tiny coral atoll that stands a kilometre off the main island, Gran Terre. This little plug is the main administrative centre and HQ of the French Foreign Legion detachment. A causeway connects it to a third, slightly larger, island, Pamandzi, and in the sheltered hollow created between the two is the anchorage.

Even from a distance we could see that this was a popular stop for the hardier yachtsmen. I used the binoculars to scan across a couple of dozen large boats, several looking as if they had seen some vigorous punishment. There were obviously characters among them too, including a large white schooner and a smaller Chinese junk. As the sun set, we motored into a position and dropped anchor about 400 yards from a small jetty.

'There is a boulangerie there,' said Per. 'They do very good cakes.'

But to no advantage for us. The port captain radioed in and ordered us to remain on our boat until he visited next day at 7.30 a.m. 'I like that,' said Per. 'No fuss. Just clear instructions. That is organisation – oh, yes. And he will be here.'

I was less impressed. I wanted to get off and wander around, not have some bureaucratic little harbour Henri tell me to sit still. No wonder Carvalho never bothered with Mayotte, I thought. If he were captain, we'd be in jail.

Fortunately a solution came quickly, a small rubber dinghy detached itself from the big old schooner and came racing across. Then a cheerful, weathered face appeared over the gunwale and an English voice called out, 'Per! Thought it was you. Come on over for drinks. Who've you got with you this time?'

'Ah, my hitchhikers.'

Lucy and I exchanged a look. We had once been described as crew, but now we were mere freeloaders. It did not bode well for our relationship with Per.

'I'm John,' said the schooner captain, extending a hand under the rail. 'Come on over and drink to a safe arrival.'

'We'd love to.'

An hour later we rowed across and climbed aboard. John introduced his French wife, Nanu, and apologised for all the timber lying on deck. 'I'm just building some seventeenth-century gun carriages. You know how it is.'

We were soon sipping whiskies and admiring the sheer awesome size of an ocean-going schooner. 'Now this is a real ship,' I said, running a hand along the lustrous timbers.

Per looked a little irritated by the remark. 'Yes, but so much repairs and headaches. It is a terrible expense to keep a boat like this going.'

But Lucy and I were in ecstasies. A ship with a professional crew, that barely moved when a wave hit it. Heaven. More guests began to arrive: a local French official, the captain and officers of a French warship who were delivered by a naval launch manned by hunky matelots in the tightest whitest shorts imaginable. Lucy became very popular. Per expressed derision: 'When their nuclear engines give up and there is no fuel, I will still be rowing and I will survive.' He loosened up a bit when one or two of the Navy men showed a knowledge of sailing. I left them to their discussion of 'Which Outboard?' and sought out John and Nanu.

'Have you been across to Anjouan lately?'

Nanu laughed. 'Have they stopped killing each other?'

John explained how they had landed at the capital, Mutsamudu, a couple of years before and promptly been arrested. 'It's not a good time to go,' he advised. 'But if you are determined, there are

[165]

boats that make the trip – mostly taking back the people who've come here illegally.'

I asked him how they managed to make a living from their own boat. He smiled wryly. 'Well, we do charters, surveys, that type of thing, and we manage. At the moment I'm just on making these gun carriages for the museum here.'

'Where did the cannons come from?'

'I found them.' His eyes twinkled.

'Where?' I thought perhaps he would avoid the question, but he did not. He pointed downwards.

'Right here. Under the ship! We were doing some surveying for the port authority when we found them: six all together, lying on the bottom, no other wreckage around them.'

He had done some research and discovered the weapons had come from a ship named the *Ruby* which had sailed for Persia in 1698, only to be wrecked during a storm at Mayotte in April, 1699. I had heard of the *Ruby* through a small mention, courtesy of Defoe, in Captain Johnson's history. Thomas White who had turned pirate after being shipwrecked with a gang of drunken Frenchmen had managed to come across to Mayotte, where he had found the *Ruby*'s twelve-oared boat soon after she was wrecked.

'We found the *Ruby* up north somewhere,' John said vaguely. 'But the puzzle was how the guns had got down here.'

John was obviously not a man to be deterred by a few hundred years and a dearth of written materials. 'Eventually I turned up a reference to a pirate ship coming to Mayotte lagoon in the summer of 1702, captained by an Englishman called North, Nathaniel North.'

He had my full attention now. North was one of the pirates who had tried to storm Zanzibar and build a pirate base, together with John Bowen, George Booth and Thomas White. Unlike Captain Misson, we have no fine speeches from North 'preserved' by Johnson, but he had undoubtedly shown himself to have that urge to find 'some Place to call their own . . . where they might enjoy the Fruits of their Labour, and go to their Graves in Peace'.

[166]

John had an interesting angle on this. 'I think it's true that they were looking for a base to use and they came here. We know they spent time in the lagoon in two ships called *Speedy Return* and *Content*, both boats taken from the Scottish East India Company.'

John took me to the gunwale and pointed to Dzaoudzi which was lit up. 'You see it's a perfect defensible position. That's why the Foreign Legion still have it. There's the coral cliffs and in those days no causeway to Pamandze, of course. The pirates must have decided to make it their base.'

Quite possibly Thomas White had told North of the position of the wreck which was conveniently lying in shallow water on the reef. The pirates had then hoisted the guns on to a barge and towed it around the island towards Dzaoudzi. Perhaps they had even used the twelve-oared boat that White had recovered.

'What happened?'

He shrugged. 'I imagine a storm, a northerly squall: it must have turned the barge over. The way the guns were lying suggests they simply rolled overboard.'

The pirates had been within 400 yards of reaching the island when the squall hit. Had they been successful, the history of the Indian Ocean could easily have been quite different and North as famous as Kidd or Blackbeard.

With the guns now lost, the pirates gave up on Dzaoudzi and turned east again, towards Madagascar. North captured several good prizes, ransacking the seas between Arabia and the Malabar coast of India. His riches, however, were short-lived. Twelve miles off the Malagasy coast his boat overturned in a storm and sank.

The belief that a better life is just around the corner is a tenacious one and Nathaniel North certainly had tenacity. As a young man he had been press-ganged three times by the Royal Navy, finally escaping with a leap over the side and a swim to freedom. Now he found himself swimming for his life, leaving behind the fortune he had made. He survived and managed to make his way to Isle Ste Marie, off the east coast of Madagascar. From there he shipped out on another venture, capturing several prizes. But the good days were gone: anti-piracy patrols were closing in and North needed that place to call his own.

I moved along the ship's side towards the bows. John had gone off to find a new bottle of whisky. As the twilight faded, Dzaoudzi had become no more than a dark silhouette, the lights of the governor's residence and the legionnaires' barracks twinkling through the coconut and mango trees. If John was right, Nathaniel North and his cronies had been here, dreaming of that perfect place to stuff with all the loot of the East and as many women as they could muster. Utopia for them was unlikely to have followed Misson's rules of no swearing and church on Sundays, but it was the utopian urge nonetheless. Like Frau Schwarz back on Shaytani, the pirates had a pretty pragmatic approach to paradise: there was hard work to be done and no illusions about it. Paradise for them was not found, rather self-made. Cannons had to be mounted and security established. North would have been in his late twenties by then, a survivor of many battles and boardings. Dzaoudzi must have seemed perfect: easily defended, sheltered from storms with fresh water and shady trees. But the dream was not to be: the storm had dashed their hopes.

North survived at least one more shipwreck before his chance to live the utopian dream came – in strange circumstances. After a successful bout of pillaging, he landed on the Malagasy east coast with his crew and several Arab prisoners. During the night he allowed these captives to get out to the boat and sail away, marooning himself and his men.

For five years, he reigned justly and soberly, according to Johnson, becoming popular with both pirates and natives. 'These men whom we term, and not without Reason, the Scandal of human Nature, who were abandoned to all Vice, and lived by Rapine . . . grew continent and sober (though polygamists).' But the paradise was disrupted by the arrival of a pirate ship and off North went, back to the Red Sea for some plunder. When he next came to Madagascar, it was at a place called Maritan where he 'prevail'd upon his Majesty's Sister to pass the solitary Hours with him'. This annoyed the king intensely and North was brutally murdered in his bed.

For some time I leaned there on the rail, listening to the music and shouting drifting across the water from a bar in the compound of that last lingering institution that seems to catch the spirit of North's times – the French Foreign Legion. I had been told that the ethos of the Legion had changed, that it was seen as a smart career move now by poor East European soldiers. The old means of entry was getting rarer: murder a man by mistake in a pub brawl, then get to Marseille and no questions would be asked. They shave your head and you discard your old life and are reborn. It was the first step on the utopian road, but one taken without expectations of heaven to follow.

9

Marooned

O my America, my new found land,
My kingdom, safeliest when with one man manned,
My mine of precious stones, my empery,
How blessed am I in this discovering thee!
John Donne, *Elegie: To His Mistress Going to Bed*, 1593–6

Next morning, after three hours of interminable paperwork, we were free to go ashore and did so immediately.

Dzaoudzi is a pretty little place with its bougainvillea bushes and palm trees. The entire coraline plug is barely a quarter of a mile in diameter and is infested with giant fruit bats, legionnaires and bureaucrats. Of these the bats are by far the most pleasant: squabbling in the mango trees by day and defecating from great heights during the night. The leathery slap of their wings and piercing squeaks are never out of earshot as they show little fear of humans – surprising, as the humans often spit-roast them as kebabs and serve them on the quayside along with deep-fried green bananas. This is the only way to eat out cheaply on Dzaoudzi, indeed on the whole of Mayotte because the three islands are addicted to a prodigal Parisian lifestyle based on a 98 per cent French subsidy.

On the ferry from Dzaoudzi to Mamoudzou, the main town on Gran Terre, this was soon apparent: snappy black dudes with bleached blond cropped haircuts driving black Italian scooters; girls with long braided hair in clothes made of lycra and velcro clutching boutique bags; then the French men in tight white shorts, plastic sandals and Raybans. It was clear that wealth and progressive westernised attitudes were inversely linked to quantity of clothing as the more traditional ladies were swathed in yards of red and white cotton while a few of the men wore capacious Arab robes. My interest in clothing was also drawn to a large red emergency box on the deck of the ferry on which the words '30 brassieres' were written. It seemed a peculiarly French thing to throw to a drowning man.

As we approached Mamoudzou, I stood by the rail and examined the town. It was a crowded little place, all clearly centred on the ferry landing point. Behind this the hillside rose up steeply, covered in a tangle of concrete and stone with some conspicuous new blocks of steel and glass. Further away the money ran out and I could see ramshackle huts with corrugated iron roofs. Often these were the houses of immigrants from the other islands, Anjouan in particular, many who had come illegally. The journey across the fifty-mile strait is hazardous in the extreme: forty-three died in one incident, others simply go missing, but still they come, and the gendarmes spend their time catching them and sending them back.

On landing, I left Lucy and Per and went off to ask about boats to Anjouan. A bar-owner directed me to a small tatty kiosk where a youth was watching French satellite television. When I asked about Anjouan, he merely flicked a newspaper towards me.

It was the local Mahorais daily and the front page exclusive was accompanied by a fuzzy picture of people running through a street in the capital of Anjouan. 'Tension high in Mutsamudu,' the story ran. 'Youths armed with Kalashnikovs erect barricades and demand the release of one of their faction.'

'Is it dangerous?' I asked the youth.

He shrugged expressively. 'They have guns. They all have guns. They are crazy. They hate each other. One side of the town fights the other side. One family controls the airport, another controls the port. And they hate each other. These two groups control all Mutsamudu and the only people they hate more than each other is those from the other side of the island – they really hate those people. Last year they fight – the two sides of the island. This year they all fight. They all hate each other.' He shrugged again and flicked through a few channels, settling on a football match.

'But is it dangerous?' I repeated.

He regarded me coolly, thinking, before he finally gave a gallic moue. 'It is crazy,' he said.

'Are there boats going there?'

He nodded. 'Maybe Wednesday.'

'Can I buy a ticket?'

He sighed and put the remote control down. 'No.'

'What is the boat called?'

'*Val de Sima*.' A smile finally came to his face. 'It is a torpedo boat,' he said. 'From the Second World War. If it goes, it will leave in the early morning from Dzaoudzi.'

Pleased to have found a possible crossing to Anjouan so easily, I wandered happily around Mamoudzou. The market was the most interesting place with perfume oils and spices. There were bundles of cinnamon sticks and vanilla, bottles of ylang-ylang and clove oil, mounds of pepper and chilli, then further on the huge jackfruits, looking like living coral heads dragged from the sea. Here the women market traders had their faces daubed with white or yellow powder and all were immensely fat. I got talking to a youth wearing a woven palm hat and a Nike tee-shirt.

'Their husbands like them very big,' he explained. 'And after they marry, he do everything to make her eat too much.' Such cosseting treatment obviously suited the ladies very well, because they carried themselves with great dignity and hauteur.

The remainder of the town was less exotic, but it was pleasant to sit in a street cafe and consume cakes and coffee while writing

[173]

up my notes for the voyage. When the sun began to dip, I decided to head back and find the others.

The dinghy was gone when I reached Dzaoudzi and I could see the cockpit light shining and people moving around. It was too far off to hail them so I waited. There was a little hut by the jetty where notices were pinned up and I sat down to wait for a lift. It was not long in coming. A grizzled old-timer appeared carrying a battered shopping bag.

'*Pardon, Monsieur,*' I said, stepping out in front of him, '*je veux transporte pour mon bateau. Elle est là.*'

He grimaced. 'What's that you're saying, fella?' His voice was a rasping growl. 'I'm a bit deaf.'

'Oh, you're American?' I shouted. 'I'm trying to get a lift across to my boat.'

'Sure thing. You come along with me.' His spectacles, I noticed, had been bound up with sticky tape and crudely sealed with a silicon gun. We walked along the floating jetty towards a shabby old rubber dinghy. In the bottom, floating in an inch of seawater, were various old canisters, ropes and pieces of wood.

'Name's Bob,' he announced. His right hand shot out faster than a fox terrier, seized my hand, and shook it like a rat. 'Don't mind this ol' rubber duck, will ya? Now when y'step inside, don't get your foot under that there metal plate – it'll take your goddamn toe off!'

I stepped down, avoiding the plate, and sat on the side. I immediately sank into the soft rubber. The sea gave my backside a sloppy kiss.

'Air-pump don't work,' he complained, fumbling with a massive and weird knot of his own devising. The rubber duck swung around and the outboard clobbered a nice new tender.

'I'll never make a goddamn friggin' sailor,' Bob grumbled throwing the rope and shopping bag aboard. 'That's for sure.'

He stepped down awkwardly and began fiddling with the outboard. 'You come across from Madagascar?'

'No, Mozambique. What about you? You live here?'

His back was to me and he didn't appear to hear. The engine caught on the fifth pull and we edged out into the harbour. Our progress was sedate: any excess of speed would have quickly swamped and sunk us.

'I'm seventy-three years old,' he said. 'I'm deaf, got me a bad ticker – one heart attack – diabetes. Reckon the old grey matter ain't what it used to be neither. But I sail. Came over from Chagos.'

This was the tiny island group several thousand miles east, bang in the centre of the Indian Ocean.

'I got me a neurosis about hospitals, y'see,' he explained. 'Last place I ever want to die is in a goddam hospital. When I sold up my business, I went down to one of those towns for old folks in Florida – them places they go when they're figurin' to die.' The sea stopped kissing and began spanking. We were taking on rather a lot of water, but Bob was into his stride.

'Well, them sons-of-bitches in there, all they ever did was piss'n'moan'n'bitch about the taxes and the government. I got so mad, I started up at 'em: "Yous the luckiest generation alive. You bought y'houses for a few bucks and sold 'em for 300,000; y'screwed up the planet and got rich – and all you do is bitch!"'

He shook his head in amazement. I moved to put more weight on my feet: the sea was slopping over the side where I was sitting.

'So I figured I'd get me outta there. Didn't wanna die in a hospital – reckoned I'd die in a boat.'

I smiled sympathetically. The inch of water had become three. Bob threw an old plastic container to me. 'Reckon it's time to be bailin', young fella.'

I began scooping water overboard. 'When you set out, had you sailed before?'

'Nope. Never. Bought me a small yacht by way of a coffin and sailed down the Mississippi into the Caribbean – slap into a hurricane. I didn't know about it 'cos I didn't know y'had to listen to weather reports.' He blinked. 'Didn't know how to operate the radio neither.'

[175]

'What happened?'

'Oh, some boats got sunk. I lay down on deck and figured I should pray. But then I never did know who I should pray to, so I figured I'd just die.'

'You survived – obviously.'

'Got wrecked on a reef in Nicaragua and lost the boat, so I went over to Mexico – Pacific coast. Fella there says to me, "I got a boat for sale, but I cain't pay the marina charges. If you pay 'em, it's yours."'

We were way off course for the *Maribel*, but I didn't mind.

'If I had known then what the Pacific would be like, I sure woulda stayed at home. Sometimes I felt my heart going, so I took me some nitroglycerine.' He blew through his teeth at the memory. 'Sixty days alone to Australia, then across to the Cocos Islands and on to Chagos, now that's as near to a South Sea paradise as you'll get. Ain't nobody there. You Brits took 'em all away. Damn fine place.'

'What about your family?'

He grinned at me blearily through his silicone-smeared spectacles. 'I always been movin' on and my wife followed me for fifty years, but I guess she don't like boats.'

He slowed the engine. 'This here's my coffin – where's yours?' I didn't answer for a moment: I was staring at his boat in complete astonishment. It was a fibreglass hull, long since unpainted and stained with algal growths. The sails hung dejected from their covers, ropes trailed in the water, bottles and bags slopped around in the cockpit. The remains of a shattered autopilot hung like a broken albatross above the tiller.

I pointed vaguely. 'The *Maribel*, behind the yellow ketch.'

He frowned. 'Okay, but I don't see too good.' We puttered forth once more. 'Where you headin' when you finished here?'

'Anjouan.'

'Ain't that the place they keep killing each other?'

'Yes, I suppose it is. But I can't find a boat going there anyway.'

[176]

'Where is it exactly?'

'It's an island about fifty miles north-west.'

He became thoughtful. 'Jeez. I'd like to take ya.'

There was a long companionable silence in which the staggering generosity of this offer was savoured by both of us.

'That's very kind,' I said, doing some bailing. 'But I'll be okay.'

We nosed our way around the yellow yacht, getting caught on their anchor chain and then set off towards the *Maribel*. Bob told me of his own plans: to round Cape of Good Hope and cross the Atlantic to South America.

'I always like Latins,' he growled. 'I think they enjoy life more: dance more, drink more, probably screw more . . .' He thought for a bit. 'But I cain't say I know that for sure.'

As we came alongside, I saw Per watching from the cockpit. Bob mistimed the manoeuvre and the outboard hit the hull with a sickening crunch.

'Hey! What the devil are you doing?!'

Bob didn't appear to hear this.

'Say, young fella,' he said as I climbed up on to the side of the *Maribel*, 'which way is South Africa?'

I hung there on the outside of the railing, looking down at him, a wonderful shambling adventurer, a Don Quixote for our times. I really wanted to help him. I lifted a hand and pointed a finger vaguely west.

'Over there, I think.'

He nodded. 'Some fella told me Richards Bay was the place to go for.'

'Was he a sailor?'

'Sure. A real ocean bunny.'

'Then I think he's right.'

Bob nodded. 'I reckon I'll find it somehow. Go west. Cain't go wrong with that.' He wobbled dangerously as he sat down. 'So long.'

I watched him putter in a great circle back to his boat, narrowly missing a French catamaran, a figure of heroic and indomitable amateurishness.

As the days passed I discovered that most of the yacht people were not interested in the Comoros at all. Mayotte was a staging post because you could buy baguettes and get air-freighted spare parts: none showed the least interest in visiting the other islands but were either heading for South Africa or to the Seychelles, then east. Boats for Anjouan did leave occasionally, all filled with illegal aliens from the gendarmerie's lock-up. No one knew when the next chance for an ordinary passenger might be. A local archivist, Vincent Forest, was helpful, supplying me with names and addresses of useful contacts in Anjouan.

'When you reach the island, accommodation will be a problem,' he said. 'Maybe these people will help you.'

Lucy too, though wary of going herself, did all she could to find me a boat. '*La belle australienne*' was soon known to everyone and we were rarely short of a lift to or from the *Maribel*. This was more than handy: Per had developed a routine of rising at dawn and leaving early to be at the internet cafe in Mamoudzou for opening at 7 a.m. Lucy and I were more interested in exploring the dives and nightclubs, rarely returning before midnight. If I had stopped to consider, I would have known that we were on a collision course. I had not really told him my plans for travel: hoping to keep my options open and, if necessary, go with him and Lucy to Madagascar. That may have rankled with him, but there were other, deeper reasons for conflict, and they would take a little longer to surface. As the days rolled by, the tension began to crackle between us.

One morning, returning from the boulangerie I found the dinghy tied up. It was a risk to take it. If Per was nearby and wanting to go back, he would explode when his beloved dinghy was gone. I got in and set off.

I had scarcely rowed a hundred yards when I was hailed by Lucy from the fine old junk that was anchored close to the shore. 'Hey, Kevin! Come and meet Ernst.'

The junk was like an old galleon from the water: huge over-hanging, square-cut stern and generous, bulging lines. There were steps built into the hull, and when I had tied up, I clambered up and over the rail.

Lucy was sitting on some sea chests on a cluttered deck between the forward holds and the stern wheelhouse. I grinned at her and glanced inside the wheelhouse. It was elegantly laid out with grass mats and cushions, the teak fittings beautifully turned and carved.

'Pretty nifty, eh?' she said. I nodded. The deck had the same well-worn practical elegance with beautifully shaped seats and lockers, some of them disappearing under a tidal wave of tubs, canisters and coils of rope. A few steps led up on to the main deck which stretched forty feet or so to the bows. There was also a steep ladder down into the hold which I could see had been made into cabins. A grizzled head emerged.

'Ja! Ve haf visitor come on board?'

The man stepped out on deck, wearing nothing but a pair of baggy underpants. In one hand he was holding a large knife, in the other a fish the size of a small torpedo. His body was lined and wrinkled by the sun, yet fit and healthy for his age – I guessed late fifties. He gave me a roguish grin.

'Help yourself to rum.' There was a large glass demijohn on a sea chest. I picked it up and saw the cloudy brown liquid had several vanilla pods submerged in it. 'You're British? Ve all haf our problems, hey?'

He began slicing the fish in two halves, fish scales and blood flecking his limbs.

'How long have you had the boat?' I asked him.

'Twenty-seven years. I bought it in Bangkok when I left the Foreign Legion. It was not like this then. I think they were using her for carrying stones. But we cleaned and repaired and sailed.' I glanced in the wheelhouse cabin, imagining the Thai sailors

[179]

squatting to eat their kao-phat-kai or bargaining with traders from Burma over cargoes of teak and sachets of uncut rubies.

'She is beautiful, isn't she?' he said, but he was looking at Lucy who grinned and raised an eyebrow at me.

'She is,' I agreed, adding after a pause, 'And all teak, I suppose?'

He chuckled and hacked the head off the fish. 'Why don't you take a look around? Go on, you can go below.'

I put my rum on a barrel and went down the steps. Lucy quickly followed.

'Not in need of protection, are you?' I whispered and she pulled a face. I think Ernst's playful teasing had brought home to me the impact Lucy was having on the male yachting fraternity. The full implications, however, would only become clear later.

Down in the cabin, the first thing I noticed was the space and the way the timber glowed as if with rude good health. Then I saw the artefacts: there was a pile of copper coins lying on the chart table and when I looked closely I could see that they were stamped VOC 1750 – the mark of the Dutch East India Company. They had obviously been submerged for a couple of centuries, long enough to bind together in a coraline matrix. On the rack above was a turtle's skull and next to it a framed collection of more coins. These were gold escudos and silver rials stamped 1564 and the label said they had been recovered from the wreck of the *San Tiago*.

We moved on through the boat, noting the bunks, the pieces of oriental statuary, the cannon balls and pieces of old muskets. Ernst shouted down at us through a hatch, bloody knife in hand. 'If you are wanting a cannon, let me know. I haf one in Switzerland. Sixteenth-century Portuguese – very nice piece.'

We climbed back on to the deck.

'But how did you find it?'

Having piled all the fish into plastic bags, he began washing himself, ladling water from a barrel. 'By reading in the library in Durban. I tell you something: if you want to find treasure, you should read the original books. There is one account of the wreck

[180]

of the *San Tiago* in 1584, you see, and I found that.' He leaned on the gunwhale and sighed. 'Ach! That wreck was my bank for many years.'

'Lots of coins?'

'Many! We sailed from Durban and we were searching a reef for this wreck. I knew it could not be in deep water because the survivors had tried to save some possessions. I was with my two boys – they were only children then – walking on the reef at low tide and one of them shouts, "Look, Daddy!" Then we saw a pot sitting in the water. I could not believe it. A big pot, trapped in the coral and sitting there for anyone to see. It had been there for 400 years. Ach, we found many things – an astrolabe, coins, a cross, guns. I will tell you a funny thing about so-called experts. When we sold some of the pots to a museum, the expert came and said, "Hey, Ernst, we found an old Venetian necklace in one pot – you missed it!"

'I was very angry with my family because I always said they had to check every pot carefully. So I ask this expert, please show us the necklace. And when he got it out, my daughter says, "Oh, Daddy, that is mine."

'You know what? Her friend had made it with cheap gold wire and a pearl only a few weeks before. And this expert was saying it was ancient Venetian! Even now they still refer to it in the museum guide, but they don't dare display it.'

He finished washing and pulled on a shirt and shorts. 'Why you come here to Mayotte?'

I explained and he shook his head.

'You vant to go to Anjouan? Are you crazy? Those people are waiting for a mercenary invasion. What will they think if they see you coming? A white man. Take my advice: I haf seen these people when trouble starts – they lose their heads and start shooting wildly. There was a Frenchman shot dead on Anjouan not so long ago.' He pulled a slouch hat on to his head. 'You see they haf so many times had mercenary invasions: with Bob Denard and the others – that is what they are waiting for.'

Bob Denard is another of the outsiders who have, over the centuries, seen an opportunity in the Comoros for indulging in a little island empire-building – Crusoe with Kalashnikovs. A French mercenary leader, he has been involved in four Comoran coups and present at the unnatural and premature deaths of two presidents. Described by journalist, Samantha Weinberg, as 'The Last of the Pirates', he was a character I wanted to know more about.

But Ernst was not forthcoming. 'I don't like to go there,' he said, 'and neither should you.' The subject was clearly closed.

He picked up the plastic carrier bags of fish. 'Okay, I am ready to go ashore. You can stay and drink the rum if you wish, but I must to go.'

Somewhat reluctantly we left in the dinghy and rowed over to the *Maribel* which was rather like getting a dose of cod liver oil after a glass of champagne. Per had been forced to cadge a lift back – like a common hitchhiker – and someone had splashed soapy water on deck, leaving a mark. He was furious. Not only that but the water tanks were empty: we were using it up too quickly and not filling the jerry cans at the jetty. There was something else too, something I didn't like to admit to, but the friendship between Lucy and myself was steadily excluding Per. At sea he had been the king-pin, we the courtiers; now he was stuck in a tedious routine, grumpily obsessed with buying technical toys for the boat, unable or unwilling to join in with our laughing and joking.

'If you are crazy enough to go to this other island,' he said, 'then you should pay what you owe me before, in case you get shot.'

He was right to ask, but I didn't like the manner of asking. 'Don't you worry, Per. I'll pay what I owe.'

His pinched unfriendly face disappeared over the side as sunset approached. He was going for a beer at the kiosk near the jetty and we were not invited. When he was gone I took out the binoculars and swept around the anchorage, hoping to see a tender coming our way. Per, I noticed, was sitting alone, staring out at the boats with a beer in front of him. Even then I knew he was simmering inside with imagined grievances. At the same time, I could not work out why, and felt no desire to placate him.

It was Bob who saved us from an evening stuck on the boat. He was meandering slowly homewards from the jetty when I hailed him.

'Sure, I'll give ya a lift,' he said immediately when I explained the situation. 'Come on down.'

We set off, gently shipping water and baling. Lucy's smile was rather fixed. Bob was a gentleman, not a single 'goddam' or 'bitch' or 'friggin'' passed his lips in a lady's presence.

'You fellas had a fallin' out with your captain?' he asked astutely.

We nodded. 'A little one.'

He gave a knowing shake of his grizzled head. 'Watch out for those ocean bunnies – single-handers – they can be awful difficult to get along with. I should know.'

We laughed, but he frowned. 'I mean it,' he growled. 'You know what? We're all just hanging on by our fingernails – and that's the truth.'

He dropped us at the jetty and we walked along the causeway to one of the small French-run bars where we bumped into Vincent, the archivist, who dragged us off to a disco called 'Animal' in the town of L'Abattoir.

That night on the *Maribel*, I woke to find myself on deck, having sleepwalked through the boat. The wind had veered to the north and was smacking the rigging against the mast with a new more urgent beat. I could only think that this change had disturbed me. A few sheets of cold rain came down, sending me quickly under cover again. The season was changing early, bringing the uncertainties and dangers of the cyclones with it. The possible dangers and all the warnings I had been given played on my mind as I lay in the darkness listening to the rain hammering on the deck a few inches above my face. It would be so much easier to give up on Anjouan and wait for Per to get his spare parts and go to Nosy Bé. Surely Ernst, ex-legionnaire, was the man to listen to.

[183]

With these anxious thoughts running through my head, I fell into a fitful sleep.

Next morning was cloudy and Per had not gone off early to the internet cafe as usual. He wanted to tune in to a radio-ham broadcast from South Africa. I didn't pay much attention until they repeated the call sign, time and date. It was, I realised, the day before my birthday.

I mentioned it when the broadcast finished. 'We must celebrate,' said Per, without much enthusiasm. 'Haf a party.'

'I'll invite some people for drinks.'

That evening I tried to smooth over any cracks in our relationship by buying freshly baked pizzas from the French-run food truck on the quayside, a couple of bottles of decent red wine came from the supermarket.

Per, however, was implacably hostile to my overtures. He munched on his food without smiling. 'It is too thin,' he complained. 'And this wine is horrible – horrible!' He turned around and threw it overboard.

I felt a restraining hand on my arm. Lucy was shaking her head, mouthing, 'It's not worth it.'

After we had finished and cleaned up, I took the dinghy and rowed Lucy ashore for a beer. The waves, even in the harbour, were splashing over the gunwales and with the north wind behind us we overshot the jetty and clipped a smart red launch. A storm was definitely brewing.

Later that night, back on the *Maribel*, we lay on deck staring at the clouds moving in across the stars. When it began to rain, Per suddenly appeared, wild-eyed and aggressive. We moved apart guiltily, watching him rip the cover down over the forward hatch. I tried to help and he rounded on me, snarling, 'Don't touch anything!'

We went to our bunks exchanging grins, but it was clear that something had altered: lines of battle had been drawn, for whatever reasons on the part of Per Willy. Then I could not sleep, wondering for the first time if those reasons were assumptions about myself and Lucy.

During the night the movement of the boat changed and I was woken by the clank of anchor chain. Per was taking in a few spare metres because we were drifting close to another boat. Later on, the rain came lashing down and I lay huddled to the side avoiding the drips.

Despite this the day dawned clear and blue without a breath of wind. Lucy and I walked across the causeway to Pamandzi, then over the hill to a small beach where we swam. Every now and again a turtle would pop its head up and take an inquisitive look at us. The turtles were protected at this beach but further along the coast we found a second beach, only accessible via a rope down a cliff. In the caves below were dozens of turtle shells and skeletons, hacked to pieces by hunters.

I had left word with various people that we would have a drinks party on the *Maribel* at 6.30 and two hours before that time we returned, laden with booze. Per was tidying in the galley.

'Can I put this beer in the fridge?'

He didn't look at me. 'Well, I don't like to open it. The cold air will escape.'

'Just a few so we can have cold beer – say, a dozen bottles.'

'You will not drink so much in one night.'

For a second I could not understand what he was implying. 'Not me, Per, the guests. We're having a party, remember?'

He placed the cloth in his hand carefully over the tap. 'That is the first I have heard about it.'

'But you suggested it!'

He went to the steps. 'I was only joking.'

'Well, it's too late – I've invited everyone.'

He gave a snort and started up the stairs. 'I don't like the fridge opened – it wastes the cold.'

I went and sat in the main cabin, thinking about what Bob had said. 'We're all just hanging on by our fingernails.' It certainly felt like it.

In the event, the birthday party went off like a bomb. Several ocean bunnies arrived and Per could chat about outboard motors to his heart's content. A manic Frenchman, Jacques, with his Malagasy girlfriend Florence joined in the fun. Vincent, the historian, turned up too, plus John and Nanu, the owners of the large schooner. At midnight I rowed some of the guests back to the jetty and we sat on the benches drinking beer, watching kebabbed bats frizzle on the charcoal burners.

It was then that Lucy dropped her bombshell. 'I overheard something on the boat. Per isn't going to Madagascar.'

This was bad news for Lucy, and for me too. I'd been banking on that crossing if the Anjouan trip fell through.

'I heard him tell one of the yachties he's going straight back to Mozambique. And another thing, he's already got the spare parts he needs. I think he wants us off the boat.'

We sat staring into space, both wondering what we should do and why he had done this. I became angry at him, but Lucy was calmer. 'We'll just ask him why he didn't keep us informed. He's the sort who won't like it if we're reasonable.'

When we returned in the small hours, he was asleep. I lay down, fuming, and waited for morning.

I woke at seven and went through to the next cabin to shake Lucy. I could see Per's legs at the cockpit table and the rustle of paperwork. When I was dressed, I stalked through and sat down opposite.

'Ah, Kevin,' he said, 'we haf some matters to discuss.' It was the same manner of clerical efficiency that I had seen on the island. He had used it to call his worker across when it was time to settle up.

'Yes, we do,' I said. 'I found out – last night – by accident – that you have no intention of going to Madagascar, and that you have the parts. Why didn't you tell us?'

He tidied his papers, quite unflustered. 'I haf kept you informed at all times. As I think I said in Pemba, I would haf to wait here for some time. Now that time is too long so I will return directly. And as my boat is not a hotel, I must ask you to leave.'

'Don't worry, I'm going.'

'And we shall haf to settle up.' He opened a ledger and I saw he had kept a minute tally of all the things he had paid for: every ferry ticket, the occasional beer – bits and pieces I thought had been in the spirit of easy friendship. I hadn't added up the beers I had bought, nor the trips to the boulangerie for cakes, nor the pizzas, nor the wine thrown overboard.

'We agreed ten dollars per day for food plus these extra items.'

'No, wait a minute. You said five to ten dollars and we have hardly eaten anything.'

The wrangling started. It was mean and petty and neither of us wanted to give an inch. Eventually I paid what I thought I owed him and went to pack my bag.

Lucy appeared. 'You're leaving!'

I nodded, grim-faced with fury. 'Are you coming?'

'But I can't afford the hotels here.'

'Neither can I, but I'd rather leave than do something painful to him. What about you?' I almost said something about Anjouan, but I knew I wanted to go alone.

She stared into space. I desperately wanted her to jump up and say, 'Yeah, let's go.' It would have been like choosing me over Per; it would have slapped Per in the face more soundly. But Lucy was far too canny for that: wise enough to see when she was being manipulated in a battle of male egos.

I went on deck. Per had the tender ready. 'I will take you ashore.'

I climbed in. Lucy appeared, and for a moment I thought she might grab her things and jump ship too. But she hesitated and Per quickly climbed down and cast off. 'Lucy, this does not involve you.' He began to row away and she stood disconsolately looking over the rail.

Suddenly, it was clear that he wanted Lucy, and I was in the

[187]

way. Not for anything physical, but simply as a trophy. Other yachties appeared with their girlfriends: an Italian had come to the party with his, Jacques had come with Florence, and there was a Britisher with two vivacious Australian girls.

We were coming in to the jetty. I wanted to say to him: all your projects end in failure – the gold mine, the aviation company, the boat charters, the island paradise. But I didn't. I just wanted to shake him up, rattle his cage. I thought about pushing him into the water, but I didn't do that either. I knew that it was ridiculous: I had wanted Lucy to choose to come with me, even though I had no intention of going to Anjouan with her, and Per wanted her to stay, even though she had no interest in him. Her decision to stay on board felt like a victory for him, even though Lucy herself was having no part in our battle. Christ, I thought, men are really pathetic. Then I started laughing. Per, however, did not. Per was grim-faced. At the jetty I climbed out and he passed me my bags. Neither of us spoke. I watched him row back to his floating island. The moment of hilarity had soon passed; now I felt cast out, unwanted. I didn't think I had behaved badly, but there was the nasty taste of doubt in my mouth. Had Alexander Selkirk spent his four years on Juan Fernández Island raking over his past, trying to decide if he had been responsible for his own fate?

When the pirates marooned a colleague, they left him with a gun, some powder and shot, and a bottle of water. I felt no better equipped, prices on Mayotte are high, worse than Paris unless you eat fried bat. The novelty of that diet had already palled.

Such reflections, however, would have to wait. I was now without a roof over my head, with no knowledge of onward transport and with a dwindling stock of French francs. Feeling rather sorry for myself, but also somehow free, I set off for the boulangerie where I knew I could indulge in several outrageously, and ill-advised chocolate cakes with a double espresso machiato.

From there I returned to the ferry and crossed to Gran Terre. Along the seafront I found a shared taxi heading across the island and got in. I wasn't in the mood to go hotel-hunting yet.

The island was much larger than I had expected and surprisingly arid. Once we reached the west coast I got out and walked along the beach. A headland forced me back on to the road for a while, a superb piste of tarmac worthy of the finest corniche and lacking only in vehicles. Once I recovered the beach, I found myself on a lovely stretch of sand fringed by vast ancient baobabs. Every so often a creamy blossom the size of a small dove fell to the sand with an audible thump.

I left my things in a pile and swam for a long long time, emptying my head of all the recriminations and criticisms that were buzzing around it. Only in utopian tracts, I told myself, do you find island communities living together in peace. The truth is always less than perfect. In 1609 the English admiral Sir George Somers visited the uninhabited Bermuda Islands and, having careened his ship, left three men and a dog as the first settlers. These four lived, apparently, in perfect harmony until the discovery of a quantity of ambergris. The sight of these potential riches threw the little community into turmoil: the men fought and the dog bit one of them. A plan to sail to Virginia and profit from the find was thwarted by the arrival of sixty more settlers who soon spririted the ambergris away from the three. The enlarged community started on a downward spiral of debauchery. Slaves were introduced to do the work and within a hundred years the islands were described by the governor as a nest of pirates.

I lay on the beach of the baobabs for a long time, until the first stars appeared. I felt myself entangled in the dreams of others, the subtle interplay of emotions between Per, Lucy and myself. Like the three settlers of Bermuda with their ambergris, we had fallen out, but over the deeper, more dangerous stuff of human attraction. Lucy and I had been steadily cutting Per from the picture and he had felt that alienation, in his own kingdom. That was what had stung him into action.

A large baobab flower plopped down by me, as soft as melting butter, and another. The dark shadows of bats moved restlessly. I would go on to Anjouan now, the great black hole of utopian

[189]

dreaming that had been drawing me towards itself all throughout this voyage. There was nothing to hold me now: no fears of Per's departure without me, nor *'la belle australienne'* either.

The beach was deserted by the time I set off, walking up the track to the road. There was no traffic and I stumbled along for several miles before a lone minibus stopped and took me to Mamoudzou. From there I caught a late ferry back to Dzaoudzi.

My plan was to try a small pension in L'Abattoir, but when I eventually got there it was full. I tried the only other place nearby and it was full too. There was nothing to do but head back to Gran Terre.

I had got about halfway along the causeway when a motor scooter pulled up. It was Vincent, the historian. 'Kevin, what are you doing with your luggage? Are you leaving?'

I explained the situation.

'No problem,' he declared. 'The hotels are far too expensive. You must come and stay at my apartment.'

Five minutes later we motored up a leafy side lane in L'Abattoir to a small white-washed apartment block. Vincent had the entire top floor with a large cool veranda overlooking the anchorage.

'Make yourself at home,' he said, putting on a Coltrane cd and pouring us both a stiff whisky. 'I'll just see what the cook has left for dinner. Oh, by the way, Kevin. There is a boat, *Tratringa*, I heard it will leave tomorrow for Anjouan.'

PART FOUR

ANJOUAN

10

An Island at the Edge

Anything but history, for history must be false.
    Robert Walpole to his son, who offered to read to him

And I had a voice within me bade me declare it all abroad . . .
There shall be none lords over others, but everyone shall be
a lord of himself.
                                    Gerrard Winstanley, leader of the
                                    communistic Levellers, 1649

It was two days later, in fact, that I arrived at the Dzaoudzi
quayside with my bags on a grey overcast morning. There was
a man sitting under a tree who accepted my money and passport:
motor vessel *Tratringa*, it seemed, would be going to Anjouan. I
went through a gate by the customs house and found a crowd
of people waiting to be let on to the boat. Here was chaos and
a mountain range of luggage to be scaled: beds, suitcases bound
with rope, mattresses, televisions in boxes, televisions out of boxes,
food in television boxes, sacks of manioc, manioc in plastic bags,
baguettes in bags, baguettes in boxes, a great wobbling woman,
her hair in curlers under a net and face caked in yellow powder,
screeching at a youth who was sucking on a rum bottle and

[193]

cigarette, a girl with the face of a Sabaean courtesan with a single pearl dangling from the septum of her nose on a delicate gold chain.

'*Monsieur?*'

I turned to see a sallow-skinned young man, wearing a smart pin-stripe shirt and carrying a briefcase.

'*Pardon. Vous êtes Monsieur Gallard?*'

'*Non, je suis Anglais.*'

He smiled. 'Ah! English touristman?'

It sounded like a rare species.

'Yes. Are you French?'

He tapped his forehead. 'We are melange. My family came from France to Madagascar 300 years ago.' A Comoran lady swathed in red and white cloth pushed us out of her way. He smiled apologetically. 'Don't worry – it is normal here.'

'Do you go to Anjouan often?'

'Every month or two. I come to buy ylang-ylang.' This is one of the essential oils which the island produces.

'You are a perfumier?'

'*Non.* My father is. I am a businessman.'

'Can't you fly there?'

He laughed. 'To Anjouan? There are no flights. The island is cut off.'

A man in a felt trilby hat joined us, grinning.

'Nzwaan is lost, hey? It fell off the edge of the world.' Nzwaan was the name I was to hear frequently from then on: Anjouan being the French pronunciation of the Comoran. For a few hundred years the island had been Johanna to outsiders, before that Hinzuan. It had also been part of the Comoros, or Comores, but no longer, politically at least. The ambiguity about the correct name seemed highly appropriate.

The men discussed recent developments and quickly disagreed about the details. 'No, no, the Sena faction will never fight for the port.'

'I am telling you: they will and soon.'

'No, my friend you are sadly mistaken.'

And so on. Others joined in. Every one of them with a view diametrically opposed to everyone else.

'Gran Comore will soon expel all Nzwaanis. And why not? It is no longer their country.'

'I can assure you, France will not allow it.'

'What do France care? Even now they are planning to invade Mutsamudu.'

'That is rubbish. The French have sent commandos to Gran Comore, not Mutsamudu. Bob Denard himself was seen in the capital.'

'Denard is in Marseille. Any fool knows that.'

And on and on they went, tirelessly wrangling. The clouds cleared and the sun came out. More passengers came with more luggage. Time passed.

'No, the point of the anti-Comoran war of '96 was to stop exactly that . . .'

A gendarme appeared at the gate and began calling names from a list. The women started pushing through towards the boat.

'Look, I fought in that war and I am telling you no one, and I mean no one, ever thought that . . .'

'*Ras Asahabi!*'

I wandered towards the gate.

'*Ras Asahabi!*' People began looking at me. I smiled back. The perfumier caught up with me. 'You see what they are like?' he asked, laughing. 'In the old days they said that sailors approaching the Comoros would smell the perfume. Now they smell only politics.'

'*Où est Ras Asahabi?*'

We stopped at the gate; the Comoran gendarme gazing angrily around for the absent traveller. I looked at the clipboard. '*Ras Asahabi!*' Only when I saw it written next to my passport number did I recognise the mutilated version of my surname.

The gendarme scowled as I put up my hand and was waved through towards the boat.

[195]

When my friend the perfumier joined me on the quayside I got a quick resumé of the recent history of the Comoros, a history which is inextricably linked to that of the French mercenary Bob Denard.

In the tangled web of Anjouan politics, the name of Denard is never far from the surface. This French mercenary leader is the modern equivalent of golden age pirates like Nathaniel North and, although an old man now, supposedly retired in France, he still exerts a powerful influence on Comoran minds.

In 1999 Denard's involvement in the Comoros came back to public attention when he was put on trial in Paris for the murder of President Ahmed Abdullah a decade before. Denard's version of events was that he had been in a room with the president when a bodyguard had gone mad and shot the leader. This bodyguard had then been killed. For some unknown reason, Denard's accomplice had then taken out a hunting knife and gutted the assailant. This version of events was decribed by the prosecution as a total fabrication.

Denard's involvement in the Comoros had begun in 1975 when he and his band of gunmen had been asked by the recently installed president, Ali Soilih, to capture his predecessor, Ahmed Abdullah, who had gone to ground after a coup d'état. This job done, Denard was encouraged to leave, something he did rather grudgingly, having taken a liking to the islands.

If the history books are to be believed, events on the Comoros now took a turn for the worse. Ali Soilih promptly disbanded the government, burned all records, legalised marijuana and put teenagers in charge.

When I came to do some background research on Ali Soilih, I could not find a single favourable comment on the man. He had, they said, gone utterly mad, enforcing a crazed Maoist cult on an unwilling population by way of a gang of zealots known as the Jeunnesse Révolutionaire. Traditional weddings were banned, as were any aspects of Comoran culture seen as backward or pro-colonial. Land was stripped from French owners and given to

[196]

peasants. Ali became a drug addict and debaucher of women who believed himself to be God. The history books were unequivocal on Soilih, lumping him together with his colleague from Parisian university days, the Khmer Rouge leader Pol Pot.

When Denard returned to 'save' the Comoros in 1978, Soilih was reportedly found watching pornographic films with three naked women. He was shot dead, while 'trying to escape'.

Now Denard, having overthrown the man he had installed, reinstated the man he had originally helped expel, Ahmed Abdullah. But Abdullah was no more than a puppet for Denard who settled on Gran Comore, married a local woman – his sixth wife – and declared the unfortunate islands as his home. So did his motley crew of mercenaries who set about ruling. It was colonialism, and one much worse than Soilih had railed against. After eleven years, Abdullah could take no more. Denard had been using the islands as a staging post for guns to the apartheid regime in South Africa. Neighbouring states were pressurising him to eject Denard and eventually the president attempted to oust his unwanted military advisor. It was then that Abdullah met his mysterious death.

In the outcry following the assassination France despatched a frigate from Mayotte, but Denard fled to South Africa where he spent the next four years. In 1993 he had tired of this involuntary exile and returned to France to face trial for the illegal invasion of Benin in 1977. For this he received a five-year suspended sentence and there was talk of retirement.

It was premature. In 1995 he once again invaded the Comoros, this time leading a force of twelve men, a Dads' Army who were all over sixty. They defeated the Comoran Army – a military body which has, in truth, rarely distinguished itself – and installed a new government. France, however, would no longer stand for this: a force of paratroops landed and arrested him. He was taken back to Paris in order to stand trial, this time for the murder of Abdullah. After sixteen days in the dock, to the general astonishment of almost everyone in court, Denard was acquitted.

Since then, he has lived in France but the threat of a return hangs over the islands. Having listened to the perfumier's version of these events, I asked: 'Where is Denard now?'

'In Metropole,' he answered, using the old colonial word for mainland France, a term still used in Mayotte.

I was thinking of Ernst's prediction of a mercenary invasion. 'Will he come back to the perfumed isles?'

The man laughed. 'Maybe. When the smell is bad, he usually appears.'

In fact, the first smell I encountered on boarding the boat was something almost as unpleasant. Two of the female passengers were throwing up into plastic bags, their yellow-painted faces rising and falling like twin harvest moons. At this point we were still firmly attached to the quayside.

In length the *Tratringa* was no larger than the *Maribel*, around 50 feet, but she was much broader. There was a central large passenger cabin, furnished with wooden benches, an open rear deck, also with benches, and a viewing deck above. I grabbed a place on the rear bench, well away from the vomitorium. The perfumier asked if I played chess.

'You have a chess board with you?'

'*Non*, but we can play mentally.'

I made an excuse and he shrugged. 'Okay, I will play with myself.' Then he went and sat in a corner, eyes closed, a position he maintained all through our departure and passage up the coast. Only when we left the lagoon did he rouse himself. By that time the boat was surging and rolling in a heavy sea and the womenfolk in the vomitorium were keeping up an impressive rhythm. Presiding over their efforts was a crazed individual in a skullcap, the high priest of puke, who giggled and tittered all the while as he ran back and forth feeding the voracious sea with oblatory bags of partially digested manioc. 'Woman she wuraaagh! Hee hee hee!' He skipped around the benches collecting the bags and heaving them out the windows. 'You?' he asked, stooping over me and patting my stomach. 'You want wuraaagh?'

[198]

'No thanks.'

But as the hours passed and the swells deepened, the men began to succumb. One poor chap, collapsed in a heap by the rail, had gone the colour of old cream – an impressively chameleonic display for a man who started the voyage as brown as a walnut. Half the passengers were shouting at him to come back and sit down – he was in real danger of being thrown overboard – the other half were roaring with laughter and miming retching.

As he threw up one more time, a dolphin exploded from the swell below him and appeared to hang for a moment in mid-air, glaring angrily at us. The man fell sideways in fright and was only prevented from slipping under the rail by a crewman who leaned forward to grab his jacket and fling him unceremoniously on to a bench.

The volcanic crag of Anjouan had come into view almost as soon as Mayotte slipped below the horizon and by sunset we were fighting our way up the eastern seaboard. One of the rum-swilling youths had adopted me and was pointing out a barren purple finger of land jutting out. 'That is Domoni,' he said. 'Very old village.'

We were probably two miles off shore and there was nothing to be seen: no lights, no houses, just an implacably hostile mountain that fell directly into the sea, its heights riven by deep ravines and its wrinkled ridges lost in cloud. For a few seconds, a long leg of golden light broke through the gloom and stepped across a lonely cluster of white buildings; then that too was gone and darkness came.

As we rounded the point and came along the north coast of the island, the rain began to fall. We could see nothing, but after an hour some lights swung into view in the distance. People began to gather their stuff, the vomiters began to smile. I went up on the viewing deck and gazed ahead.

There was precious little to be seen in the thick darkness: the dim outline of triangular concrete shapes stretched out towards us like an abandoned giant's puzzle. Passing this breakwater, we

[199]

came to the harbour wall where a crowd of several hundred people was gathered awaiting our arrival. Of the town, I had the impression that it rose up on the hillside immediately beyond the port's perimeter wall and that the houses were densely packed – no more than that. There were no lights. This was the spot where the East India ships would have dropped anchor and where many were caught napping by the pirates who lurked behind every headland.

A young man, Yakut, appeared at my elbow. 'Mutsamudu,' he declared, 'capital of Nzwaan.'

I looked down at the crowd: men in white Arab robes or jeans and tee-shirts, all the women in the red and white cloth – the shiromani, tied like a sari. There were no uniforms, no soldiers, and surprisingly, as far as I could see, no guns. As we inched alongside the wall and touched, a spurt of energy passed through the crowd which had been quiet as we approached. Several of them suddenly sprang forward and jumped on board, others pulled open the windows of the cabin and began climbing in while passengers tried to climb out. Some men were trying to stop people getting aboard, others were trying to stop people getting ashore. Some who had got aboard now wanted ashore and those ashore who had been aboard wanted back on board for their bags. A chaotic scrum developed from which a lunatic dressed only in shorts, his face sweating and smooth, broke free and made a dash for the wheelhouse. Yakut and I were pushed back down the steps by the force of people. 'Passport! Passport!' someone was yelling in my ear. Foolishly I managed to get it out and instantly the precious book was snatched away from me. I tried to follow it but failed. Then I spotted my perfumier friend, already ashore and getting into a car. He did not hear my call.

A small wiry man with a beard and a grin was pulling me back up on to the viewing deck. I could see the captain grappling with the lunatic in the wheelhouse. 'Jump,' said the bearded man. I looked down at the people and the narrow glint of water between boat and wall. He pushed me off.

Somehow the crowd parted, just sufficiently for my arrival not to kill anyone. Immediately I was elbowed aside. Suitcases, beds, children – all were being passed overhead. A hand snaked through and took hold of me. I was pulled out. 'My passport,' I bleated. I was lost and alone. I had never had an arrival like this. My sense of direction was shot. I had lost my bag, my passport, and my one friend. I tried to head one way and two powerful arms grabbed me and span me around. '*Non, non!*' said a voice in my ear. '*La barrière est là. Vite! Vite!* It is okay.'

I tried to get back on the boat but was blocked. I could see no one in charge, no officials, nothing. Two men suddenly grabbed my elbows and turned me to the gate. 'This way!'

I stopped struggling and began to laugh. 'This is crazy,' I shouted in English.

One of them turned, a gold tooth glinted in the darkness. '*Non, mon ami,*' he said, 'this is Anjouan.'

We passed through the big gates and I glimpsed, momentarily, a street of whitewashed and dilapidated colonial buildings and the leaves of the breadfruit tree spreading above like giant green hands. Then I was bundled into the back seat of an ancient Renault 5, its engine wheezing and roaring in desperate gasps. The two men piled in on either side, squashing me up. The doors were tied shut with string and I noticed what appeared to be a bullet hole in the windscreen three inches above the level of the steering wheel. The driver turned and grinned. I recognised the beard of the small wiry man on the boat. Then he let in the clutch and we shot forwards.

I can remember narrow winding streets in darkness, people sitting in candlelit doorways, the heat and the rain; I can remember repeatedly asking where I was going and who they were, questions they thought hugely amusing and repeated back at me. On all the walls was old graffiti: '*Anjouanais demandent le départ des mercenaires!*' We rose up and up through the town, then stopped and got out. The road here was above the town and there was a wall with a gap. The men stepped through the gap and went

[201]

down, shouting at me to follow. I went to the edge and found a steep staircase going down to the Arab medina, looking like nothing but a dead coral reef in its minute complexities and ruin. The steps were broken and uneven and dangerously steep so I had no chance, nor time, to examine my surroundings properly. These men who had practically kidnapped me were now my only hope and I was suddenly afraid I might lose them. They had turned at the base of the steps, waving at me, and set off down a dark alley.

When I arrived, they had disappeared. I plunged forward, desperately, hand on the wall to my right. It was utterly black in these cracks of alleyways. I found I was on a ledge and must clamber down steps that were crumbling. Muttered words came from below as if the stones themselves had tongues. There was a door, and from inside a dim electric light. I saw the carved wood of the frame, dusty arabesques, withered and cracked by the sea air. But there were no voices from inside. I stepped forward and felt only air, then jarred my knee as I hit ground. When I straightened, there was a disembodied white shirt floating in front of me. I reached out and touched it. A set of teeth gleamed. 'Hey, brother,' the teeth said. 'Cool to cool. Take it.'

A hand searched for mine. I understood that he was swaying and drunk. 'Take it, man. Bob Marley. We are inna Babylon, baby. We are inna Babylon.' The red tip of a giant spliff lit his face for a second, creased and shiny like a well-worn funeral suit.

The spliff was pushed into my mouth. 'Hey, brother, keep it loose. Passss the duchy. Par-take of the 'oly 'erb.'

He was pulling me down the alley. We turned a corner and I scraped my temple on a rough stone cornice. Bob Marley was talking to me, 'Observe the hypocrites, man, Trenchtown. What is this but a Babylon!'

Above us I saw a lighted window and there were steps up from the alley. Bob pulled me up after him towards the light, still keeping up a steady stream of 'seventies reggae lyrics, re-spawned as conversation. I began to laugh uncontrollably and we stopped in the darkness. He too was laughing: laughing at me laughing. Tears were streaming down my cheeks which were held in a rictus by the chemicals.

'Hey, brother,' he howled, 'you is one skanking cat.'

There was no way to stop this laugh. It was downhill laughter with no brakes, passports, or luggage and we stood there, helpless, supported by the narrow walls and let it run its course.

After a minute we collected ourselves and carried on. The steps led to a landing and there I saw shoes lined up on a rug by an open door. Inside there was a black leather sofa, a television and a poster of a football tournament. My giggles stopped for the moment, but I felt my face was like water that is about to boil. The wiry man with the beard who had driven the Renault suddenly appeared and embraced me. 'Ras Asahabi! Welcome, welcome. My name is Ladre and this is my house. You drink gin?'

Bob Marley removed his Cuban heels and headed for the bottle. 'Brother, there is no hi-iding place for dat stuff.'

I stepped out of my shoes and inside the room. Yakut, the youth from the boat, was there.

'Ras Asahabi. We got your room ready. Your bag is there.'

'Passport?' It felt almost ungentlemanly to ask after my suspicions.

He shrugged. 'You will get it – but not now.'

A glass full of gin was put in my hand. Bob Marley had turned up the music and was dancing around with a huge slack smile on his face, knees bending slowly – a mantis does the mambo.

On the other walls of the room I now saw that there were photos of football teams and a large formal portrait of a severe individual in a fez, looking like an Turkish dictator. Underneath was printed: Ahmed Abdullah.

'You know dis brother?' asked Bob Marley, his finger describing circles as he attempted to point.

'The ex-president?'

'Right. He was from Domoni in Anjouan. Assass-inated. Say what!? By Uncle Bob.'

[203]

They all paused to gaze reverently at the portrait for a moment, then I was shown the football pictures. My host, the wiry bearded man, had played for the Comoros in his youth and had even once scored a hat-trick against Madagascar. As the rain siled down outside, we discussed David Beckham, Ronaldo and Zidane – France's victory in the 1998 World Cup was fresh in their minds. Bob Marley rolled his herbal cigarettes and danced. I asked about recent events. Had anyone been killed?

There was consternation and horror. 'Killed! My God, no!'

'But there was shooting?'

Smiles. '*Ah, oui!* A lot of shooting because everyone has a gun. But then everyone is very useless at shooting.'

The weight of history was behind them on this point. In 1995 Denard's force of twelve men had easily defeated the 4,000-strong Comoran Army without any losses. Two years later, they told me, Anjouan had decided to secede from the Comoros and the army had been defeated again, this time by a rabble of football fans, shopkeepers and drunks. Subsequently a battle had been fought between the two sides of the island, then between the two sides of Mutsamudu and finally, only a week before, between two factions. Casualties at all times were minimal, often zero. The Anjouanais love war but hate bloodshed.

'Peace, man, Natty Dread!' urged Bob Marley, dancing across the floor as though he had messed his pants. 'Gin finish, we lost in a Babylon. Now we go roots – discoooteque!'

But there were few as enthusiastic as he: the rain was coming down in vertical lines. Ladre the footballer fell asleep on the sofa. Yakut showed me a bed in a room and I lay down, suddenly exhausted by it all, and fell asleep.

I awoke with a start. Sunshine was pouring in the barred window and my watch said nine. There was a brief moment of panic in which I could not find my money belt, but then it came to hand. Everything was there: my bags, money, camera – only the passport still missing.

[204]

From the window I could see the tops of the houses below, a messy patchwork of dirty concrete and stone punctuated by mosque minarets and the occasional breadfuit tree. It all seemed very Arab and yet the voices coming up from the street spoke in Nzwaani, a language more akin to Swahili than any other.

I dressed and went out on to the landing. The house was rather peculiar in that the public alley and private landing were not marked by a boundary. Quite where the house began or ended was a matter of some vagueness. I found a bathroom where there was a barrel of cold water and a scoop for washing. The toilet was in the old Arab style of stepping stones for the feet and separate channels for liquid and solid wastes.

When I came out, there was a man sitting on the stairs. He was slightly built, neatly dressed and with a quick, intelligent look about him.

'Hi,' he said. 'You must be Ras Asahabi?'

'Kevin,' I said. He stood up and we shook hands.

'I'm Abdulkarim. They said you're American?'

'British.'

'And a doctor?'

'Writer.'

'And you want me to translate some medical work for you?'

'No, I don't think so.'

He began to laugh.

'Where did you learn English so well?' I asked.

'In the States. I was a student in Knoxville, Tennessee, for four years – long time ago.'

'What do you do now?'

He laughed. 'Like everyone here, not much. Nothing is happening. I have a shipping agency, but there're no ships. No one knows what will happen here – not even those guys in charge.'

'Who is in charge?'

'I don't know, man. No one knows. Whoever it is, they don't know anything. I hate politics.'

[205]

I put my head into the living room and glanced around. There was nobody to be seen. 'They seem to have gone out.'

'Come on, man,' he said. 'Let's go walk somewhere. I'll show you the medina. Later there is a barbecue in the jungle and someone you must meet will be there.'

We went down the steps and into the alley. Negotiating its obstacles was considerably easier in daylight, but navigation was hopeless. Never more than three feet wide, the alley burrowed through a maze of houses, whitewashed stone walls, patched with concrete and blocks. Men sat in elegant carved doorways drinking glasses of tamarind juice or smoking; some played cards in small groups – the loser of the last hand forced to wear a crown of leaves. Barefoot children scampered through our legs, laughing and wild-haired. We took several turnings, squeezed through narrow archways, clambered down precipitous flights of steps. After a while Abdulkarim stopped. 'Are you lost?'

'Of course.'

He grinned. 'Those in power hate the medina. Even in the days of the mercenaries, they would only enter by day.'

'You remember those times?'

'Sure. We were kids and the mercenaries were like gods for us.'

'You liked them?'

He gave a dismissive snort. 'I did then, but not now. They brought many bad things. Before the mercenaries people did not drink too much, or smoke ganja. It was very quiet: no theft or crime. But we kids thought they were wonderful and we learned some bad habits.' He shrugged. 'We got rid of the mercenaries, but the habits stayed behind.'

We carried on through the maze, Abdulkarim pointing out some of the older houses and features. 'This house belonged to my great grandfather, Sultan Abdullah, and before that to his grandfather Sultan Alawi.' There was a broad flight of stone steps leading up to magnificent ancient double doors, which we found locked. Abdulkarim touched my arm. 'Wait here. I'll ask my cousin who has the key.' He went down the steps and disappeared into the alley.

I sat down on the steps and remembered James Prior who had arrived here with the frigate *Nisus* on 25th August, 1812. It seemed astonishing that I should run into a descendant of the very same man who Prior had been brought to see on landing in Johanna, but it was my first day and I had yet to realise that Anjouan is positively Elizabethan in the way everyone knows or is related to everyone else, both living and dead.

Excepting a few bits of concrete and some wires, Prior's description was as accurate now as it was when the Johannese emissary had led him through the alleys to the door. 'The residence of the king is situated near the centre of the town, in one of the principal streets, or rather alleys, for they are so narrow that two persons can scarcely walk abreast. It is an irregular stone-building of some extent, partly enclosed by dead walls, and not remarkable for shew or neatness. Part projects over the street, forming an arch, one front of which represents the head of a ship, the other the stern.'

The arrogant young Englishman found much to amuse him in the 'burlesque grandeur' within, the king proving to be an amiable old codger who praised his 'good friend King George' and demanded that the visitors perform various 'wonders'. Happy to impress with his scientific knowledge, Prior singled out a young nephew of the monarch who had a serious head wound, and according to the latest advanced techniques, opened a vein. Several ladies fainted away at that point, but after a judicious blood-letting, Prior confidently declared the youth to be 'out of danger'. His subsequent fate is not mentioned.

Once out of the palace, Prior found himself inundated with requests for medical help, many from the fair sex. 'These calls being of course irresistible, I complied, with the greatest pleasure.' He finds the sequestered women handsome though languorous, and quite determined to examine him as minutely as he does them. In the house of the sultan's secretary, he finds two particularly

[207]

vivacious and attractive lasses, one of whom takes the opportunity to seize his hand. 'I could do no less than kiss hers in return. Far from being offended, the lady seemed as if she would not dislike a still warmer repetition of the salute, but just at that moment the trusty guardian of the castle returned.'

Unfortunately, I was not to see the interior of the building as Abdulkarim returned with bad news. 'The caretaker has gone to Gran Comore with the key.' He shook the hefty ring latch. 'Nobody lives here now. When we fought Gran Comore, they locked the prisoners inside. Come, let's visit my uncle: he knows a lot about the history of this place and our family.'

We strolled out of the medina and took the road east through the tumbledown 'modern' suburbs. Now I could see the spectacular peaks of the island soaring up above us, all covered in brilliant green. Apart from a few plantations of cloves, however, the hillsides looked untended.

'Nobody wants to be a farmer these days. They come here to sit in doorways and talk politics.' We nipped up a side road to get some green mangoes off a tree.

'That is the good thing here,' he said. 'Nobody is ever hungry: you just go and pick something off a tree. Not like the States, man. I couldn't believe the poor people there: they only have television and drugs! Better to be poor here.'

The houses by the road were mainly simple white boxes, most of them with a scrappy palm-thatch hut on top. This, Abdulkarim explained, was a 'den', traditionally provided for teenage sons – a kind of halfway house for them to run wild in before the responsibilities of marriage.

'That seems like a good idea.'

He sighed wistfully. 'Ah, it is a very nice time.'

As we walked further, there were some ruined houses; others were marked by gunfire. 'This was where they fought,' said Abdulkarim. 'The two halves of Mutsamudu. One group controls the port, the other the airport – so they fought.'

We came to a two-storey house where neat bright blue cotton

curtains flapped in the open windows. Abdulkarim knocked and a moustachioed middle-aged gentleman wearing sarong and white vest appeared, looking like a date merchant from the souks of Baghdad. They greeted each other warmly and I was shown in.

'This is my Uncle Kassim,' said Abdulkarim. 'He says sorry that the house is so empty, but everything was looted in the fighting.'

Three ornately carved armchairs had survived, however, and we sat down. Abdulkarim explained my interest in history and Uncle Kassim looked pleased. With a grandiose gesture, he reached behind his chair and produced a large roll of paper which he proceeded to unfurl, then unfold. Eventually we were looking at something the size of a bedsheet – appropriately for a family history. 'This is a copy of our family tree,' he said in Nzwaani with Abdulkarim translating. 'The original was lost in the war.'

I saw that this tree, unlike English geneologies, really was a tree, branching and growing towards the top of the page, not rooting down to the bottom. That in itself, I decided, revealed a certain confidence about one's past. What was in doubt was not where the family came from, but where it was going. And when I traced it back down, through various sultans, most of whom were named Abdullah, I came to a line of names which led around the corner and up the side to the top where it ended with 'Anli Fatumat bint Rassoul Allah' – the daughter of the prophet Muhammad.

'In Anjouan,' the uncle began, 'there were two sultans . . .'

And there I will stop him, because I understood nothing of what he related, except to say that a large number of Abdullahs were involved. The exposition continued for some time with much tapping of the family tree. Finally, he sat back.

'So which sultan is your ancestor?'

Kassim and Abdulkarim exchanged a glance. 'Abdullah.'

'Right. And when was that? When did he rule? Where did he come from?'

There was an awkward silence. The sort that greets, in other cultures, sudden explosions of flatulence. Quite clearly, in polite Anjouani circles, one does not require dates of one's host. Kassim waved a hand in the air.

'From the Yemen, many generations ago,' he said. This was the key: if someone asked how far back the family went, they would say, 'Thirty-two generations to the Hadhramaut in Yemen.' What mattered was not the actual dates or their antiquity, but the lineage itself, stretching like a ship's rope across the ocean and tethering the family to the shores of Arabia.

Abdulkarim courteously covered my *faux pas*. 'Abdullah was a very bad man,' he said. 'They say he did black magic.'

Kassim nodded. 'By his magic he started a war between Gran Comore and Nzwaan. Since that time the two peoples have hated each other.'

'So your ancestor started all these problems between Gran Comore and Anjouan?'

He nodded. 'And now the government there in Moroni want to expel all Nzwaanis, because they hate them. Why do they hate them? Because of Abdullah.'

I could feel the urge rising within me again, the terrible urge to ask when.

'And . . . approximately, when did he live?'

'Once,' said Abdulkarim, 'he built a palace and buried some slaves alive in the foundations to protect it.' He laughed. 'I don't mind if my ancestor was evil.'

'But very roughly – I know it's difficult to be precise, but was that, shall we say, a hundred years ago . . . or two?

'It doesn't mean I am like him, does it?'

'No, no, not at all.'

Kassim began folding the genealogy up. 'And the war last year, between Domoni and Mutsamudu, that was because there used to be two sultans and they were always fighting.'

'That is interesting,' I said. 'It would be nice to know, more or less . . . I mean, obviously we are in the Islamic period, pre-colonial, so somewhere between, let's say 700 and 1800 AD. But could we be more accurate?'

Kassim finished rolling the bedsheet of history and dropped it behind his chair with a flourish. 'It was,' he said, with an air of rather grand disdain, 'a long long time ago.'

So concluded my lesson in Anjouani history.

Our day continued. We ate green mangoes at one house, drank tea at another, met dozens and dozens of relatives and friends. It was quite standard practice to wander into someone's house say hello, discover that there was nothing more to be said, and wander off again. Familial duty had, at least, been done. Between meetings, Abdulkarim reminisced about Tennessee.

'They always took me out to the mountain – hiking they called it. Why do they do it? We walked and walked and carried all our food until we stopped and ate it. Then we came back to where we had started. There were no houses on the way at all – I mean, man, it was way out in the bush!'

We were passing the great mosque of Mutsamudu for the third time. 'You're meant to enjoy the exercise.'

'No way!' It was strange that he could have picked up the language so well and left the culture adrift.

We strolled along the seafront, an elongated rubbish tip delicately picked over by small pretty cattle. The sun was lower now and Abdulkarim decided it was time to go to the barbecue. He claimed it was out in the jungle somewhere and there would be drink, plus the man I had to meet. I had visions of a little patio with a sack of charcoal, a selection of salads and a glass of Chablis.

Once again we climbed up through the medina, squeezing past the drunks who were being pulled by gravity down the alleys. At the top we came out by a river. The lower reaches were choked with plastic bags and refuse, but as we went higher, we entered a gorge where the stream tumbled over big smooth boulders. A brilliant blue kingfisher flashed across the deep green pools, its plumage catching the last rays of the setting sun. There were many trees here: coconuts, cloves, mangoes, breadfruit and jackfruit, the huge yellow fruits budding from the trunk of the tree. I wiped the sweat from my forehead. Without the gentle sea breeze, the heat was oppressive and gangs of mosquitoes whined around us.

We crossed the river with some care, jumping from boulder to boulder, then scrambled up a bank to a thorn hedge. Beyond was a steep field, neatly cultivated with manioc and sweet potatoes.

'This belongs to Ben,' said Abdulkarim quietly, 'but I can't see if he is there.'

In the far corner was a thatched lean-to where a group of men were sitting around on stones. Smoke curled up into the gathering dusk. They had stopped talking and were watching us. Abdulkarim called out in Comoran and they answered.

'It's okay,' he said, starting over the fence. 'Ben is there.'

The mosquitoes were biting now and there was an oppressive atmosphere of decay. We passed the rows of vegetables: lettuce, tomatoes, aubergines and flowers.

'Ben is a gardener?'

'Ben is many things.'

The men were all in varying stages of drunkeness. Large, loosely rolled joints, smouldering like compost heaps, were being passed around. One man, wearing only shorts, stood to greet us. His eyes were blurred by alcohol, but he spoke clearly.

'You are welcome, friend. I am Ben. Come and sit next to me.'

I made myself as comfortable as I could on a seat made of river stones. Overhead giant bats were gliding silently up the gorge.

'What do you think of Anjouan?'

'It's very beautiful.'

He wasn't interested in platitudes; he wanted politics. 'But the future – what will happen?'

He had a slow thoughtful manner that made me wary. 'The people of Anjouan will decide.'

'Some want France to come and make us like Mayotte – with a

French governor and new roads paid for by the European Union.'
The other men had gathered around us, listening.

'Anjouan fought for independence. You shouldn't give it up too easily.'

This, apparently, was the correct response.

'Ben was one of the leaders in the battle to throw out the Comoran Army,' said Abdulkarim. He leaned closer and whispered. 'Give some money to this boy and he will bring wine and cigarettes. That will be good.'

I slipped a few notes to him – Comoran money. Anjouan has yet to get any of its own.

'We cut ourselves off from Ngazidja,' said Ben, using the Comoran name for Gran Comore. 'Now we cut ourselves off from each other. Our problem is that we have a fertile island with ylang-ylang and cloves and other perfume oils, but the merchants buy at low rates. Sometimes they insist on paying with food, not money.'

'You should organise the farmers.'

'We have tried, but the merchants are fat and the farmers are thin. They need rice to live.'

Someone had blown the fire into life and was throwing lumps of chicken meat on to a grille. The smell of sizzling meat filled the air and made my mouth water.

'So what would you do?'

Ben did not think for long before answering. 'Someone will come.' There was a long pause in which all the men pondered his words. It had the ring of prophecy about it. At that moment the boy returned, clutching two American cigarette packets and three bottles of French wine. No one appeared to take this as a sign.

'And if they do not?' I asked.

'We will kill the merchants.'

'More fighting?'

He gave a secretive smile and, lifting his glass, offered it to me. I took it and drank. It was rough red wine.

'Were you a soldier?'

He nodded. 'But now I plant vegetables.'

A plate of grilled chicken came our way and Abdulkarim whispered to me, 'Ben is a leader, ask him about Denard.'

The chicken was scrawny but welcome. We opened our wine and began to drink. The others were downing toothglasses of Malagasy rum in single, suicidal, gulps.

'You were a soldier?' I said again.

'When I was small, my father beat me and made my life into a routine. Get up and go to bed at certain times. Jobs to do at certain times. More beatings. When I ran away from home, I missed the routine. What could I do? I was trained for nothing. So I joined the army.'

'When was that?'

But Ben liked dates no more than any other Nzwaani. 'It was with Denard. I was his bodyguard for five years.'

'What was he like?'

'Very greedy. He would kill his own grandmother for money.'

'They say he sold guns and drugs to South Africa.'

Ben smiled and said nothing. Abdulkarim whispered in my ear again. 'He keeps his secrets, man. Don't ask like that.'

The chicken was finished and I could feel the effects of the wine hitting me.

'Bob Denard's dream was to be president,' said Ben. 'He built many houses, married a Comoran woman and had children.'

But unlike that other self-made king, Rajah Brooke of Sarawak, Denard had never really established himself. The India-born Englishman, James Brooke, had used East India Company fire-power and a loophole of opportunity to establish himself as ruler of northern Borneo in 1841 – a kingdom which lasted up to the third rajah, exactly a century later. Denard, less successfully, was the last in that line of colonial era characters who saw themselves in the same mould as Brooke: blasting their way to paradise. They were pirates all the same, but their prey was entire countries.

'When did you last see him?'

'I was sent to France for military training with another man.

He was Denard's favourite, but I came higher than he in the examination. From that time Denard hated me.'

He glared at me as he said this, as though trying to convince me he was telling the truth. It didn't work. 'What happened?'

He played with his wine bottle. His silences were like the gaps in a censored letter. One picked up the story somewhere down the line.

'The mercenaries chased me,' he said. 'I ran to the medina to hide, then they came inside the medina. They wanted to kill me. When I heard them in the house, I climbed on to the roof and escaped.'

'Where to?'

'The medina. I ran from roof to roof. They cannot find you when you hide there.'

Abdulkarim drank from our shared glass. 'It's true he fell from favour,' he said, adding under his breath, 'But I don't know why.'

Ben continued his story. 'I took a small boat to Mayotte and stayed there until the mercenaries were gone. Denard still wants to kill me to this day.'

We sat back. Some of the noisier drunks had left and I could hear the sound of the bats: the wind on their wings, then the squabbling as they landed in the trees. The smells of earth, dung and vegetation grew stronger as the fire burned down. Trees creaked, as though with growing pains; there was an incredible fecundity to this volcanic soil, plant stems squeezed out of its belly like toothpaste from a tube, including the vigorous marijuana bushes. The night had enveloped us now.

'What happened in the end for Ahmed Abdullah?' I asked quietly.

'I was not here,' said Ben, 'but I know the true story. The president had gone to Iraq to meet Saddam Hussein and Saddam told him, "I will give you some finance, if you expel Denard." Abdullah signed the agreement and came back here. But there was a French spy in Iraq and he sent a message to Denard warning

[215]

him. So Denard took Abdullah's daughter hostage. Still Abdullah refused to capitulate. Denard then sent a message saying he wanted to talk. Then they met and Abdullah was murdered.'

'Denard killed him?'

'Who knows? There was Denard and his friend Marquès in the room with the president. They say that some presidential fingers went missing during the interview. Denard says a bodyguard burst in and he dived out the way. The bullets hit the president and killed him, then Denard and Marquès shot the bodyguard.' He smiled. 'This is Denard's story. In Metropole at the trial they believed it, but not here.'

We sat in silence listening to the river.

'Do you worry the mercenaries will come back?' I asked eventually.

Ben shook his head. 'Those men were manipulated by France. It was colonialism – just as Ali Soilih predicted. They are not interested now.'

'You know who Ali Soilih was?' asked Abdulkarim.

I nodded. I had been waiting to ask about the Maoist dictator. 'Did you meet him?'

'No, not me,' said Ben. 'I am too young.'

'I heard him,' said Abdulkarim. 'He came to speak to us when I was in school.'

'What was he like?'

'Totally wild, man. He hypnotised me. He hypnotised everyone. He talked for four hours. Can you imagine! Four hours. But we never noticed the time passing and when he finished we wanted more.'

'He made many schools,' said Ben. 'Even now most of the schools here are from Ali Soilih's time.'

They talked about Ali Soilih's presidency, their voices imbued with wonder as if it had been a golden age, a time of hope and of hard work. I was astonished: I'd been expecting bitterness and bad blood – the bloodcurdling memories of a holocaust. Surely what I had read could not be so completely wrong. I asked about

[216]

his claims to be a prophet and even God. 'French propaganda – he was a good Muslim.' A drug addict and deflowerer of girls. 'More French lies.'

But both had been too young to be involved. I wanted more information; I wanted dates and times and names and faces. History belongs to those who write the history books. Could the murderous despot have been someone completely different to the monster of the written accounts? These were events within living memory, I reminded myself, and surely could be corroborated.

The wine had soon been finished and Abdulkarim took me back to the medina in search of drink, staggering through the alleyways to a ruined merchant's mansion, now a bar. By the candlelight I could see traces of grandeur in the carved timbers, despite the drunken figures slumped in pools of urine on the floor. In one of the roofless rooms a girl was following her profession – a sailor came staggering out. 'You should try her!' he bellowed at us, encouragingly. 'We all have.'

With the darkness and the alleyways, the faces hardened by strong weather and bad drink, I was reminded that this waterside area was where the English pirates had often divided up their spoils. In one particular case, the notorious Edward England and his henchman John Plantain had urged the men to murder a captive East India Company officer, only to be foiled by the intervention of a fearsome old brigand who insisted they let the man go. Captain Johnson described the old pirate: 'with a terrible pair of whiskers and a wooden leg, being stuck around with pistols, like the man in the almanack with darts'. It was from this brief sketch that Robert Louis Stevenson developed the character Long John Silver.

Between shots of rum and red wine, Abdulkarim's life story spilled out: a history like the history of Anjouan, dramas and disasters interspersed with periods of total inactivity. As a youth he had repeatedly fought with his father and been thrown out of the house before winning a grant to study in the US. Once there, he met a Japanese girl and married her. Four blissful years later, he went to Japan to meet her parents. At the welcome dinner he had

[217]

left the sushi uneaten. This was the worst, the most disgraceful, insult that a son-in-law could make. His shocked in-laws threw him out; his wife miscarried; the marriage fell apart.

He came home to a plum job which lasted until he had refused to accept his boss's nepotistic advancement of an incompetent relative. The superior threw him out. He set up a shipping agency and the island promptly declared independence, strangling his budding enterprise at birth.

We started on another carton of wine. An old man, his grubby vest plastered in detritus and vomit, began to roll around the floor singing: 'John Brown's body lies a moulderin' in the grave.' Faces loomed up out of dark corners: ugly, sweat-soaked drunks who wanted fights, others who wanted only to hear their own voices. 'That man over there,' said Abdulkarim, 'he is making a lot of money and no one knows how. You see Anjouan is cut off from the real world so the unreal world takes over.'

Talking to these men was like trying to catch eels by hand. Scraps of rumour and gossip glittered in the muddy mess of their addled conversations: a Chinese ship stuffed with cocaine landing its cargo by night, a top Malagasy politician seen with money launderers, an unmarked plane that came and went in the small hours. Abdulkarim was right: Anjouan was adrift and losing touch with any kind of recognisable reality, even the basic facts of its history had become uncertain.

I told him about the pirates who had been here and he nodded. 'Go to Domoni,' he said. 'It is the oldest town here on Anjouan. They say a Frenchman, also a pirate, was there and made a treaty with the queen.'

'Who was he?'

He frowned drunkenly. 'Christ, man, I don't remember. Mission, Mansion – something like that.'

A drunk came staggering towards us and landed on the table, destroying it, but Abdulkarim saved the glasses. We ordered more. The talk span away from English and French into Shinzwaani and I could no longer follow. Wishing I had not drunk quite so much, I lay back on the bench and looked up beyond the bare rafters to where the giant black bats were playing languid games of dot-to-dot with the stars. Beneath me the earth was corkscrewing crazily through space. The next day, should I see it, I would go to Domoni and search for Captain Misson.

11

The Year Zero

For sweetest things turn sourest by their deeds;
Lilies that fester smell far worse than weeds.
William Shakespeare, Sonnet 94

I am monarch of all I survey;
My right there is none to dispute;
From the centre all around to the sea,
I am lord of the fowl and the brute.
O Solitude! where are the chasms
That sages have seen in thy face?
Better dwell in the midst of alarms
Than reign in this horrible place.
William Cowper, 'Verses supposed to be
written by Alexander Selkirk'

When I woke up, I was back at the house where I had stayed on the first night. It was morning and I had a raging thirst. Once again I stumbled out to find the place deserted, but this time there was no Abdulkarim to orientate me. I found some paper and wrote a note explaining that I was going to try and find transport across the island to Domoni and thank you for the hospitality. I left it on the bed.

The Place Moroni was full of life at this early hour. Under the shiny dark leaves of the breadfruit trees, men with little carts were selling baguettes, women in the red-and-white shiromani were on their way to market, and dozens of taxi brousse were waiting for travellers. These are the main form of transport: nothing more than a pick-up truck with a crudely made iron cage on the back containing two bench seats.

I found some tamarind juice for sale and having downed several glasses, ate an unappetising breakfast of boiled meat. The flies in the restaurant were so slow and drowsy that waving my hands over the bowl only succeeded in knocking them into it, and there they stuck, waving their legs in the air.

On my way out I was accosted by a smiling young man. '*Bonjour, monsieur*. You are Ras Asahabi, the English who drank three bottles of wine and one of rum last evening before fainting?'

Did I mention that Anjouan is shaped like an equilateral triangle with sides about twenty-five miles long? A small place.

'You want your passport?' asked the young man. I nodded enthusiastically and he led me to a small office up an alleyway where a man in sunglasses rummaged in a drawer for several minutes. Eventually the passport was produced and handed over with a flamboyant gesture. 'Have a nice day,' said the man in sunglasses.

Soon I was safely aboard a taxi brousse to Domoni, watching the road unwind behind us as we motored out of Mutsamudu. The road followed the coast to the small town of Ouani where we started up the hill, rising quickly through a series of hair-pin bends.

It was a glorious day with vast panoramas over the Indian Ocean. Next to the metalled road were plantations of clove trees: the spices laid out for drying on the tarmac in neat patches of red and brown. Occasionally our taxi brousse encroached too near the edge and gave them a gentle crushing, sending clouds of the delicious sweet scent up into the cabin.

Despite its relatively small land area, Anjouan rises to almost

5,000 feet in height and it took almost an hour to reach the pass at the top where we were stopped by an army road block. Even here I saw no guns, despite everyone's assertion that the island was full of them.

From the pass we began to drop down a valley, the sea far below, its surface wrinkled with ocean swells. It was an exquisite place: brilliant green trees, the sound of running water, and villagers waving at us from tidy little huts. Soon we came to a ylang-ylang plantation, the source of much of the island's revenue. With constant pruning over the years, the trees are kept low and manageable, but the resulting strange contortions and twists of the trunk give them the appearance of weird woodwind instruments waiting to be played. The valuable flowers are large but well camouflaged: the long narrow petals being the same pale yellow-green as the leaves. When crushed, they exude a thick soapy fragrance and a tiny quantity of essential oil – a tonne of flowers producing one kilo of oil.

Lower down we crossed a tumbling river and the roadside was patched with sheets and clothes drying in the sun. In some pools young men were washing shirts, in others girls were doing their sarongs. The river laundry is a traditional meeting place for courting couples.

The east coast of Anjouan is in many ways a harsh environment: the steep forested hillsides drop to a dark stony foreshore which is often pounded by powerful storms. There is no harbour or sea defences, only the strange finger of purple volcanic rock that projects into the ocean about halfway down the east coast. Here, the original settlers built the first town, Domoni.

The town is only small, but it has spread beyond the original defensive wall which encloses the old medina. I climbed down from the taxi brousse at the market, a few hundred yards before the wall. In Mayotte Vincent had given me the name of a schoolteacher living in the town called Ibrahim Djae. Now I set about finding him. It did not take long.

I had just sat on a wall to gather my thoughts when a very

dapper man in tortoiseshell spectacles came hurrying up to me. 'Mister Rah Shabby? I am Ibrahim Djae.'

We shook hands. 'Kevin,' I said. 'Kevin Rah Shabby. How on earth did you know I was looking for you?'

He smiled. 'No secrets in Anjouan! Someone came from Mutsamudu yesterday. Did you tell someone there about me?'

I had indeed mentioned his name in passing when I was telling a relative of Abdulkarim's where I planned to go on the island.

'Come, come,' said Ibrahim Djae. 'You may take your rest at my house.' He was constantly moving and talking, with a ready smile and gentle manner. As we strolled out into the suburbs, he stopped to exchange words with many passers-by, introducing me as, 'My writer friend, Kevin, from England.'

'I run the Islamic League school here,' he explained, in between introductions. 'But because of this political situation, nothing is happening. No diplomatic relations, you see, it has frozen all these projects. Nothing is happening.'

We came to the garden gate of a late 1960s villa: its walls a patchwork of mock crazy-paving under a sloping concrete roof. Ibrahim breezed inside. 'Come, come. It is hot, isn't it? No electricity for the fan, I'm afraid.'

The interior was clearly unchanged from the time of building: oranges and browns in bold concentric circles, bare stone, minimalist furniture. It must have once been a palace by Anjouani standards, a monument to someone's success. 'This will be your room,' said Ibrahim. 'Why not take a rest? I will come back for lunch later on and then I can show you the old town – my family are there.'

I was grateful to him for sensing my weariness: the exertions of the previous night combined with the heat had suddenly overcome me. When he had gone, I threw myself down on the bed and fell instantly asleep.

It was almost four o'clock when Ibrahim woke me. 'Kevin, would you like lunch now?'

I realised, rather guiltily, that he had been waiting to eat. Throughout the meal he spoke enthusiastically about his home town and the impossible decision he was facing: 'If things do not change, I will have to accept a job in Mayotte. I don't like it there, but I am getting married next year.'

We set out for the old town as soon as we had finished, making our way along the main road. 'This wall was built by the Shirazis,' said Ibrahim, pointing to the high rubble barrier through which the modern road has crudely punched a hole. 'They suffered very much from pirate attacks.'

These had been the Betsimisiraka pirates, a fearsome tribe from the north-east of Madagascar who appeared off the Comoros from around 1795 onwards. In fleets of war canoes, they spread fear and terror amongst the coastal communities. The irony was that these communities had done very nicely from the slave trade for centuries and only objected now when the tables were suddenly turned. It was to suppress these attacks that James Prior and the *Nisus* had been despatched, duly delivering a hundred muskets, 10,000 musket balls and ten barrels of powder to Sultan Alawi. 'That a nation of savages,' wrote Prior, 'nearly ignorant of navigation and of the military art, should have assembled fleets and armies under our eyes during many years past, committed themselves to the ocean, and attacked and ravaged distant islands, is so strange an event in modern history as scarcely to be believed.'

'The British helped build part of the wall,' said Ibrahim, 'to defend from sea attack. I will show you.'

We walked past a huge modern mosque which, a plaque declared, held the tomb of President Ahmed Abdullah, then skirted the old medina to emerge at the foot of a steep gravelly incline. Unlike the main town where the houses were neatly stone-built and whitewashed, on this barren spit there were simple shelters of straw. At the top, where the volcanic promontory started, there was a high defensive wall.

'This was the British wall. They gave some cannons too.'

The attacks were sustained and savage. Usually the war canoes

[225]

would be spotted from lookout posts and warning fires lit. The people then ran into the town, but anyone caught would be enslaved. Those inside the walls faced siege and possible death by starvation or thirst. Even the smallest expedition would consist of 300 war canoes, sometimes as many as a thousand would be seen. 'What will the politicians in England think of this?' wrote Prior. 'Thirty years ago we thought it vast things to send out an expedition of 10,000 men: how mortifying to be told we were even then excelled, in numbers at least, by African savages!' He might have been even more mortified had he known the true origins of these savages – something I was to discover only later on my journey.

We left the barren scene and walked back towards the town. Beneath the mosque I could see a steep cliff and a narrow stony shore where men were manhandling canoes from the sea. Ibrahim led me up a lane into a small square. On our left was a graveyard where strange pyramidical tombs stood untended in the long dry grass. 'We do not know who is buried here,' said Ibrahim. 'But they were the first settlers from Persia. Over here is the oldest building.'

He led me across the square to a large house, a two-storey structure built with fortress-like walls. A flight of steps ran up to a beautiful carved door. 'It is tenth-century – the oldest of its kind here.'

He pushed open the door and we went inside. Surprisingly the house was a series of small rooms, linked by intricate passageways and stairs, all doubling back on themselves. There were few windows: light was provided by a central courtyard on the second floor where we found the inhabitants. 'My future in-laws,' Ibrahim explained. 'They are descended from the first sultan who built this place.' Throughout Domoni I was to find that successive sultans and sultanas had built palaces and left descendants who had spread out around the original palace, but were still there, often camping in the ruins.

Ibrahim and I delved deeper and deeper into the Domoni medina.

[226]

This place was even more enclosed and narrow than Mutsamudu, and with far more old carved windows and doors. Inside various houses, some infested by jinns Ibrahim claimed, we wandered along windowless corridors open to the sky above, down twisting staircases and through gloomy vaults. I felt we had been drawn into one of those perspective puzzles of the Dutch artist Escher: stairs that went up, only to emerge below where they had started.

I asked Ibrahim about Captain Misson. Had he been here?

'There is a story,' he said thoughtfully. 'A French pirate who came and stayed here when Halina was queen.' He turned up an alley. 'Come, I remember now. I will show you something.'

We entered a grand old house through elegantly carved doors. Inside was a large room, beautifully decorated with stucco painted mint green. Two children watched us from the floor. Ibrahim ignored them and led me down through a series of winding stone corridors and stairs.

'This family are descendants of Halina,' he explained. 'And this was her house. The pirates came here to negotiate with her.' There were no windows in these lower reaches of the house. The houses here were accretions of rooms, ant heaps that had grown and over-grown with the passing generations. As we delved further and further down it was like passing through the geological strata of human occupation.

'They were, of course, not allowed to see the queen. She was hidden at all times.'

'So they would have talked here in this house – through a veil?'

'Yes. They came here to make a deal. The pirates would protect Domoni in return for a base.'

We came to a low courtyard, the sky at dusk far above the walls, one or two stars beginning to show.

'And what happened?'

'The pirates did stay some time, but this coast was not good for them.'

So Libertalia had had its first failed outing here. I wondered

[227]

how Halina and Misson might have conversed: probably in that melange of language which any resident of the region would recognise, but which outsiders called Misson's universal language. Captain Johnson claims that the Frenchman went to war on behalf of the queen, defeating the sultan of neighbouring Moheli before marrying the queen's sister. Several other liaisons further entangled the pirates with the Johannese women, both groups apparently besotted with one another. When one pirate was killed in a battle, his comrades found his distraught lover had laid him on a bed of flowers where she proceeded to stab herself fatally. With such tales, true or not, Johnson was stoking the fires in romantic loins and furthering the idea of a lover as a utopia.

Ibrahim had gone off to fetch a torch and I waited, listening to the distant whine of an electric drill. When he reappeared I asked him about it. 'Oh, the mosquitoes – not a problem.'

Crouching down we entered a low tunnel. Clouds of mosquitoes rose in glee. They probably didn't get many good meals in this bit of the house. At the end of the tunnel, Ibrahim shone the torch through a dusty hole in the wall. There was a tomb.

'Queen Halina,' he said. 'There are other sultans and sultanas of the family over there.' He motioned that we should go on, but I backed out. If I stayed another minute, I decided, all that would be left of me would be a skeleton too.

Frustratingly, there was no other information to be gleaned on Misson or any other pirate visitors. According to Johnson, the pirates decided that Madagascar would be a better spot to settle in and left Johanna – in Misson's case, never to return.

Out on the street it was now dark and we wandered along, meeting and greeting at every turn.

'Gégé?'

'*Djema.*'

I met Ibrahim's mother, a former fiancée and dozens of friends. The whole impressive network of relationships was as tight and intricate as the medina's own construction, and that network was serviced by simply popping in and out of houses to say hello. Other people simply stopped to find out who I was. One old man was particularly interested.

'What is this?' he asked, Ibrahim translating from Shinzwaani with a grin.

'It is an English.'

'Ah! Does he need special food?'

'No, he eats what we eat.'

Astonishment. 'By God! And what does he speak – the language of the Muzungu?' By which he meant French.

'Yes, but his own language is Shingrez.'

'Marvellous. Ask him to say something in Shingrez.'

I said, as fast as I could, 'She sells sea shells on the seashore.'

The old man, eyes wide, fell back in horror. 'I seek refuge from the stoned Devil! Is that a language! God's creation is a wonderful thing!'

He held Ibrahim's arm and put his head closer. 'Go on – tell me truthfully. What do you feed him?'

'The Ingrez will eat anything,' Ibrahim asserted stoutly.

The old man shook his head in disbelief. 'I'll bet you don't feed him tamarind juice?'

One was brought and placed in front of me. I sniffed suspiciously, toyed with the glass a little. A hushed expectancy fell over the crowd that had gathered. I put the cool glass to my lips and drank it down in one gulp. The old man yelped. 'There is no God but God,' he declared. 'I will go now and tell my wife, but as usual she will say I am a liar.' To the laughter of the others, he trudged on his way, stick over his shoulder.

It was while we were still laughing at this conversation that I heard the drumming. Ibrahim noticed my interest. 'There is a wedding,' he said. 'Come, I will show you.'

We found the procession in the main street: two lines of male dancers all dressed in their best suits and ties, with embroidered skullcaps and over their outstretched arms a silk scarf. The dance was deceptively simple: two shuffling steps forward, one back, then a sudden swoop forward, spin around and back. While they

[229]

did this they sang in Comoran, but this time Ibrahim could not translate. 'Some words are very old and I cannot find a meaning – we do not understand ourselves.'

Women leaned out of upstairs windows above and let loose startling volleys of ululation. The dancers slowly moved down into the heart of the medina, taking an hour to cover a few hundred yards – one very important aspect of any Comoran traditional wedding is that time is not of the essence. As Ibrahim tried to explain above the din of the passing drum troupe, a wedding should last three weeks to meet the standards of basic decency.

We were now in a street barely wide enough for the two lines of men. Children wormed around their legs and the calls of the women overhead were deafening, but there was no escape; I was hemmed into a little alcove.

'Getting married is very very expensive,' Ibrahim shouted above the racket. 'Sometimes two million Comoran francs or more. Men can spend years saving for this.'

He pointed to the groom and I could see he was not a young man.

'But the wedding is important to us,' he went on. 'Every part of Comoran life – our past history taken from Arabia and Persia and India – all this comes together in the wedding. Come!'

He dived off after the dancers who had now changed their rhythm and were dancing in a small square outside the mosque, singing very beautifully: '*Usiriwa! Usiriwa!*' which translates as, 'You are called.'

Ibrahim led me around them and into a house up a small alleyway. I found myself in a front room where a rather nervous young lady was sitting alone in an armchair.

'This is my cousin,' said Ibrahim, introducing us.

The bride looked stunning. She was dressed in heavy silks tied with a broad band at the waist to look like a geisha's kimono. In her hair was a fragrant halo of intricately-woven jasmine and orange blossom. Her face had been painted white with flowers across her forehead, a style that reminded me of Balinese dancers.

[230]

In fact, the entire effect was oriental. Curiously, studies have shown that the women's culture of Domoni has strong Indian and South-East Asia influences while the men's tends toward African and Arabian sources. The dancing I had just witnessed was strongly reminiscent, in its swooping circling motion, of the bara', the Yemeni dagger dance.

Suddenly the bride leaped to her feet and dashed from the room. The men were coming. The front door burst open and in they danced, forming up in a semi-circle facing the drummers. The rhythm changed again and a pair of men came shuffling forward, swayed back, then pounced down with a great shout and leaped up, spinning. Not everyone was quite as proficient as the first pair, however, some men fell over in the attempt and Ibrahim did a little coaching on the side.

I was intrigued. Did they know the dance or not? 'We do not know so well,' admitted Ibrahim when I asked later. 'You see Ali Soilih banned the weddings and so many men never learned. Then afterwards it had become very expensive and people never bothered. Only now we are trying to re-establish our culture.'

A full traditional wedding in Domoni was a crazed alchemist's concoction of rituals and ceremonies drawn together from every Indian Ocean culture. They had bullfights, blood-stained rags, transvestitism, ritual bathing, ritual eating, ritual plucking of pubic hair; they paraded in chairs, they bathed naked in mud, they had food fights and processions of gifts; they danced in lines; they danced in circles; they danced by day and by night; they danced on beds of flowers and they danced while wafted by youths dressed as maidens; they consulted astrologers and necromancers; they sacrificed goats and watched whirling dervishes mutilate themselves with daggers; then on the appointed day for deflowering, they had an old woman under the marital bed shouting sex tips to the bride. In short, the indomitable Domonians included every aspect of nuptual ceremonies known to humankind – with the possible exception of confetti.

As we wandered along the main street again, I asked Ibrahim if he wanted the full wedding. He nodded. 'Yes, at least with all the dances done correctly. It's important we keep our culture.'

'People here must have hated Ali Soilih – for banning the weddings.'

Ibrahim did not answer for a while; we had stopped to watch some school students who were playing handball by the light of a few dim electric bulbs.

'He came here,' he said eventually, 'when I was at secondary school.'

'To speak to the students?'

'Yes. I remember him arriving in a taxi brousse, just like anyone else, and when he got out there were some workmen mixing cement – they were still building part of the school. Ali Soilih took off his shirt and began to work with them.'

'Did they like that – a president joining in?'

'Yes, but we were all amazed at it. This man did not behave as was expected of the president.'

'Some people must have said it was wrong?'

'Traditional people said that, especially because he was stopping the weddings.'

He turned and we began strolling down the street, passing out of the town walls towards Ibrahim's house. 'I can say I loved Ali Soilih because he came as a simple man and spoke to us. He loved young people: "You are the future," he told us. And when he spoke we forgot about time – we only wanted more. There was real justice for ordinary people at that time. He taught us not to feel superior to the villager because we were townspeople with an education. "You are all brothers and sisters." He taught us that to eat rice and sugar was foolish because neither of those things can grow here. He taught that to spend all your money on a wedding will beggar your children. He took land from the French colonialist and gave it to the people. In three years he did more for us than any other president.'

'But what I read of him is all bad. Surely he cannot have been so popular?'

He waved a greeting to a friend across the street. 'Many hated him. The intellectuals hated him; the French hated him; the conservatives hated him. But the young loved him. I don't believe any of the bad things they say.'

'Was it a shock when he died?'

'No. He told us that he would die. He knew that France would not allow him to govern for long.' He leaned closer to me. 'He said, "This is only the first page in the history book of our country." That is what he wanted it to be – the first page.'

'And when Abdullah replaced him?'

'Pah! Corruption. Mercenaries. Drunkenness. Abdullah would come with a big fleet of cars all with sirens and no one could speak to him. It was the opposite. They all began to steal from the government. Under Ali Soilih that did not happen.'

The towers of Abdullah's mausoleum were still visible, flood-lit above the trees, a monument to the capricious nature of reputation. His were the fine marble halls, the fortune and the stature of the man who died standing up to Denard; he even had the honour of a trial for his alleged murderer in Paris, though not a conviction. Ali Soilih had been shot 'while trying to escape' and hurriedly buried in his mother's front garden, leaving only a few transcripts of speeches. His utopian dream had been taken to be a Marxist one, but to me he had more in common with those seventeenth-century dreamers who had imagined paradise as a fresh start on a distant island.

Ali's arrival on the scene in August, 1975, came in typical Comoran manner: together with a few helpers and armed with four rusty shotguns, he drove up to the palace in a clapped-out Renault 4. Using umbrella spokes, they punctured the tyres of Abdullah's vehicles. No one was shot and the government capitulated.

Abdullah, knowing the game was up, escaped to Anjouan, hiding out in his home town of Domoni. Unable to dislodge him, Ali Soilih contacted a friend who managed to put him in touch with an ex-French Army man with the right sort of experience – Robert

Denard. The arrangement was a simple financial one: for a fee, Denard arranged the capture of Abdullah.

Ali was proud of his achievement, a bloodless takeover at the cost of a few flat tyres and an umbrella. He refused to countenance the assassination of his rival. Instead he demanded an oath, sworn on the Holy Koran, that Abdullah would retire abroad and never re-enter politics. That done, a cheque for about £600,000 was written and Abdullah retired to Paris where he could best plan his immediate and vengeful re-entry into Comoran politics. It would, however, be three years before his chance came.

Like all utopian despots, Ali needed a clean slate to work on and vast powers. He ordered the veils to be torn from women and burned, government archives went the same way. His belief was that young people did not have the baggage of the past and so could be taught new ways. When a delegation from Germany arrived after the coup, they found illiterate teenagers 'running' the ministries while their erstwhile masters stumbled blindly around the streets with sacks over their heads.

The islanders' tendency to withdraw and isolate themselves now went against them. With the French gone and other foreigners snubbed, aid money and trade deals were hard to come by. Added to these economic hardships were a number of disasters: thousands of Comorans living in Madagascar fled home after horrifying massacres took place; then the only active volcano on Gran Comore erupted, causing widespread devastation. But more humiliating for Ali was the failed invasion of Mayotte.

The French island had voted to continue as a dependency of France in 1975, much to the annoyance of some French economists who saw it as little more than a money drain. When the Comorans threatened to invade, to claim their 'lost' island, the French seem to have given the impression they would be happy to lose ground gracefully. With high hopes then, Ali Soilih and fifty men set out to capture the prize. It was not to be.

From the first, the reception was hostile: local people began to shower their liberators with stones, spitting at them and shouting insults. The one factor Ali appears not to have considered was whether Mayotte actually wanted to be free of the colonial yoke. It clearly did not. Several local market women decided to take the offensive: they lifted their skirts and bared their bottoms. Judging by the size of some women in Mamoudzou market, it must have been an awesome sight, and the effect on the invasion force was devastating.

Some time later, the small French garrison, who had been packing to leave, received word that their liberators were pinned down in the market place. Reluctantly, flights were cancelled and they headed across the narrow straits to rescue them. One can imagine the scene as shocked survivors, comforted by burly legionnaires, were helped on to a boat and sent home. Ali's great dream of a liberated Mayotte and free Comoros Islands had been decisively squashed.

I left Domoni two days later and took a taxi brousse around the island to the south coast. Ibrahim had told me about a place where there was a hotel: the only one outside of Mutsamudu on the island. I could tell he didn't really approve of hotels. Like other Anjouanis, he became rather anxious at the prospect of letting a defenceless foreigner fall into the clutches of a paying establishment.

At the top of the pass the taxi stopped to let me out: they were going up a side track to their village. It was a bright day and the forest was sparkling with fresh green. I walked along quite happily, getting occasional views of the ocean far below. Anjouan is so tropically fertile and so remote that it is hard to believe it was not the setting for all island paradise tales, from More's supposedly-idyllic *Utopia* itself to the hellish dystopia of *The Lord of the Flies*. Uniquely perhaps, under Ali Soilih, the place appears to have somehow contrived to be both simultaneously, depending on one's viewpoint.

For myself I was happy to be far from Per and the intrigues of the yacht. I was a recovering utopian. On Anjouan, I told myself, no one knew a damn thing about me: I could be whatever

[235]

I wanted – just like Soilih wiping the slate clean and declaring the Year Zero. The claustrophobic atmosphere of Mayotte, particularly Dzaoudzi, was replaced with bright clean mountain air and ocean winds.

After an hour a taxi brousse came grinding down the road and I held out an arm. This ride proved to be a stunning spiral down through thick jungle towards the sea. Between the trees were glimpses of steep forested ridges plunging into a boiling mist of sea spume.

Before the bottom of the hill, the car stopped and the driver gestured up a muddy track. I could hear the muffled roar of the ocean but not see it. The path burrowed downwards between fences of split canes hung over with fanfares of morning glory, then a path lined with flowers led to several thatched shelters on a bluff above the ocean.

I saw immediately that there was another guest: a slim blonde-haired woman, sitting with her back to me at a table covered in papers. I strolled down to her past a line of small thatched huts, each with a bed and mosquito net inside. The woman glanced up, obviously as surprised as I was to see another guest. '*Bonjour.*'

She was a middle-aged Frenchwoman with an engaging smile, but it was the papers in front of her that caught my attention: they were photocopies of hands – twenty or thirty pairs spread out before her, some with scribbled notes attached.

'You are English,' she stated. 'Isn't it wonderful 'ere?'

It certainly was. To the right of the belvedere where I stood, a path led down to a small beach enclosed by two headlands a hundred yards apart. Some outrigger canoes were drawn up, but there was no sign of any fishermen out at sea. To the south stretched the vast and empty ocean, its surface creased with swells moving like the involuntary muscle spasms of a giant beast, building and growing as they approached, then rolling and barrelling with great plumes of spray whipped from the tops. About two hundred yards out the wall of water appeared to divide, held back by a narrow flooded sandbar that projected from the beach. Then the two fronts, began to roar as the foaming upper lip reached a critical mass, too heavy to hold its height but slow to break until with a dull crump it exploded in on itself.

'Look at those waves!'

'I count them,' said the woman. 'But there is no pattern.'

'Have you swum here?'

'Yes, but only here, near to the beach.' The water on the sandspit was choppy but shallow.

'I want to go in.'

'Wait,' she said. 'Have some tea with me and I will come too.' She called across the lawn to the kitchen and a tray of tea was brought. I arranged to take one of the huts and accepted the offer of a fresh lobster for lunch.

'I think a person can be very 'appy 'ere,' said the woman, then remembering that we had not introduced ourselves, we shook hands. Her name was Nicole and she had come to Anjouan, she said, in order to escape distractions and do her work.

'I am palm-reader,' she explained. 'People send me a photocopy of their hands and I tell them something.'

'Their future?'

'Not exactly.' She took my hand and turned it over. 'You see I look at the shape of the hand, the way the fingers divide or stay together. I see the type of person, what they have done so far with their life – all this is in one hand. In the other I find their potential, what they can do, or what could happen. It is not fixed, you see. But sometimes I see quite accurately how their past was and their future will be. Like you . . .'

She took the other hand and frowned. 'That is interesting.'

I had a strange cold feeling, wondering what might come next. The past always goes with you, she was saying, etched clearly enough for those who know how to look. No wiped slates or Year Zeroes, you cannot erase the past, nor hide it.

But she put my hands down on the table. 'Not now. Let's drink our tea and swim first.'

I went and dropped my bag in my hut and changed into some

[237]

shorts. Nicole reappeared wearing a sarong over a black bikini and carrying a face mask, snorkel and flippers. We walked along the path, then scrambled down a steep track on to the sand.

The beach was backed by what appeared to be jungle but was in fact fruit trees: coconuts, jackfruit, bananas, lychees and mangoes. Vanilla creepers twined around old stumps. There was little here that was not useful or edible in some way.

'It is a garden of Eden,' said Nicole, untying her sarong and entering the water. 'Do you want to try snorkelling?'

We splashed around in the shallows for a while, but even here the water was so turbulent that visibility was zero. Eventually I handed the equipment back to her, shouting over the roar of the surf. 'It's no good – too much sand in the water.'

She put on the mask and flippers. 'I will try over there near the rocks.'

I almost warned her then, but she seemed so sure of what she was doing and no one, I told myself, would be so foolish as to get into those huge breakers.

She set off parallel to the beach and I waded out further. I wanted to get into the medium-sized waves, have some fun with them. When I got into waist-deep water, there were sudden impish little wavelets slapping at me. I looked across to where Nicole was swimming: she had reached the point and stood up. She waved to me and I could see her shouting, but it was impossible to hear anything. She put the face mask back on and began to swim towards me.

I swam a little further out then stood up again. Immediately a wave knocked me off my feet. There was a moment of panic. Which way is up? I was spun around, arms flailing, touching nothing, no bottom. Then I righted myself and came up for air, spluttering and laughing. Surprisingly, in those few seconds I had been carried 30 or 40 yards out. I tried to put my feet down.

I think it was then that I felt the first real doubt. I've always been a strong swimmer but never reckless; a near miss when swimming across a river in flood a decade before had cured me of any over-confidence. I knew my limits and I had deliberately stayed within my depth. But when I tried to put my feet down, the undertow simply clubbed them away. It was the sheer power that had caught me unawares. And every second that my feet were off the bottom, I was moving swiftly out towards the big seas. Suddenly those huge waves seemed dangerously close. I put my head down and began to swim hard for the shore.

Seconds later I took a mouthful of seawater and had to stop. I was making progress, but only slight. I could no longer see Nicole, the waves around me were too high. Then I caught a glimpse and she was waving at me from far away to my left. I waved back, pointing at the shore, but she seemed to be coming on. 'My God,' I thought. 'I hope she knows what she is doing.'

Even in the moments that this took, I had lost all the ground I had gained. Now I really swam. A wave caught me and I managed to body surf in a little, all the time pulling as hard as I could. Every now and again I glanced up, but I was still in the thick of it. I was at my limit now. I knew I couldn't swim like this for much longer and, though I never doubted I would get out, I was already thinking of Nicole. What if she was not in control? What if she had to be rescued?

When I reached the sandspit, I managed to stand in the waist-deep water, feeling the sand ripped from under my soles. Anxiously I scanned the horizon. Nicole had disappeared.

I turned towards the shore. A figure was running along the bluff and down the track. More appeared from the trees, running on to the sand, then stopping to watch. But I could see nothing. The waves and spray were too high.

After these crises are over, you look back and marvel at the mind's ability to compress thoughts and feelings. I should think I hovered there for a fraction of a second, but an avalanche of unconnected thoughts passed through my mind. How to rescue her. Who is she? I might die too. Where is she? Will they fly the body back to France? I must go back for her. But the truth was, I could not. I could not even see her.

[239]

I began to struggle back towards the shore, heart pounding. The words of Stevie Smith's poem running in my head like a silly love song that gets stuck there when you least want it. '*I was much too far out all my life.*'

For an agonisingly long time I could not move quickly, the weight of water was too great. But then I was into the shallows and found I was so tired I could barely jog. The youths who had run on to the beach were standing staring while an old man from the hotel ran up and down, desperately holding his head in his hands. '*And not waving but drowning.*'

I got on to the sand and moved as fast as I could up the beach, past the discarded sarong and towel left there only a few minutes before. I wasn't thinking. I had no plan of what to do. I remember the frightened faces of the villagers, the fatalistic stillness of them as they watched the tragedy unfold. Nothing can be done. She's dying. Oh shit! Shit! Shit! Where is she?

A youth pointed and I saw her now. Way out in the huge waves, still afloat but not moving, face down, then an arm came up and over, exactly as if she was lounging in a hotel pool and for a ridiculous moment I almost thought she was in control, that everything was going to be all right. Then she disappeared under a mountain of water.

That broke the spell for me, the awful reverie that had come over everyone. I shouted, '*Le pirogue! Le pirogue!*'

But the old man grabbed my arm. '*Non, monsieur! Pas possible.*'

I pulled away from him and ran along, waving my arms like a madman at the empty ocean. Some older youths had come now. 'Rope!' I shouted, forgetting the word in French, so it meant nothing to them. 'Rope! Get a rope!'

But no one moved. They were used to this: the greedy ocean snatching someone away. There was nothing to be done. How could you fight such a beast? They watched me in the way we watch the aftermath of a car smash from the other side of a motorway, wishing something could be done but knowing nothing can, except to accept what has happened. Was that woman this man's wife, or his mother? A muzungu without a name who came with that inexplicable desire of theirs to sun that white skin and swim. Now he is alone. The beast is fed.

'*Il n'y pas de chance, monsieur. La mer là-bas est très mal.*'

Then, way out in the swell, a distant pale figure could be seen, no longer struggling. As we watched, the head slowly lifted and I knew she was looking at us. I don't remember if anyone shouted, or who moved first. Next thing, I was pelting down the beach and four of the older youths came with me.

When we hit the water, she was out of sight, but I knew she might have seen us coming. It might just lift her for a last effort at survival. Not only that but a couple of minutes with water rushing off the sandbar had made an important difference. We could run almost fifty yards before we had to wade. And then we were five. The strength and confidence of numbers supported us: we joined hands as the undertow grabbed at us and we could steady ourselves.

As we left our depth and had to swim, a pale bloodied figure appeared, waving weakly, scarcely able to lift her head to breathe. By a miracle she had managed to get to the edge of the big breakers. Now one caught her and spat her out towards us. The tide had turned. With one of the youths I got to her and we took an arm each. With a few strokes and some pulling by the others we were able to stand. She was saved.

At first, Nicole could not stand up. Her bikini had been torn off and there were bloody scratches on her, as though she had been clawed. We half-carried, half-dragged her into the shallows, then I fetched her sarong and wrapped it around her.

'*Merci, merci,*' she kept gasping, but it was a few more minutes before she stopped shaking and could walk unaided. When she finally did manage to shuffle up on to the sand, a youth with a box in his hands came sprinting down the track, leaped on to the beach in front of her.

'Madame,' he panted, opening the box with a flourish. 'You like to buy souvenir? Ylang-ylang oil. Very good quality. One bottle last one lifetime.'

The old man who had been close to tears only minutes before, recovered himself sufficiently to try and chase the boy away. Nicole started to laugh weakly. 'One lifetime? And how long is that?'

PART FIVE

MADAGASCAR

12

To the Pirate Coast

Walker there is no path,
You make the path by going,
And on looking back,
You see steps you will never retrace,
Walker there is no path,
Only trails in the ocean.
                    Antonio Machado

There was Frank (the owner), plus Robert (the crew), André (a
Pole), and me. We sailed for Madagascar in a varnished tub that
had been built as a fishing boat in Sweden in the 1930s and
converted by Frank. After the narrow elegance of Per's yacht,
this boat felt huge. It had a broad curving deck with little to stop
the waves breaking except the wheelhouse and smokestack at the
stern. Access to the cabins was via a hatch and ladder just behind
the stubby foremast.

Frank had ripped out all the old fish-containing gear and
replaced it with cabin space for passengers. Nevertheless, the
guts of the boat shone with the honeyed glow of old timber
and brass. The toilet required the operation of several levers
and stopcocks, all found in a tangle of fine old tubing. In the
bow was a master cabin, something of a bachelor's love palace

by the look of it. Moving astern was a modern galley, then a large cluttered communal area with two cabins, both with bunkbeds. A gangway led through to the engine room under the wheelhouse. Frank was very proud of the engine. 'Sixty-seven years old,' he shouted, wiping his hands on a rag. 'Twenty-two-litre cyclinders with direct drive at 800 revolutions per minute. That engine noise never changes, no matter what speed.'

André recounted his life story between bouts of vomiting – the weather wasn't so good. He was a stocky young man with plenty of tattooes, a military haircut and an interesting array of scars. He told me how he had been discharged as an invalid from the Foreign Legion after being blown up by a mine in Zaire. He had only survived the explosion because his best friend had partly shielded him, dying in the process.

'Will you go back to Poland?'

He shook his head. 'There's nothing for me there. I want to see the world. I'll stay in Madagascar as long as I like – maybe not in Nosy Bé though, not with this cholera epidemic. Haven't you heard? Over 300 have died.' He shrugged. 'No problem for me. I go somewhere else. The Legion will send my pension wherever I want. It's not much, but enough to live somewhere cheap like Madagascar.'

'What were you doing in Anjouan?'

He shrugged. 'I wanted to see it. That's all. But I got caught up in some fighting. I was asleep when it started. I heard the shots and went to the door. Then they pulled me out into the street and then took all my stuff.' He made a face. 'So I'm travelling light now. No problem. I have my passport and my credit card – they were in my jeans pocket. What about you? Why Madagascar?'

I told him about the pirates and how I'd been chasing their shadows across the ocean, heading for the place that they had finally called home.

He grinned. 'Like us. The Legion. We are like pirates, no?'

I didn't want to disappoint him. He was a strong-looking fighter, but the answer was no, the Legion were hired guns, the pirates had been free. He had to stop talking then in order to rush to the side and vomit. It made me feel queasy to watch him so I went to my bunk. If I lay with my eyes closed, the motion soon settled and I could doze.

In Mutsamudu, Abdulkarim had worked things out for me, between drunken bouts at the roofless bar where the owner lay on the floor singing 'John Brown's body lies a moulderin' in the grave'. I had come down from the other side of the island, having parted from Nicole: 'Kevin, you and I are connected now. We are blood brothers.'

I had even felt sufficiently comfortable with her to ask the most difficult question: 'Didn't you see it in your palm?'

She was not put out by this at all. 'Of course, I see in my cards – great danger – only three days ago.'

I didn't say that I would have been more impressed had she mentioned it earlier, but I was soon to realise that for Nicole, proving herself was not an issue. She didn't just believe in her palm-reading and her cards, she knew it to be a fact. If someone disagreed, then so what? Having discovered how deeply the irrational utopian myth was rooted in me, I could hardly object to her own belief. When she listed the features and the meanings, it seemed almost logical itself.

I had returned to Mutsamudu and to Abdulkarim, hoping he would find me a boat to Madagascar. We spent the days doing very little. I bought food. He and his wife cooked. I felt that I had taken over their lives: how had they filled their time before I had appeared? Abdulkarim talked to me of his ex-wife, the Japanese woman he had met in Tennesee, and his current wife sat and watched his face as he recreated that golden age which he had lost over a sushi supper.

Utopia in a person, the most ephemeral and illusory of paradises, and yet the most compelling. Nicole had leaned over my hand and seen that belief, teased it out like a surgeon taking out a thorn.

When I woke first, it was dark and waves were breaking on the porthole. I was disoriented, having fallen asleep thinking of

[247]

Abdulkarim and woken with the memory of a dream. I had been standing on a seashore, hearing the song of the whales out in the swell. The flukes of the creatures were black against the sky, rising and falling and rising again, but this time becoming figures of men: two sea captains in black frockcoats and tricorn hats, beckoning to me.

I lay for a long while, drifting in and out of sleep. At one moment I was imagining, with peculiar clarity, walking on Per's island once more. Odd, discarded images came to me: the smile of the man we had left there as he turned and walked away; a small hole in the forest path that I knelt to peer into and saw a cave of twisted ancient coral leading down; the way the forest closed off the sea after only ten paces.

When I woke again it was still dark, and we were still rolling. I climbed off the bunk and, holding on all the time, shuffled out into the saloon. The other cabin held the sleeping figures of Frank and André.

At the stern, hanging on to a rope, I peed over the side and wondered if a person overboard would stand any chance. Not because of shark attacks which were unlikely, but from exhaustion and thirst, and perhaps, despair. The swells were too large and broken to allow any clear sight. I imagined what it might be like: to watch the boat heading away, shouts unheard. There was a feeling in me, like that when standing on a clifftop, of wanting to jump. It wasn't a death wish, simply a desire to experience something so completely and utterly extreme; to take an irrevocable step. That's the negative face of the utopian urge, I thought, to chuck yourself out there and smash up what is left behind. The wiping of slates that seems so beguiling and yet is so difficult to achieve.

Anjouan was drifting away from me: its significances and symbols moving beyond my grasp, becoming no more real than the dream I had just had. Steinbeck had described a friend of his as a sceptic with a mystical approach to life: I saw myself watching Nicole's face as it peered into my hands. I would have rejected all she said if it were not that the ocean had tried to snatch her away before saying it, then made us blood brothers. Looking for utopia in the palm of your hand, in the tea leaves or the crystal ball. Looking for a decision to move on, move back, or stand still – or jump. The madness of Anjouan had infected me, the madness that kills presidents and abolishes government on a whim. I had the feeling that I could suddenly do anything, no matter how bizarre: throw myself off a boat for no reason. Jump.

I pulled back with a start. The bizarre hypnotic effect of the ocean's movement was broken, yet I still felt feverish and edgy, hanging on that rope for far too long, feeling the delicious thrill of the vast ocean, the vast and magical loneliness of it, 6,000 miles wide and three miles deep. The rail was so low and the roll of the boat so violent, a single moment of hesitation on the rope and I could go over. Then within seconds, they would be beyond shouting, a further minute to be out of sight. Would I start swimming after them? Nathaniel North would not have seen land when his vessel sank under him. Had he struck out blindly? Or were there stars to guide him? Before he struck out for the shore, he had saved a young negress from drowning and put her on the upturned hull. Had he the least idea of how far he had to go? The man's sheer, bloody-minded, physical refusal to die was immense. I pulled back on the rope and staggered around the wheelhouse.

Back in my bunk, I switched on the light and tried to read about the island that we were slowly approaching. But the words did not stick in my mind. I could hear the waves smashing against the porthole and feel the lurch of the boat digging into the hollow swells. I put my head down and closed my eyes.

It was my brother who woke me. I got up, noticing that the boat had ceased moving and that it was sunny. We were in a newsagents buying Sunday papers, but there was nowhere to pay. I wandered through a bulkhead door and found myself in a village fete. The Rolling Stones were there. I asked Mick Jagger about the papers and he sent me to Keith Richards who was busy tattooing cabalistic symbols on the inner lower lips of beautiful girls. He sent me onward to the others, each passing me on around the stalls, until I came to the last. By this time I was panicking about being accused of stealing. The woman at the stall looked up from her cake display. It was Nicole.

'Where do I pay?' I asked desperately.

Nicole took the papers from my hand and replaced it with a slice of home-made cake. 'The papers are free, Kevin,' she whispered. 'Now it's time to eat cake.'

As I bit into the cake, there was a great bang on my head and I reached up to feel the roof of the cabin. It was light outside, but the ocean was still throwing itself against the porthole. I swung myself down from the bunk and lurched along to the galley where I drank a glass of water to try and get rid of the metallic taste in my mouth. On deck I found André and Frank standing at the prow, watching the islands around Nosy Bé as we approached.

'That is the sugar plantations,' said Frank, pointing to a large patch of pale green on the lower slopes of Nosy Bé itself. 'Over there is the sugar refinery and rum distillery.'

'Where's Hellville?'

'Around the back in a sheltered bay.'

We passed an inlet where several yachts were anchored: the sailors steer clear of Hellville, Frank explained, because of its reputation for theft. I took his binoculars and examined the fleet and sure enough, tucked away among them, were the long elegant lines of the *Maribel*.

After a further hour chugging along we rounded the point and saw the town. Given that all I had to go on was the name and some travellers' tales of robbery and prostitution, Hellville was a big surprise. The name itself is misleading: rather than an appelation earned after years of misbehaviour, it is merely the name of a French admiral. Viewed from the sea, you could not imagine a more peaceful, sleepy town. A few serviceable colonial buildings, all slatted shutters and cool verandas, peeked over the tree tops. A pleasant breeze blew. People smiled and waved at us.

Leaving Robert to guard the boat, we went ashore in the tender and took a taxi to the immigration headquarters. The ragged boulevard was lined with lace tablecloths that the women were making.

Having got ourselves stamped into the country, André elected to stay at a small bordello where the rooms were little stable boxes with a choice of girls, all wrapped up in towels. He's probably still there. Much to his surprise, I opted for a small hotel around the corner – twice the price and no girl included with breakfast. I was careful to drink clean water, but there was no visible sign of the cholera epidemic.

Two days later I left and took a plane across the island to the east coast feeling strangely free. My entire trip up to that point had been a series of individuals who had linked me to the next. Now I was facing the last leg without clues: I knew no one; I had no addresses; I had no guide; I had never been to this place before, nor met anyone who had.

This was what Crusoe loved, I told myself, to be set free by solitary travel. Rousseau wrote of Robinson Crusoe: 'The surest way of rising above prejudice and ordering one's opinions according to the real relations of things is to put oneself in the place of the solitary man.' Yet somehow, given this solitary start, I had to find the descendants of those early pirates and the forts they had haunted. It seemed a daunting task as I gazed down at the vast expanse of Madagascar, the fourth biggest island in the world, its surface area as large as the Iberian peninsula.

I changed planes at Antananarivo, the capital, and by late afternoon I was in the eastern port of Tamatave, or Toamasina as it is officially known. I liked the place immediately: the centre boasts a boulevard of royal palms whose pale trunks swell gently, like furled umbrellas. At one end is the city hall, at the other the broad blue ocean with the occasional rusty freighter manoeuvring out of port. The streets were slow-moving, partly because the favoured transport is the pousse pousse, the simplest form of rickshaw – two wheels, a red-painted cart and a stick-thin man between the traces. The passengers were mainly schoolchildren or ladies with shopping.

[251]

In the market the mixture of foods was wonderfully varied: cola nuts next to breadfruit, tamarind and strawberries under the umbrellas. The women favoured big straw hats with artificial flowers and ribbons; the men chose straw trilbys, baseball caps or wilted panamas, like old pancakes tossed up there and forgotten. Women's hair was exquisitely braided to the small of their backs, their blouses were church-going white, worn with a long colourful sarong; their faces held every feature found east of Suez: Khmer, Dayak, Chinese, Malay, Polynesian, Javanese – I had no doubt the majority had been born within a few miles of the spot. There were others who held themselves apart for religious reasons: quite a few Ismailis, their men with big black beards and robes, the women demurly Victorian in linen shawls and ribboned caps. A new Mercedes Benz sat parked up amidst the pousse-pousses while couples swept past on Chinese bicycles, the lady always elegantly poised on the backrack with a shopping basket on her lap.

I spent a night in a hotel and next morning caught a shared minibus north up the coast: my goal was the small island of Ste Marie, one of the pirates' main haunts. There was no virgin jungle along the way: where roads go, loggers follow – modern day bands of pirates who have stripped the land north of Tamatave entirely. All that remains are scrubby hills covered in traveller's palms, the fan-like plant which gives the locals a thatching material.

We crossed big rivers where dugout canoes slid under the narrow clearance of pontoon bridges. The wreckage of previous bridges was never far away, whole generations of construction methods, almost always finishing with the practical solution to cyclones – a temporary wooden pontoon of railway sleepers. The concrete hopes of the 1970s lay beside them in great useless chunks, good for nothing but blocking the river. Set well above the flood levels were villages of woven huts on little stilts surrounded by stands of bananas, lychees and jackfruit.

I got out at Foulpointe, a single strip of wooden huts and cheap hotels, then walked the half mile to the sea. What I found was wrinkled French men with whiskery white chest-hair, strolling along the beach, their blotchy arms around teenage Malagasy nymphettes and their deflated buttocks in black swimming thongs. There were a few small-scale tourist developments here, run mainly by Chinese families and catering for French people from Réunion Island. In the evening the men gathered to bitch about ex-wives, while their local girlfriends disappeared, no doubt to spend their sugar papa's money on something pretty   like a local boy.

Next day was wet, the clouds as static and heavy as the air. There was a very distant whining noise in my head, as though a thin, slightly roughened wire was being drawn across a violin bow somewhere between my ears. I skipped breakfast, heading out of town on the main road towards the ruined fort which I had heard about. No sooner had I started than a youth attached himself to me. We exchanged a few words and then lapsed into silence. A mile north of the town there was a lane going inland and a sign: 'Fort Manda'.

The structure was almost lost in undergrowth but still standing: a circular defensive stone wall, about fifteen feet in height with cannons poking from the crenellations.

'*Voilà*,' said the youth. 'Give me 20,000 francs.'

I think it was the smug little grin that did it: as if he had conjured a white rabbit from his trousers. Whatever it was, a deep red mist enveloped me. I heard a voice climbing from a growl to a roar. Next thing I was chasing him around the fort, quite determined to beat his head to a pulp.

When we got halfway round I stopped for a breather, and having restored some oxygen to my brain, I began to laugh.

'You're going mad,' I said, thinking I was alone. 'You really are.'

There was an oppressive atmosphere here that weighed on me: the clouds sagged, the lush vegetation hung limply all around, and there was a dank foetid smell rising from the ground. I wondered if I was falling ill: I felt so thin and unbalanced.

'Easy, boy,' I said loudly; then rather taken with the idea of myself as a frightened stallion, blew air out my lips with a flapping

[253]

noise. I asked myself if I should continue the hunt, and answered my own question aloud: 'Neigh, lad. Nei-ei-eigh.' I felt much better for neighing, it helped me forget the whining noise between my ears. I did it again.

It is as well that I saw the man at that moment, before I cantered in a circle or stooped to graze on the long grass. He was looking down on me from one of the cannon emplacements. When I glanced up, he dodged out of sight.

I walked around to the front gates of the fort. There was a tunnel entrance under an arch which twisted around to the left. The chased, and chastened, youth was standing well away behind a tree, and in the archway were two older men.

'Why won't you pay him?' asked one in French.

'I didn't ask him to be my guide.'

'He showed you the fort.'

'No, that is not correct: the sign by the road showed me the fort.'

They held a discussion in Malagasy. I recognised one word: 'rats', which is easily remembered as it is Malagasy for 'bad'.

'If you want to enter the fort,' said the older man. 'You must first pay me 10,000 francs, and him, and him.'

That was about five US dollars, but to put it into context, I had paid only 20,000 for a decent chalet the previous night. I sat down on a rock. I felt sweaty, tired and obstinate.

'I won't pay him anything.' My hands were shaking uncontrollably and I wanted to lie down. For some time I didn't say anything: I was starting to worry about malaria. The first time the disease had caught me, I had felt this way: suddenly tired and fractious. Within five minutes I had blacked out, waking up twenty minutes later in a gynaecologist's waiting room next to five pregnant Kenyan ladies. This had not helped my reorientation, although it was not as bad as it sounds – I was in Kenya at the time.

'Here,' said one of the men, offering me a Good Luck cigarette. I didn't want it, but accepted to be sociable. I smoked in silence and felt better. The moment of doubt had passed: it was not malaria, I told myself, just a touch of some fever allied with an empty stomach.

'Look,' I said, feeling better disposed to him. 'I'll give you the 30,000 after the tour. If you want to give some to him – that is your problem.'

He gave me a hand up and we went inside the tunnel, leaving the other two behind. The fort was sturdily built with coral stones which my guide pointed to. 'They used egg white to make the cement. Every family had to provide eggs.'

The entire fort was no more than a defensive soufflé. 'So the Malagasy people built it?'

'Yes – with the British. Sir Robert Farquhar came here in 1811 to stop slavery by the French traders. The commandant was James Hastie. Very good men.'

We climbed up on to the walkway and admired the cannons, most of them still in position. Afterwards I remembered the tour in sudden patches of vivid clarity. The walk up had exhausted me and wriggling black maggots were flying across my vision.

The guide led me down past a tree where glasses of flies pickled in rum sat as offerings to the spirits. There was a tunnel to a rear door and a large stone over a hole.

'The royal family hid in there when the French came,' he said. 'My ancestor, my great great great great grandfather, was there fighting. His name was Letafika.'

'What happened?'

'There were forty-four French soldiers with guns and eighty Senegalese. Inside the fort were 500 Malagaches.'

'No British?'

'No, they had gone. The French used their guns well and killed many people before they rolled stones up to the walls and climbed inside. There was terrible fighting by hand and my ancestor was killed.' He mimed bayoneting.

The British had actually made a treaty with the French and withdrawn, leaving their erstwhile allies in the lurch.

We walked out the gate and back down the lane to town. The

other two had disappeared. In the town we parted and I walked on, past the church where a choir was practising. When they sang, I stopped to listen and it was so beautiful my eyes filled with tears. I was shivering too, and when I reached my beach chalet I fell on the bed and drifted into sleep.

The nightmare must have started much later because when it woke me it was dark outside. I had been walking across a desert when I found a manhole cover. Sweeping the sand from its surface I saw it was the lid of a World War Two tank. It opened easily and inside was a grotesque pile of mangled corpses.

I got up and wiped the sweat from my body with a towel then slept again. At seven next day I was up and feeling light-headed. To move further north I would have to wait for a passing car or minibus on the main street, so I strolled up there.

People rise early in the Malagasy countryside. All the shops were open, selling bolts of bright cloth, tools, Chinese radio batteries, 'BonBon' English lemonade, and Old Guard Whiskey. There were wooden counters bearing glass jars filled with cakes and sweets, men gazing longingly at new bicycle saddles, and women taking their time over purchases. I bought a glass of Negrita Cazenove dark rum and a hard cake over the hardwood counter of the Chinese general store. Thus fortified I was ready to face the road.

Three hours later I got a lift in a packed minibus to Fenerive where the legend of a pirate fort did not stop me hopping on a pick-up truck heading further north. I was in a hurry, keen to get across to Isle Ste Marie, trying to ignore the fever.

It was a wet journey: rain poured down from a grey sky; the villages of bedraggled thatch were silvered with great puddles and the people squatted in doorways staring out. Drips came through the canvas roof of the pick-up but there was no escaping, all movement was precluded by the crush of passengers. This coast has two seasons: wet and wetter. In some places, over 3.5 metres falls in one year. There are many big rivers and they get increasingly frequent the further north you go, until at Soanierana-Ivongo, the economics of bridge-building fail and there are only makeshift rusty barges.

We reached the town in the mid-afternoon and I soon discovered that all boats to Isle Ste Marie were cancelled due to the conditions. I left my bag in a small clapboard hotel and walked around the town.

The largest and tallest building, apart from a radio mast, was the Protestant church, set on a hill over the river. On impulse I asked in a small store and was shown to the pastor's house. It was much like all the other houses: a wooden hut, neatly built, with flowers in tins on ledges and lace curtains in the windows. I was shown into the parlour by his wife, a room obviously kept for best, with its doilies and vases of artificial flowers. The pastor was a young man and enthusiastic about his mission, though his talk was mainly of the capital, Tana, and the theological college.

'Church funds are a problem,' he said. 'The building is only seventy years old, but with this weather it ages very quickly.' We went on to the veranda and he pointed out the dilapidated roof of his church.

'You see?'

'Yes,' I followed him down the steps. 'Is there a cemetery nearby?'

He nodded and led me along a side track. The rain had eased to a few drips: the jungle gleamed and exuded a thick dank breath. Many trees were festooned with orchids, but the pastor was surprised I should notice: 'Just wild flowers,' he said. He turned off the track and pushed through the undergrowth. 'I have never been here before,' he said.

This struck me as rather strange. Was it some political gesture? Traditional cults in Madagascar are closely associated with death. Perhaps the church felt it expedient to distance itself from the business of dying. But there were Christian graves here, mixed in with all the others. 'Died about 1932' read one inscription. Had they been unsure of the year, or of when the death occurred? The air was full of mosquitoes, as big and ponderous as jungle flowers.

[257]

'Don't you bury the dead in this graveyard?' I asked. But he turned away with a non-committal smile.

There were many Chinese graves, as cracked and overgrown as the others. Trees had taken hold; long twining creepers had spun themselves around headstones; roots had pushed and elbowed for space; leaf litter had gathered and rotted, then smaller plants had grown. The European attempts at posterity, with its stone and inscriptions, could not bear such an attack. Nothing was old or ancient here, a century was as far back as history could leave much mark, beyond that all was swallowed up by the jungle and the rain. Even concrete could seem no more durable than timber in such a place. Green algae had crept across it before it was barely dry, tendrils crept into tiny cracks and worked them open. The huge panting jungle seemed to awaken urges within inanimate manmade objects to rebel: they sprouted, they shifted, they went AWOL and never came back. Standing in that graveyard, I began to see the impossibility of any hopes for lost pirate forts filled with cannons and inscriptions. This was a place where the past left few traces, obliterated by the remorseless forces of nature. History became rumour and hearsay. Perhaps this was why such a place had suited both the pirates and utopians, the people most in need of obliterated pasts, of a Year Zero.

In one corner were some thatched shelters. 'Local graves,' said the pastor, meaning non-Christian.

The coffins were positioned on low trestles under the thatch, not in the ground. Each was a section of tree trunk hollowed out like a canoe, a boat to take the deceased on a last voyage. It reminded me of Bob, the American, and his floating coffin – which I fervently hoped was still floating. Perhaps this was some cultural relic of the arrival from Java by the original inhabitants of the island.

The pastor had gone back to the road. I could see he didn't like being here, but perhaps it was just the dripping trees and mosquitoes. I went and joined him.

'How many services do you have in a week?'

'Twice on Sundays,' he said. 'Then on alternate Wednesdays we have Bible study or exorcism.'

'Exorcism?'

He shrugged. 'Oh, yes, there are so many people here who are possessed by the Devil.'

'Why is that?'

'There are many traditional cults you see and people usually come to the church for help.'

'How many in a week?'

He thought. 'I suppose we have twenty new cases per week.' He was quite matter of fact about it: as though more than a thousand fresh cases of diabolic possession per year was a typical small town average. He started down the track once more. 'Shall we stroll into town?'

We took in the post office and the river frontage. 'I'm afraid the seasons have changed very early,' he warned me. 'And the sea only has to be a little bit rough to deter these sailors.'

'Is it dangerous?'

'Very. At the river mouth they must break through the surf and there is a danger of turning the boat over. Last year several people drowned.'

I began to take an anxious interest in the weather from that moment, but by dawn next day the skies had cleared a little, enough to encourage the boatmen. Together with six French tourists who had appeared in a minibus, we boarded an ex-Japanese Navy lifeboat and set out downriver. Isle Ste Marie has become something of a tourist destination lately, but most arrive by air from Réunion. This was the traditional method and it was not pleasant. We survived the surf, then romped and rolled across a choppy sea.

Watching the low island come closer, I wondered how the pirates could have ever chosen such a weather-beaten corner as a sanctuary. It is, in fact, a tribute to their seamanship and confidence because even with modern navigation aids the coast is largely avoided by sailing boats.

[259]

Ambodifotatra, the capital of Isle Ste Marie, proved to be a single street of houses, mostly devoted to tourists. My heart sank when I saw the 'Filibustier Cafe' with its gaudy placard, but a few steps away from the jetty it became a normal, peaceful Malagasy village. I walked northwards along the coast road, hoping to find a room, but eventually the relentless rain drove me to find shelter in a shop.

The manager was bored and keen to chat. 'Why not stay here?' he said when I explained what I was looking for. 'There is a spare room we can rent to you.'

Jackie and his wife had been in a music group in Tana before they had opted to try their luck here, running a shop for a local businessman. At night I bought bottles of Three Horse beer and they sang Jackie's songs, melodic and rhythmic love duets with an edge of melancholy. At times the rain on the tin roof was so loud I could barely hear them. When it stopped, I went out and found the shadows beneath the trees were spangled with hundreds of fireflies.

For two days I searched for pirate history in the pouring rain. I went to the supposed pirate cemetery and other cemeteries. Everywhere seemed to be decrepit graveyards: one epitaph announced that the deceased had died '. . . after creating the new colony at the price of six years work and perils, not for fortune only for glory'. I sat on verandas talking to old men and I wandered jungle paths. If the rain ever stopped, it was as if only to take breath before renewing its assault. The sea came up and the beaches disappeared. Dugout canoes floated around the trees and bright blue parrot fish swam through the garden gate.

At Jackie's house I lay on my bed, slapping at the mosquitoes and reading about the pirates, particularly Misson.

The Frenchman had been in Ste Marie at least once but seems not to have bothered himself overly with the island's speciality: the burgeoning world trade in stolen goods. His life was too busy with noble deeds and fine speeches. Having constructed an octagonal fort defended by forty guns on the Malagasy coast, he recruited the English pirate Tom Tew, who was something of a leader himself. When Tew's men voted to follow him, they are said to have cried as one: 'A gold chain or a wooden Leg, we'll stand by you.' Tew was friendly with several unscrupulous notables in the Americas including Governor Fletcher of New York and Isaac Richier, Governor of Bermuda. No doubt such connections helped the finances of the burgeoning Libertalia.

If Johnson/Defoe invented Misson, then combining his story with that of the very real Tom Tew was a typically clever touch. The trade with Manhattan is also a verifiable fact. Frederick Phillipse, a New York merchant, would send homely essentials for the pirates such as needles and buttons, plus more predictable items like wine, tobacco and rum. In return, the pirates despatched ivory, silks and other luxury items for the New York rich – most of them unwillingly provided by the English East India Company and the Great Mughal.

Both ends of the long trade route did well: Phillipse bought a 90,000-acre estate on the Hudson and built the church in Sleepy Hollow; his man in Ste Marie, Adam Baldridge, sold rum he had bought for two shillings per gallon at three pounds and became as powerful as any petty potentate. In 1697 he retired, to New York, living out his days in peace and luxury.

At Libertalia, however, the pirates were far more concerned with higher matters. Tensions between Tew's men and Misson's led to the founding of a parliament with the Frenchman voted in as Conservator. The tentative steps towards democracy almost foundered, however, on Misson's generosity. Urged to kill prisoners by more cautious souls, the captain demurred, preferring to release them with a promise never to return. The result was much the same as that experienced by Ali Soilih when he sent Ahmed Abdullah into exile: the prisoners returned with a force of Portuguese men-of-war which were narrowly beaten off.

Nevertheless, the damage had been done. Libertalia was fatally weakened by loss of men, and when the natives attacked they destroyed the settlement, killing the priest, Caraciolli, and others.

[261]

Misson and Tew escaped and turned their noses towards America. They had plenty of money and planned a quiet retirement. Unfortunately, they were caught by a storm and Misson's ship disappeared, never to be seen again. Tew struggled on, making it to Rhode Island where he settled down for a magnificent dotage.

Initially it went well, but after some time, his crew came back to haunt him. Predictably, they had quickly squandered their share of the loot and now began begging the captain to take them on one last great adventure. He held out for a few years but finally, desperate to shut them up, he agreed. It was a bad decision: somewhere in the Red Sea, a cannon shot took most of his belly away, so bringing to a close the whole Libertalia story.

Isle Ste Marie had certainly been a key pirate stronghold, Nathaniel North was said to have been leader for a while, but it was always too busy a place, too wrapped up in the trading of loot, to be anything like a pirate utopia. The forts and settlements which had generated those stories back in the drinking dens of Deptford were to the north-west, across the narrow straits on the mainland. Every day I splashed my way down to the jetty and asked if a boat might be heading that way. Every day I trudged back to Jackie's flooded garden and looked through the rain to the dark smudge of jungled mountains on the mainland. That was the region where the pirates had spun their dreams but, unlike the tourist island of Ste Marie, it had remained a remote and wild place. The roads were said to be terrible and the jungle still untouched. I had no intention of searching for Libertalia, others have tried and failed many times. (Perhaps the best place to find it would be in London's Stoke Newington where Defoe is buried.) But I did want to reach that coast and maybe get to Rantabe where John Plantain had built his fort.

One morning at the jetty in Ambodifotatra, I discovered a motorised canoe that was leaving next day for the village of Manompana across the straits. The captain was about sixteen years old and wore, rather proudly, a *Titanic* tee-shirt.

*   *   *

We left far too late in the day. It was noon and we immediately started smacking into a choppy sea. Captain Titanic had grabbed for himself the only life jacket and a huge black oilskin. I sheltered under a scrap of tarpaulin. The anchor, I noted, was an old wheel hub and the bilges were full of water.

We motored north up the coast, hugging the shore and riding any large swells with great care. Isle Ste Marie is forty miles long and about halfway up a wooded sandspit reaches out from the mainland like an umbilical cord and leaves a gap of no more than five miles. North of this we turned away from the island and started across. Then the engine stopped.

There was no cover on top of the small outboard and the rain was sluicing down as Captain Titanic struggled to start it. Rain squalls moved across the straits like galleons in full sail preparing for battle. The surface of the sea became puckered, throwing up sudden sharp waves that snapped at the sides and sent deluges of cold water over us. I picked up a plastic container and began bailing. Other storm fronts were rolling in now, blackening the sky like a bruise until it was as though night was coming.

Eventually, the engine caught again and we were moving. I was shivering with cold, soaked to the skin. We reached the tip of the sandspit. This was known to the pirates as Charnock's Point, and often rumoured to be a place where the pirate John Plantain buried his treasure. The white beach curved away to the north from here, tucking itself into the feet of the jungled mountains.

We were just following the shore, perhaps a hundred yards clear, when I heard the sigh. It was behind us. Two humpbacked whales had surfaced, so close to the beach that a good throw with a stone would have hit them. A cloud of spray drifted gently down the wind and the two low dark shapes hung there, not moving at all, even by the swell, perfectly balanced. It was a mother with a young calf, still a massive beast, but scarcely a quarter of her size.

Captain Titanic span the boat around and raced towards them until we came alongside. I smelled the breath, unsurprisingly fishy,

[263]

and saw the blowhole pout expressively, probably annoyed by the buzz of the engine.

'Switch it off!' I shouted and at that moment, as the engine died, the whales sank down. The flukes came up lazily and hung there for a fraction of a second, then slipped away. Through the clear water, I glimpsed the huge bulks sliding underneath us, then the mother's flukes swayed gently to one side and the surface became a boiling cauldron of water. We were spun right around, the helmsman standing up and roaring with laughter, the black oilskin wrapped around him like an old frock coat. The memory of the dream came at that moment, the sea captains walking on the water. I hung on to the side and prayed the creature would not capsize us.

We survived the scare, but now the weather was becoming worse, the wind stripping spray from the wave crests and flinging it down on us. At times, huddled in the bows, I could hardly see the other end of the boat. Captain Titanic was proving himself worthy of the task, somehow steering for a narrow gap in the reef. Then we were safe.

The coast, I realised, was not as straight as it appeared: there was in fact a small bay beyond the reef which curled around behind a hook of forested land and formed a perfect hidden lagoon about 150 yards across.

'You want to go to Wen Ki's place?' asked the boatman.

'Who is he?'

'He runs a hotel – the only hotel.' He pointed across the ruffled green waters to the beach where I could see a distant figure coming down to the narrow beach. As a potential visitor, I had been spotted.

'Will you stay here?' I asked the youth.

He grimaced. 'Storms are coming. No boats will go.'

I paid him and waded ashore to meet Mr Wen Ki, a small wiry Chinese man in shorts. He was pleased to see me, not having had a guest for over two months and with a large brood of children and grandchildren to support. I had my pick of the neat slatted cane bungalows, each on short stilts, then went to sit with him in the restaurant hut and drink hot tea.

He had built the site himself, he told me, and was sure that one day the tourists would discover his little place. Until then he cleaned the beach every day, swept the rooms and played with his grandchildren in the dark cave of a kitchen.

That afternoon, between rain squalls, I explored along the coast to the village. The beach was lined with cycads, their fruits like strings of pale brown eggs between the top of the straight trunk and its plume of fern-like leaves. Orchids grew among them, sending sprays of white flowers out, and these were shaded by larger trees. There were a few dugout canoes and chickens picking around the fallen leaves – the storms of the last few days had brought many down.

Wen Ki was helpful when I asked about local history that night. We were sitting together in his bamboo restaurant watching the drifting constellations of fireflies under the trees. The wind was picking up, however, and slowly the tiny lights went out, the insects clinging to leaves for shelter as another storm came charging in from the ocean.

'I myself do not know much of the history,' Wen Ki admitted. 'My family have only been here since 1898. We are newcomers. But Monsieur Colobali is the one to talk to. He is very very old and knows everything here. I will send word to him.'

'And your own family? Was it your grandfather who first came?'

'Yes. He came to Tamatave by boat from China. You see there were many wars and bombardments in Canton, so he left. At first he was a coolie, but later he got a shop. The family moved up here and began selling things to the Malagache people in the forest. I was a boy then but the whole family would go along.'

He smiled at the memory. The ceaseless singing of the cicadas was gone now, drowned out by the urgent sound of the wind in the trees. A shutter slammed back and Wen Ki went to secure it.

[265]

When he returned, I asked how the family had travelled in those early days.

'By canoe. It was the only way. We took soap and pots and pans. In exchange the forest people gave us baskets and jungle things – roots for medicine and strange animals and birds. Later, my father started a general store here in Manompana.'

'Is he alive?'

'No, he was assassinated in 1981.'

There was a silence. The word itself seemed so inappropriate in such a setting.

'Here?'

'Near here. I was staying seven kilometres away when a boy came running. He said come quick because your father is injured. I ran all the way in the night along the beach, but when I got there he was already dead. Some men had broken into the store and when he woke up, they stabbed him through the eye with a spear.'

'Did they catch them?'

It was the one moment when he showed any emotion: an expression on his face and a movement of his hands, a small gesture of despair, as if to say: In this place? What do you think?

'It seems so peaceful,' I said, not knowing what to say. I was wondering if he knew the murderers: this was a small community. Or had it been something like a pirate attack, a sudden and violent visitation, that came, caused havoc, and went away.

'There was another murder here not long ago,' he said. 'But he was French so they took him to Réunion for trial.'

A dog started barking nearby. Wen Ki fetched a candle for me from the kitchen. 'Nowhere is safe,' he said. 'Go sleep now.'

I walked back to my hut, attempting to shield the light from the wind, but it flickered and went out. It was an utterly black night, the storm that had threatened to rage all day now began in earnest. During the night, I woke to hear rain lashing down outside and a loose window shutter slamming back against the hut. I got up and grabbed at it. Lightning flashed inside the clouds, transforming them into great globes of phosphorescent gas against which the coconut trees were starkly exposed, bending and weaving like beaten boxers on the ropes, trying to escape the killer punch.

13

A Drink for the Dead

Our revels now are ended. These our actors,
As I foretold you, were all spirits and
Are melted into air, into thin air:
And, like the baseless fabric of this vision,
The cloud-capped towers, the gorgeous palaces,
The solemn temples, the great globe itself,
Yea, all which it inherit, shall dissolve
And, like this insubstantial pageant faded,
Leave not a rack behind. We are such stuff
As dreams are made on, and our little life
Is rounded with a sleep.
                    William Shakespeare, *The Tempest*

Monsieur Colobali arrived after breakfast: a stooping ancient man dressed in broad-brimmed straw hat, white shirt and trousers. He was carrying a walking stick and a file of papers which he hung on to grimly. At dawn the wind had dropped to nothing, but already it was picking up again, bringing sudden cold clouts of sea spray across from the beach.

'Monsieur Wen Ki has sent word that you wished to speak with me.'

I went down to shake his hand, liking him immediately and

feeling slightly embarrassed that I had not set out to find him as soon as breakfast was over.

'Yes. I'm interested in the history of the place – especially the pirates.'

'I know a little, although I am from Tana originally.'

I gave him a helping hand up the steps to the chair and sat down on the floor in front of him. 'The pirates came here in the seventeenth century, didn't they?'

He donned a pair of spectacles but said nothing.

The big question had to be asked.

'Do you know of anyone . . . ? I mean, is there anyone in Manompana who is descended from those times – descended from a European pirate? I would like to meet that person and talk to them.'

Monsieur Colobali scrutinised me in a puzzled, slightly bemused manner. He reached out a long, dessicated finger and tapped the table thoughtfully. 'Well, monsieur, I don't understand. If you want to talk to such a person, why not do it?'

I wasn't sure he had understood me correctly. 'But to find him – or her?'

He waved his twig-like fingers vaguely in the air. 'Then go to the village.'

'And what is his name?'

He began to chuckle, still bemused, as if unsure quite what game I was playing but keen to play. 'How do I know his name? You tell me.'

'But I don't know it. I thought you might.'

He drummed his fingertips gently, trying to be patient. 'What kind of a man is he?'

'A man descended from a pirate.'

He smiled encouragingly. 'And what else? Tall, short, young, old?'

'It doesn't matter. All I want is a man descended from a pirate.'

He sighed, his exasperation was showing. 'But monsieur,' he

said, 'don't you know? Everyone here is descended from a pirate.'

A flock of chickens, anxious to escape the mud, attempted to climb the steps and Monsieur Colobali absent-mindedly flicked the tip of his walking stick at them. I asked him to repeat what he had said – not that I hadn't heard him; it just seemed too incredible to take in. He repeated the assertion, qualifying it slightly. 'Let us say, the majority. Not I, nor Wen Ki, obviously. But most of the others. They are all descended from Imballe.'

'Imballe?'

He sighed. 'Imballe was a French pirate who died in 1813 – in a fight over a woman. They buried him along the coast at Teinteingue.'

'And Manompana was Imballe's base?'

He pointed out across the lagoon to where the beach curled around into a scorpion's tail of a sandspit. 'You see how that land with the forest hides us from the sea? Imballe could bring his boat here and not be seen. It was an excellent hideout.'

He stopped.

'Is there anything else? Legends? Stories? Wrecks?'

'Yes, there is a wreck.'

My heart leapt.

'But you should speak to Sese, the boatman, about that.'

'And Ranters Bay – Rantabe?'

'Yes, there are stones of a pirate fort there.'

'Guns? Inscriptions?'

He shook his head. 'Nothing but stones.'

When he had left, I went and found Sese who was tipsy but agreed to take me out wreck-hunting. He was a tall cadaverous smoker, with a laugh like a cavern, his conversation veering off into wild yells and snorts of laughter. A large dugout canoe was unearthed from a pile of palm leaves and a paddle, carved from a single piece of wood, borrowed.

A stiff cold breeze was bustling in from the sea when we set out, and once we got to the point, progress became even more difficult against the choppy waves. Sese sang with gusto and asked me about England.

'Do you have merchandise there?'

'Yes.'

'Aaaah! *C'est bien.* Cigarettes?'

'Yes.'

'Rum?'

'Yes.'

'Marmite?'

'Yes.'

'Mmmm. *C'est bien. Très bien.*' What more could anyone want?

Eventually, he was satisfied that we had found the spot. I donned the snorkelling gear I had borrowed from Wen Ki and jumped overboard.

The water was cold. Without the sun to warm it, and with the wind driving ocean swells inshore, the temperature had plummeted. The wreck was easily spotted: there was an iron boiler standing in about three fathoms of water with other parts of the ship scattered around. A few shivery angelfish hung about next to the boiler, as though hoping it might spring to life and warm them up. This was certainly no pirate ship.

I clambered back into the dugout and we set off towards the point.

'Is there no other wreck?' I asked.

'You want Surcouf?' asked Sese. 'He was a pirate and his boat sank in the lagoon.'

'Robert Surcouf was here?' I knew of him: a dashing French pirate who had nettled the English by seizing a twenty-six-gun Indiaman with only a four-gun vessel, the *Emilie*. But his famous command was the *Confiance*, an eighteen-gun ship renowned for her speed.

'Do you know the place?'

'I have never dived down, but an old man showed me the spot.'

[272]

We paddled around to the quiet corner where the water was green and very still. Sese manoeuvred us to within a few yards of the beach.

'Here.'

Once again I dived over the side. But this time I could see nothing but a thin yellow soup. I went vertically down, paddling hard with the flippers. Expecting to be in no more than ten feet of water, I had not prepared for this.

I surfaced, gasping. 'It's deep!' This set Sese roaring with laughter.

'*Ah, oui!* Deep! Very very deep!'

My second attempt also failed to establish any bottom. I began to concentrate, taking several deep breaths and swimming hard downwards.

Slowly the yellow soup faded to green, then darker and darker. I felt the edge of panic that I always have when underwater and without vision. My hands were stretched out in front of me, but I could not even see my elbows. The water seemed to coagulate coldly around me, I could feel my hands sinking into denser and denser layers of silt, but still nothing solid. The mask was hard against my nose and I had no more breath to equalise the pressure. I turned and swam as hard as I could upwards, watching the light appear, then the black shape of the canoe.

I could not speak at first, or climb out. Instead I swam to the beach and crawled out. The edge was astonishingly sharp: a gentle incline of pure white sand, then a sudden descent.

'It is a strange thing,' agreed Sese when he came over. The beach fell away so abruptly that he used it like a landing stage.

'Surcouf used Manompana as a base,' he said. 'He was very clever. You see he would lure boats to chase him, then come through the gap in the reef and hide here. It is very narrow there at the entrance. When they ran aground, he could attack.'

'But his ship, the *Confiance*, sank here?'

'I don't know the name but it was right here.'

I looked around. Maybe the sandspit itself had grown up

[273]

on top of a boat. It did seem peculiar that it was so sharply defined.

'How did his boat sink?'

'It is not known.'

Quite possibly the story holds some truth. The coast must have been littered with wrecks at one time, the pirates often running them aground before plundering. But the nature of the coast is to smash and destroy such things, leaving precious few traces of what had been.

'You know,' said Sese, 'if you want pirates, you must go to Fenerive.'

'Why?'

He laughed. 'There were too many pirates at Fenerive. You must ask when you get there.'

The wind was rising again and he was keen to get home. To the south the mountains disappeared behind a grey wall of rain. I seemed no closer to evidence of pirates, reaching down into the mud but never able to grasp anything solid or definite. As we paddled back the showers started, bringing whoops from Sese and a song, a crazed outpouring of war-cries, screeches and growling which he later claimed was 'une ballade' concerning our 'voyage'.

The storm intensified as evening came. I sat in the Chinese-owned general store on a sack of grain watching the villagers buy simple things: a scoopful of cooking oil, a paper twist of salt, or a tot of Old Nick rum. The people I spoke to had heard of Imballe but knew nothing of their ancestor.

That night was the wildest so far: the floorboards vibrated and rain was driven through the slatted canes. If I lit a candle, it was immediately blown out. All I could do was shift the bed as far from the leaks as possible and huddle under the sheet. The fever that had left me for a few days now returned and I lay half-awake, half-asleep, snatching at dreams and moments of lucidity, the pale ghostly surface of the mosquito net rolling and shaking with the draughts.

The next day I spent shivering on the veranda. The rain had become loathsome; I couldn't bear any more of it. I couldn't recall a single day in Madagascar when it had not been pouring down. This was not the short sharp bursts of joyful precipitation that tropical downpours were meant to be. This was low pressure and Manchester in November. When Wen Ki passed I asked about transport: were there boats north to Rantabe? He laughed. 'There are no boats to any place.'

And cars?

'There is only one here but he will not go. The storm is too bad.'

When the wind came that night, it kicked open the door and lifted the mosquito net right off the bed. The net held on by a single string to the ceiling, flapping and dancing, until I managed to get the door shut.

Later I dreamed I was in a television studio watching the making of an arts programme. Several fashionable set designers were discussing the problems they had faced in a particular production. The cameras swung around and showed the scene in question: a kind of tableau vivant of three African men on a plinth. Their bodies had been painted to look like grey stone and there were dead leaves and sticks thrown over them.

As I watched, the walls of the studio and the cameras fell away and the graveyard came to life. The Africans jumped down and began to run up a field. They were terrified and not without reason. The set designers had become hunters, brandishing spears, and they chased the three back and forth across the grassy field. The first was brutally slaughtered in front of me with a spear in his eye, the second caught in a net and garotted, but for a long time the third eluded them. Like a frightened hare, he criss-crossed the ground at great speed, but eventually he tired and they roped him, just a few feet away from me. I stepped forward, shouting: 'Stop this! Stop! Let him go!'

One of the designers, almost unrecognisable now in blood-splattered peasant costume, came striding down with a pitchfork, ready to deliver the final blow. I stepped in front of her, but she simply passed through me. I felt a peculiar shiver, then heard the horrible squelch as the fork went into the body. I woke shaking and disorientated, rain was lashing down and the wind had risen to a scream. When I got out on to the veranda, I could see the silhouettes of palm leaves against the sky as they were flung over the bungalows. Sticks and other bits of vegetation were crashing into the thatch, then a shutter broke free and smashed itself to pieces against the frame.

Dawn came as no more than a slit of light, the rest of the sky was black and pelting rain. Sweat was running off me and I stumbled down the steps and out on to the flooded lawns. Tiny zebra fish squittered away through the beds of flowers and out into huge lakes that had appeared overnight. The cycads had thrown off their load of curious egg-like pods and they floated in like some alien seed released from the deep.

The restaurant was closed up and I went out towards the track into the village, feeling the rain hammer on my skull. The misery of jungle rain. I was back in southern Sudan as a twenty-something teacher, pushing my bed around the mud hut to find a place where no drips fell, watching a black mamba skitter across the flooded yard in front, its eager eyes on the weaver birds' nests in the mango tree above. Rain meant mud and mosquitoes and malaria. It was sleepless nights and empty days with nothing to do but wait. I couldn't bear it. I had to get out of Manompana. The awful memories of those weeks and months in the rainy season, when I'd lay on my grass rope bed hallucinating from malarial rigors and wake to find snakes crawling around the room. I'd jumped out of bed and sliced the head from a spitting cobra once, then slept and woken, thinking it was a dream, only to discover its corpse being eaten alive by safari ants. Feelings of being trapped in the endless season of mud, the civil war having cut the roads out to Juba. Suddenly I was running down the track to Wen Ki's, aware that I was doing something very strange but unable to stop myself. I had to get a car. I had to find that car and get out of Manompana. I had to be in a building that could withstand rain, where humanity did not cling to its mean shelters like drowned rats, waiting for God to end his Flood. Utopia would never be a tropical island for me, nor the simple tribal life I had once admired. If this was pirate paradise, then I wanted out – and quickly.

It was when I reached the track that I heard the chanting. It was the sort African soldiers sing when they jog in groups, a sound that once sent shivers through the ranks of redcoats when the Zulus were approaching. I stopped.

It was coming from the right, from out of the village. And now a group of people appeared from around the corner, running in the flooded track and sending big splashes of water over one another. Some carried umbrellas, others carried a long pole with something slung beneath. None looked at me, they were so busy concentrating on not falling over and on singing. As the bearers came alongside I saw that what they carried was a sort of hammock made of palm leaves and inside lay a figure all wrapped in grubby bandages. It was only a glimpse and then they were past.

As I watched them go, I thought to follow, but then there was a hand on my elbow. Wen Ki had an umbrella and was looking, concernedly, at me.

'Mister? You okay?'

'What was that?' I looked back and they had gone. For a horrible moment I thought he would say he had seen nothing. Instead, he smiled.

'They take their ancestor for drinking a glass of rum.'

'Somebody died?'

'No, no. He is dead for many years already. They dig him up!'

'They believe he is not dead?'

'Sure he is dead, but he is still part of the family, no?'

He gently tugged at my arm and we started back up the path towards the restaurant hut. The dead were not dead in this place. Like the border between land and sea, that of life and death was undefined and porous. The pirates still got out of their graves and drank rum with the descendants who had forgotten all except their names.

I pulled away from Wen Ki. 'I'm okay – really. But I must go after them – to see.'

Rain coursing down my face, I hurried along the flooded track into the village where miserable dogs and bedraggled children stared out from their huts. I had left it too late and the sound of the rain drowned any clues as to where they had hidden themselves. Convinced I had missed them and they would be somewhere back up the track, replacing their ancestor in his grave, I returned and left Wen Ki's place behind me.

I walked for miles, crossing muddy torrents and following rainswept beaches. It was a wild and magical place, full of signs of nature's violence with trees torn down and huge boulders smashed on the beach. There were orchids too, more than I had ever seen before, decked in the trees as though by some unseen gardener.

Eventually the track was pressed closer between mountains and sea, climbing a little, then going down to a narrow strip of land where I found what I had been searching for: the graveyard.

It was a strange and deserted place: canoe-like coffins standing on little trestles under thatched shades. At the far end I found a special place where the skulls of sacrificial bulls were driven on to poles and surrounded by offerings of rum. This was the no-man's-land where the living and the dead might meet. I sat on a boulder and watched the sea pounding in, thinking about my own journey and those I had followed.

Death had never been far away for those men, and it surrounded me too as I sat next to the disturbed graves. From the cholera epidemic in Nosy Bé to the murders here, all I had heard of was death. This coast, a paradise to the pirates, had an atmosphere of death around it which the relentless rain did nothing to dispel. I felt like a man on a cure: a bizarre behaviourist experiment to rid me of all those myths – Utopia, Crusoe, tropical beach paradise, and any lingering liberal nonsense about Noble Savages. But take away the underlying myths and people don't travel any more, they simply go from A to B. I didn't want that, or the cure. I simply wanted out.

For all that was written of the primitive pirate democracies, I had seen and heard nothing to confirm it. Perhaps, after all, they had been no more than anyone could expect: nasty, brutish and short on ideals. They seemed to have come and gone leaving no trace as to the manner of their passing beyond a few babies.

I looked at my fingers which were trembling with cold. The skin was wrinkled and sodden; it had been either wet or damp for days. My feet were beginning to rot between the toes. I was evolving into some semi-aquatic beast. I no longer cared about Rantabe, a pile of algae-covered stones in a dripping forest probably; I would trust the judgement of Sese, the village drunk, and head south to Fenerive and civilisation.

Back in Monompana I found the car that Wen Ki had mentioned. It was outside the general store being loaded. Yes, the Chinese driver told me, he too was sick of the rain and would attempt to go that day. He promised to pick me up later at the hotel.

There were several other passengers already on board when he arrived. I squeezed myself among them and, after the usual tour of the village searching for extras, we set out.

The car moved slowly, grinding through deep mud and puddles, to a river mouth where we waited for the tide to lift the rusty barge off the bottom. Then we were poled across. Further rivers were more difficult: once the wind caught the car like a sail and blew us far upriver against the current until we were almost shipwrecked in a flooded banana plantation. We finally reached Soanierana-Ivongo at sunset. Rain was falling and I had little hope of further transport that night, but as I walked along towards the hotel, a car pulled up.

'You want a lift?' asked the driver in English.

'To Fenerive?'

'No problem.'

I jumped in. He was a Belgian roadbuilder who had lived most of his life in South Africa but was now on a European Union project in Tamatave. Without the usual stops for passengers we made good progress and pulled in to Fenerive just after eight.

'Where do you want to go?'

I shrugged, squinting out at the few lights. There was not much to be seen except some wooden stores and a few people braving the downpour.

'Is there somewhere by the sea?'

He thought. 'I don't know. I think there's a track heading that way just after the town.'

We motored through and found the track. It curled down to the sea then followed the beach, a pale glimmer of sand in the darkness. There was a place with a few beach chalets that looked closed and the track became rougher. He stopped.

'You want to go on?'

'Maybe a little. Do you mind?'

We ground up a slope and the track turned through a gate. Fireflies signalled from the bushes and there was a house there, overlooking the sea.

I jumped out and walked towards the light. On the side facing the sea was a spacious veranda laid out with rattan furniture and potted plants. Rainwater gurgled in the drains. In one of the chairs a French woman was sitting smoking a cigarette, a middle-aged and motherly figure. She looked up with a quick smile.

'Can I help you?'

We shook hands. 'I'm looking for somewhere to stay.'

'We have a spare room in the house for 40,000 francs, or there are some bungalows – are you alone? Ah, I see you are two.'

The Belgian had appeared, shaking the rain from his hair. 'No, no, not for me,' he said. 'Unfortunately I cannot stay: you have a beautiful place.'

'I'm Dominique,' the woman said. 'Sit down. Can I get you a beer?'

While she was away, I glanced in the living room: a simple white-washed space decorated with family pictures and books.

[280]

'Are you a tourist?' asked Dominique when she had set the beer down on the coffee table.

I explained what I was doing – how my search for piratical ancestry had led nowhere.

She grinned. 'And how did you come here?'

'By chance. We saw the road and followed it.' I explained about Manompana, the relentless rain, the mud, the fever, how I wanted to sleep in a room that was dry.

She whispered something to the Belgian who laughed. 'Boy, you landed on your feet.'

I nodded. 'Yes, I can see that.'

They were both laughing. 'You don't understand,' he said, 'Not the comfort thing. You'll get that for sure. Your project about pirates.' I sat up and he clapped me on the knee. 'This woman is a direct descendant of an eighteenth-century pirate. She's even got a family tree to show you.'

'Mister Kevin?' A smiling Malagasy face appeared around the door. Light flooded in. I could hear the sea rolling on to the beach below. 'Breakfast?'

I got up and went out on to the veranda. For once the sun was out, rapidly drying the broad-leaved tropical grass and the sandy track. The woman who had woken me appeared once again and pointed down the path into the garden.

I walked down, noting the various trees: cinnamon, breadfruit, coconut and jackfruit. On them grew orchids and below were clumps of lemon grass. By the white sand beach there were barringtonias, a low and shady tree that throws off a profusion of floating four-lobed fruits. They had also colonised the small island which lay a quarter of a mile off shore.

Dominique was taking breakfast at a large round table under a thatched roof. This was the centre of life at Paradisa Kely – Little Paradise, as they all called it – the circular table at which everyone ate and drank. And they all ate, more or less, the same things: not the pirate favourite, salmagundi, but sometimes combinations

[281]

equally strange such as the starter of camembert and manioc which appeared one night.

With her jet black hair and infectious laughter, there was certainly something piratical about Dominique. But there the similarities ended: she was far too kind and amiable. After I had drunk some tea, I asked if the place had changed over the years.

'The place, yes, but the people, no. If you get up at dawn, you will see the local women come to the water and pray to the sun. Then they take seawater in their mouths and go back and spit it out on the sick people. They are animists: they respect every tree, every animal – even the sand on the beach. When I was a child here, you could see big rainforest trees everywhere. Not now.'

'So what happened?'

'The road came, and then outsiders. That is why the road stops at Soanierana-Ivongo. The people to the north saw what happened here and they don't want it.'

'And how did your own family come to arrive here?'

'His name was Adam James and he took the boat in Ostend when he was seventeen. Come up to the house because I have the family tree there.' We transferred to the comfortable rattan chairs and the whole story emerged.

Dominique's ancestor, Adam James, had shipped out of Ostend as lieutenant to a pirate called Clayton and arrived off Fenerive around 1720. James took a liking to the place and struck up a friendship with a local chief, Ratsimilaho, who claimed to be half-English, his father having been an English pirate from Plymouth called Thomas White.

I smiled at this: White was the man who had found the twelve-oared boat of the *Ruby* at Mayotte and had gone to Zanzibar with Nathaniel North and John Bowen. His name ran like a golden thread through Captain Johnson's narrative: he had even met Captain Misson when they were both at Isle Ste Marie. Most fascinating of all, Johnson reported that he had died of 'flux' leaving a son by a 'woman of the country' who he asked to be sent to England for his education. Suddenly I had the feeling of enormous satisfaction – and relief – Johnson's tales were not all lies and exaggerations. Here, at last, was living confirmation of it.

'Adam James and Ratsimilaho swore a vow of brotherhood,' said Dominique. 'They cut their wrists and mingled blood.' A proper blood brotherhood then, mine and Nicole's had been sealed with saltwater.

The alliance was a strong one: Ratsimilaho married a local princess from Fenerive and founded a tribe.

'His tomb is here,' said Dominique pointing across the narrow straits to the island. 'You can go by pirogue to see it.'

I twisted in my chair and looked out through the cinnamon trees across the sea. There were men in canoes heading out to fish.

'Who were they?' I asked. 'That tribe founded by the Englishman's son.'

'They became terrible warriors,' said Dominique, 'famous for their raids in big canoes all up the coast. Later they went as far as the Comoros and Mozambique.'

I frowned. 'What did they call themselves?'

'Betsimisiraka,' Dominique said. 'Their chief lives next door if you want to meet him.'

I almost felt like laughing. Poor James Prior in the frigate *Nisus* and his 'ignorant savages' mortifying the English politicians with their bloodthirsty excesses and vast war fleets – Ibrahim Djae had shown me the defensive wall built to repulse them at Domoni. As they rampaged on across the channel and down the coast of Mozambique, their presence sparked off the panic which would give the British an excuse to send Prior's gunboat and embrace a new role as world's policeman. Now here was an extra layer to add to the irony: the revolting natives traced their line back to a publican's son from Plymouth.

'You can see that the alliance of Adam James and Ratsimilaho was strong,' said Dominique. 'Because we are still here!'

In the afternoon, I went down to the beach and waited. Eventually two youths came along and I asked if they had a pirogue: would they take me to the island?

They were unenthusiastic. Could I wait till morning? We stood watching the waves smash into the two rocky headlands at either end of the beach. There was a narrow gap through which to manoeuvre, but beyond that the water was less choppy. I offered 10,000 francs. They wavered. I made it 15,000 and they agreed.

The outrigger canoe is often cited as an example of technology brought from Java by the early immigrants to Madagascar; it is certainly hard to imagine the dugout being a viable vessel without the long balancing arm – not in such temperamental waters. We pushed off and I sat, gripping the sides that had been so skilfully cut to finger thickness, trying to keep upright as we wobbled over the waves.

The island was a thickly wooded low outcrop surrounded by a beach of broken coral. When we had landed, I followed my two guides along the shore, climbing over fallen barringtonia trees and listening for the calls of lemurs. There were two species, Dominique had told me, both easily approached if you went slowly and quietly. This was not so easy once we turned away from the coral strand and entered the shaded forest. Here the leaf litter crunched underfoot and the cycad trees were tied together with spiders' webs that gently wrapped themselves around my head like widows' veils. The creatures themselves, often a handspan wide from toe to toe, scuttled into the safety of the dark dank recesses of the cycad's hairy trunk.

The island was much larger than it appeared from the mainland and I realised that it contained an untouched sliver of rainforest – a natural world just the same as that the first explorers had found. When they had arrived, the entire coast would have been covered in this magical and alluring forest.

In the centre we found the grave: a simple block of stone with a plinth and a few glasses of rum, each with a complement of inebriated insects. King Ratsimilaho, born 1700, died 1750. I regretted not bringing a little tot to leave for the man, but I did what others had done and left a few small coins. The two youths hung back, crouching in the shade of the cycads and watching me.

[284]

When I rejoined them, one led me into a little glade of cycads.
There, sitting on the ground, was a large iron pot.

'*Les forbans!*' he hissed. 'The pirates. They make their soup
in this.'

It was a stout cauldron indeed, and had survived its exposure
to almost 300 years of the elements surprisingly well. Shaped just
like a witches' cauldron and around three feet in height, it had a
thick lip which had been chipped and eroded.

'Pirate Clayton brought it here,' explained the youth. 'People
like to take pieces – for good luck and to keep the Devil away.'

There was no trace inside of what had once been cooked, no
dried salmagundi which the insects had refused, just a few inches
of brilliant yellow water seasoned with mosquito larvae. I took
some photographs and sat on a lump of coral nearby.

The two youths had wandered away down the beach to the
pirogue. The sun was setting and they clearly did not care to be
in the vicinity of the old pot and the tomb after dark.

The journey had brought me here: to the place where those early
Europeans had, at long last, left some mark. The place where the
revered ancestors, sons and grandsons of the pirates, were taken
out for a glass of rum and a change of bandages.

The pirates had come expecting very little: their motivations
had been as base and greedy as any other's, but the manner of
their living had left its mark, creating new myths of democratic
utopias that had reverberated all the way to the founding fathers
and the US constitution. And of all the sorry blood-thirsty bunch,
they had found something and left a mark, though it was not
great architecture built on classical dimensions, nor any kind of
civilisation; what they had left was some children who had kept
their memory alive and an old iron pot, the symbol of their freedom
and equality. No doubt some of the tales of utopian settlements
were dreamed up by Defoe, but they had begun here with some
small simple truths. The pot from which all men shared the same
food and the blood brotherhood between the local chief and the
pirate – a brotherhood that has survived three centuries. Truths

[285]

such as these had been carried back across the oceans to places such as Deptford and captured the imaginations of others.

The pirates themselves could not go back. Some accepted pardons – Adam James too, eventually – but like hopeful utopians everywhere, they had obliterated the past and thrown themselves into the future. Perhaps they knew that the secret of heaven on earth was not to search at all, simply to recognise its existence when you landed in it.

In *Robinson Crusoe*, one of the books that had fed my own boyhood desires to travel, Defoe had always been rather vague as to Crusoe's reasons for wandering the globe, referring darkly to some 'original sin' against God and his own father. The crime appears to have been nothing more than wandering itself, the refusal to follow the profession chosen for him and lead a good decent life. In two less celebrated books, Defoe followed his roving hero towards some sort of self-knowledge. He buys a farm in England, marries and has three children. But the contented middle way does not last. Crusoe cannot leave alone the idea that there must be something better. He embarks for his island once again, now a colony, but he does not settle, preferring to wander the globe. His crew abandon him in Bengal and he sets off for Siberia, his restless spirit unquenched despite all the impediments thrown at him by his own creator. The reader finishes with the impression that the arch-conservative Defoe does not know how to stop this man, that no amount of lecturing on the nobility of honest toil will kill the wanderlust.

My own experience duplicated the fictional one: I'd burned out – or perhaps drowned – any lingering pretensions to savage paradises and island idylls. I was left with the safety net of an English home. Now, like Crusoe, I would go back, and like him, I would wonder how long it might last.

From above me came a strange cry and when I looked up into the trees, I saw a black-and-white lemur, big-eyed and slow, come edging down the branch then stop.

If I had been prepared, I would have brought a hand of bananas from the market. Instead, I'd raided a sorry single fruit from the kitchen, all blackened and squishy in my pocket. But the lemur's liquid eyes showed interest I placed the banana gently on a branch near my head. The creature waited, clucking to itself, then it descended, very slowly, to the fruit. He paused, then picked it up and ate it, dropping the skin. He waited.

'I haven't got any more,' I said, spreading my arms, open-handed. The eyes seemed so huge and intelligent from close distance. When no further bananas were forthcoming, he very gently, very slowly, withdrew up the branch, exactly as if he was taking care not to frighten the human.

Index

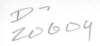